PRAISE FOR *NO FASCIST*

"Smash fascism! Read this book!"
—Tom Morello, songwriter and guitarist from
Rage Against the Machine

"*No Fascist USA!* is not only timely, but also essential in the present period of accelerated white supremacist activity and anti-racist organizing to combat it. In telling the story of the John Brown Anti-Klan Committee, the authors, without romanticizing or condemning, draw important lessons from the fifteen-year history of the group."
—Roxanne Dunbar-Ortiz, author of *Loaded: A Disarming*
History of the Second Amendment

"With its savvy blend of youth culture and street confrontation, the John Brown Anti-Klan Committee tried to stop Trumpism before Trump. They confronted the rise of white nationalism in prisons, workplaces, and music scenes when precious few paid attention to it. If more people had grappled with their warning decades ago, we might be in a better place today. While I wish we did not need this book as badly as we do, I am grateful that Hilary Moore and James Tracy have gifted us this urgent read."
—Dan Berger, author of *Captive Nation: Black Prison Rights*
Organizing in the Civil Rights Era

"Yes! This book is right on time! As a Black woman supporting Black liberation struggles, it has been terrifying to grasp the resilience and reach of fascism in the U.S. and around the globe, and disheartening to see how many White people want to sign petitions and express discontent with current political conditions, but won't acknowledge that there is an ongoing race war that they're benefiting from, and who won't put their actions behind their beliefs. This book is about an imperfect effort to be brave, to be committed, and to risk the privileges of Whiteness in order to relinquish the entire construct of white supremacy.

And from where organized people of color are sitting, this kind of work is absolutely necessary. Studying the John Brown Anti-Klan Committee will give readers an understanding of the complexity of deconstructing the weapon of white supremacy from the inside out. Thank you, Hilary and James, for the precision of this analysis, and the true north of this star."

—adrienne maree brown, author of *Emergent Strategy* and *Pleasure Activism*, and facilitator of Black liberation movements

"This riveting and deeply researched new book, Hilary Moore and James Tracy's *No Fascist USA!*, brings us the unromanticized, and largely untold story of the John Brown Anti-Klan Committee. Through the stories of those who were part of this critical anti-fascist and U.S.-based group, we learn how their work exposed the complicity of the state—all the way to its highest levels—as well as the media's role in the spread of white nationalist ideology. This book is a 'must read' for anyone wanting to understand the roots of what happened in Charlottesville, and the burgeoning white nationalist membership lists in the U.S. today. We cannot possibly take on the challenges we face without learning from the past. This book is a necessary and long overdue contribution to inform the way forward."

—Carla F. Wallace, co-founder of Showing Up for Racial Justice

"The history of the John Brown Anti-Klan Committee is important because it explains the historical roots of the current struggle against American fascism. In their timely book, the authors of *No Fascist USA!* place the role of the state in proper perspective. Moore and Tracy remind readers that white supremacist terrorism thrives partly because the United States government embraces and benefits from it. Therefore, they indicate, the organizations and individuals are not just a Southern problem. No! They live, work, and attempt to dominate in every part of the United States of America. Equally important, there have always been dedicated White opponents of fascism. Refusing to sit idly as their Black and Brown comrades place their lives and freedom on the line, the people who joined JBAKC attempted to carry on the spirit of John Brown, just as Malcolm X suggested."

—Dr. Edward Onaci, author of *Free the Land!: Territorial Nationalism and Lifestyle Politics in the New Afrikan Independence Movement*

"James Tracy and Hilary Moore deliver a searing, bold new work that examines another painful and complicated chapter in American race relations. In an eye-opening account, they are able to connect the dots of the John Brown Anti-Klan Committee, a band of contemporary predominantly white activists, and their efforts to expose white supremacist organizations. With a fresh eye and new research, their book uncovers with stunning precision how these groups remain active and exposes some of their unlikely alliances."

—Laurens Grant, filmmaker, *The Black Panthers: Vanguard of the Revolution* and *Freedom Riders*

"I've waited for thirty years for this book! Our emergency hearts have always driven uprisings to stop white terrorism, but it always takes more than black bloc tactics in the streets to stop fascists. *No Fascist USA!* firmly connects today's militant antifascist street-fighting movements with important living radical histories to disrupt the cycles that keep the specter of fascism alive in the modern era. The struggles faced by the John Brown Anti-Klan Committee continue today in our difficult arc toward collective liberation."

—scott crow, author of *Setting Sights: Histories and Reflections on Community Armed Self-Defense*

To Felix,

May the record show that you are in fact part of this book's process. From hardcore promises in HMB to mountain lakes in Innsbruck, from heartbreak to friendship, get ready to never get rid of me. "We're all going to die. The only question is how."

Love,
Hilary

NO FASCIST USA!

The John Brown Anti-Klan Committee and Lessons for Today's Movements

Hilary Moore and James Tracy
Foreword by Robin D.G. Kelley

City Lights Books | Open Media Series
San Francisco

Cover photograph: Protesters demonstrating against the Aryan
Woodstock, circa March 1–5, 1989. Printed with permission of Napa
Historical Society.

Cover design by Herb Thornby

Open Media Series Editor: Greg Ruggiero

ISBN: 978-0872867963
eISBN: 9780872868007

Library of Congress Cataloging-in-Publication Data
on file

City Lights Books are published at the City Lights Bookstore
261 Columbus Avenue, San Francisco, CA 94133
www.citylights.com

Hilary Moore dedicates this book to:
Hans, for your good company as we wade through history.

James Tracy dedicates this book to:
Felix Shafer, Rest in Power!

CONTENTS

FOREWORD
Robin D.G. Kelley

"No Trump, No KKK, No Fascist USA!" has been a popular protest chant since the New York real-estate mogul and former reality TV star became the 45th president of the United States. This was no mere rhetorical flourish. We saw a surge in the ranks of white nationalists and the "alt-right," an escalation of domestic terrorist attacks on Black and Brown people, immigrants, Muslims, Jews, and the LGBTQ community. The road to a "Fascist USA" took a deadly turn after Trump indirectly condoned the Unite the Right rally in Charlottesville, Virginia, in which an assembly of Klansmen, "alt Knights," neo-Nazis, and white nationalist militias inspired one of their number to mow down anti-racist protesters with his car. A consensus took hold that Trump's election, along with the campaign to remove Confederate monuments following the 2015 massacre of nine Black worshippers in a Charleston, South Carolina, church, had emboldened militant white supremacists. Books, articles, and blog posts linked Trump's ascendance directly to white nationalism, even reminding readers of his daddy's ties to the Klan.[1]

A fair share of liberal intellectuals and pundits set about explaining the roots of contemporary white supremacy by tracing the events in Charlottesville to the history of the Ku Klux Klan in the 1920s.[2] This is understandable. The "second Klan" enjoyed a high degree of legitimacy, and its xenophobic slogans—"America First" and "100% Americanism"—were echoed by the Trump administration. Besides, most of the recent scholarship on the Klan focuses on the 1920s, precisely because, in spite of its virulence, its values and ideology were not far from the American mainstream.[3]

But why go back to the 1920s when the militant white supremacists of current generation are either products of, or influenced by, the "third Klan" of the 1970s and 1980s? Between 1974 and 1981, Klan membership grew from about fifteen hundred to more than ten thousand. In the course of a decade, a resurgent Klan formed paramilitary units, burned crosses, organized rallies in cities such as Chicago, Washington, D.C., and Meriden, Connecticut, and prepared to patrol the U.S.-Mexico border as an auxiliary to the Immigration and Naturalization Service. Their leaders also attained enough legitimacy to enter mainstream politics and run for public office. In 1980, Tom Metzger, the "Grand Dragon" of the Ku Klux Klan, garnered enough votes to win the Democratic primary in Southern California's 43rd Congressional district. Similarly, in 1989 David Duke, former Klansman and founder of the National Association for the Advancement of White People, was elected to the Louisiana House of Representatives.

The spectacular rise of the Klan, the American Nazi Party, skinheads, and various white Christian nationalist militias opened the floodgates for a reign of terror by adherents and lone wolves targeting African Americans, Jews, and Mexican and Vietnamese immigrants. Homes, churches, synagogues, and schools across the country were firebombed. Between 1979 and 1980, two dozen Black people and two white women in interracial relationships were murdered in seven different cities. In Buffalo, New York, two Black taxi drivers were found dead with their hearts cut out, and two weeks later in that same city a white sniper took the lives of four African Americans. Meanwhile, between 1979 and 1981, twenty-eight children, adolescents, and adults were mysteriously murdered in Atlanta. Other murders were not so mysterious. In Mobile, Alabama, in 1981, members of the United Klans of America kidnapped, tortured, and hanged a Black teenager named Michael Donald.[4]

Why, in an effort to understand the Trump era, have the pundits, the press, even some of our finest historians ignored this crucial period of white racist violence?[5] Why do most Americans believe that such virulent expressions of white supremacy died with Jim Crow, leaving in its wake more indirect or benign forms of racism—employment and housing discrimination, a biased criminal justice system, the dismantling of affirmative action, and the like? One recent exception that has garnered significant attention is Spike Lee's Oscar-nominated *BlacKKKlansman*, based on the true story of how a Black undercover cop, Ron Stallworth, infiltrated the Klan in Colorado Springs in 1978. But Lee's film elides the fact that Stallworth also infiltrated the Klan's chief opposition, the International Committee Against Racism, a mass organization formed by the Progressive Labor Party. By transforming an undercover cop into a Black freedom fighter and presenting the police as the first line of defense against white nationalists, *BlacKKKlansman* fundamentally distorts the history of the Klan, the police, and the period.

Fortunately for us, Hilary Moore and James Tracy have written a magnificent book that not only corrects the record but helps explain the mercurial rise of white supremacist organizations in the 1970s, how the Klan was (temporarily) defeated, and why this period has been largely ignored. *No Fascist USA!* is not a history of the Klan, per se, but rather a history of anti-racist, anti-fascist resistance in the United States, from the post-1968 insurgencies through the Reagan-era counterrevolution. We learn that opposition to the Klan was militant, uncompromising, and effective, mobilizing more white people to confront violent white supremacist organizations than at any other time in history. And, contrary to popular stereotypes, the Klan was no joke. Its members were not poor, frustrated, ignorant outcasts out of step with modernity but often men and women of standing who held positions of power and authority in state institutions—police forces, prisons, jails, and local government.

No Fascist USA! radically shifts our perspective, challenging the prevailing wisdom that racist terrorism rises in response to economic downturns, because of white downward mobility, or in a vacuum created by a lack of progressive alternatives. On the contrary, the Klan's resurrection was a *reaction to* the radical insurgencies of the era: Black and Brown rebellions, struggles for gender equality and sexual freedom, the defeat of U.S. imperialism from Vietnam to Tehran—real movements for democracy and social transformation. The same can be said for the original Klan, formed in 1866 as a reaction to Emancipation and the struggle of formerly enslaved people to establish a real democracy in the South. With the military defeat of the first Klan in 1871, the Southern Bourbon Democrats reverted to the reign of terror, though it took them another three decades to crush abolition democracy and install the Jim Crow regime. And even then, Black resistance to white supremacy persisted. Indeed, the resurrection of the Klan in 1915 and its growth in the 1920s ought to be seen as a reaction to a new wave of democratic insurgencies—notably Black, immigrant, pro-labor, and feminist.

Its initial inspiration derived from a national campaign to erase the history of Reconstruction. "Colonel" William Joseph Simmons revived the Ku Klux Klan after seeing D.W. Griffith's 1915 masterwork of racist propaganda, *The Birth of a Nation*. The film was historical alchemy, turning terrorists into saviors, rapists into chivalrous protectors of white female virtue and racial purity, and courageous and visionary Black men and women into idle, irresponsible ignoramuses, rapists, jezebels, and sexually depraved mulattoes. By circulating old racial fabulations and new fictions in the service of New South capitalism and modern white supremacy, *The Birth of a Nation* attempted to obliterate all vestiges of the Black struggle for social democracy during Reconstruction. Respectable white supremacist groups such as the Ladies' Memorial Associations and the United Daughters of the Confederacy waged their own soft power campaign of building Confederate monuments throughout the region and around the nation's capital. One of the most elaborate statues, erected at Arlington cemetery in 1914, depicted an enslaved Black man marching into battle alongside his master, and a faithful "mammy" caring for her charge as the child's uniformed father heads off to fight the dreaded Yankees. In a particularly ironic twist, the myth of "mammy" was weaponized by the federal government to buttress the hard power of Jim Crow. In 1922, the U.S. Senate approved a monument dedicated to "Mammy" in Washington, D.C., just weeks before allowing a Southern filibuster to defeat an anti-lynching bill. Not surprisingly, Black leaders not only excoriated the Senate's failure to pass the bill but thoroughly rejected commemorating a stereotype. The *Chicago Defender*, a Black newspaper, proposed an alternative monument to the "White Daddy" showing an adult Black woman ("mammy") looking on helplessly as the white master assaults a small child—presumably his child with "mammy," born of rape.[6]

The truth is, neither the soft power of historical revision and erasure nor the hard power of lynch law could keep Black people down. Despite the Klan's best efforts, Black people fled the old plantations for the industrial plantations of the urban North. They founded new organizations, exercised the franchise, continued the fight for democracy, and called themselves "New Negroes." These New Negroes refused Griffith's racial and national fabulations; fought back with pickets and boycotts, speeches and editorials, scholarship and art, and outright rebellion; called on their country to get out of Haiti, the Dominican Republic, the Philippines, and Mexico; and exposed the United States for what it was—the tyranny of white supremacy masquerading as enlightened democracy.

The new Klan hoped to make America great again by purging it of un-American (read: radical) influences—Negroes, immigrants (except for those of Anglo and Scandinavian stock), Catholics, and Jews. The Klan's pursuit of severe immigration restriction was driven not only by xenophobia but by anti-communism. Immigrant workers from Europe, the Caribbean, Latin America, and Asia populated the burgeoning socialist, anarchist, and communist organizations and were often outspoken opponents of the First World War. The Second Klan emerged against a backdrop of state and federal anti-sedition laws, the Mexican Revolution, the Bolshevik Revolution, and a wave of deportations of immigrants accused of subversive activities. In January 1920 alone, some four thousand people were rounded up all over the country, held in seclusion for long periods of time, tried in secret hearings, and deported.

So we should not be surprised that the Third Klan arose at the height of insurgent movements in the United States, when the FBI's Counter-Intelligence Program (COINTELPRO) and local police red squads surveilled and jailed key leaders just as prison organizing reached its apex. According to Moore and Tracy, the catalyst for the John Brown Anti-Klan Committee (JBAKC) came from Black activists *within* the prisons, who warned that the Klan was not only growing but occupied important positions within prison administration. The call to resist the Klan galvanized white radicals on the outside who engaged in prison solidarity work. In other words, the Committee was formed not by naïve do-good liberals but by folks associated with the organized Left. Many of their principal leaders came out of cadre organizations committed to the larger project of socialist revolution and self-determination for oppressed nationalities. They saw themselves as comrades, not allies, in a life-and-death struggle to stop fascism in its tracks.

The perils of fighting the Klan were made abundantly clear on November 3, 1979, when the members of the Communist Workers Party (CWP) held an anti-Klan march at a predominantly African American housing project in Greensboro, North Carolina. As the demonstration was about to begin, a nine-car caravan pulled up carrying thirty-five armed members of the United Racist Front, an umbrella organization consisting of Klansmen and Nazis. In the space of eighty-eight seconds, they emptied more than twenty rounds of ammunition into the multiracial crowd, wounding a dozen people and killing five of the march leaders: Dr. James Waller, William Sampson, Sandra Smith, Cesar Cauce, and Dr. Michael Nathan. Three of the victims were white men, Cauce was originally a Cuban immigrant, Sandi Smith was an African American woman. All were veterans of the student anti-war and Black liberation movements, and all but Nathan were members of the Communist Workers Party. Despite the fact that a local news station captured the entire ambush on camera, two all-white juries acquitted the Klan-Nazi defendants of criminal charges in the Greensboro murders. In a civil trial in 1985, a third jury held two Greensboro police officers, the Klan–police informant, and four Klan-Nazi gunmen liable for wrongful death. The trials exposed not only the complicity of the local police but the fact that a federal agent of the Bureau Alcohol, Tobacco and Firearms, Bernard Butkovich, who was working undercover in the American Nazi Party, encouraged members to come to the demonstration armed and never informed the police or FBI of their plans. As a consequence of the civil suit, the city of Greensboro paid a paltry $351,000 to Dr. Martha Nathan, widow of Dr. Michael Nathan.

How could this be? Why, as we prepare to commemorate the fortieth anniversary of the Greensboro massacre, is this incident not part of our collective memory, our national trauma? For the same reasons that so little is known about the John Brown Anti-Klan Committee. In the political culture of the Cold War, Communists spouting "Death to the Klan" were the principal threat, not armed white supremacists. Indeed, Klan-Nazi defense in the second trial rested on the argument that they were fighting communists, and therefore their actions had no racist intent! Members of the Communist Workers Party, like their counterparts in the John Brown organization, would not play the victim or turn the other cheek. They believed in armed self-defense and famously refused to testify in the first trial out of principled opposition to a criminal justice system that targeted them.

The John Brown Anti-Klan Committee showed unfathomable courage. Their numbers were always small; unlike Antifa and other anti-fascist protesters today, they rarely outnumbered the racists. The Klan and local police could identify them by name, knew where they lived, knew what kind of cars they drove. Committee members endured potentially deadly attacks—cut brake lines, slashed tires, burglaries, rocks thrown, and even gunfire were not uncommon. Moreover, in exposing the depths of the Klan's paramilitary operations and the level of violence that members of the John Brown Anti-Klan Committee were up against, *No Fascist USA!* overturns one of the most common narratives of the era: *that the Black freedom movement's presumed shift from nonviolence to violence led to its downfall*. Instead, the 1970s and early 1980s were marked by the *unabated escalation of violence perpetrated by white supremacists*, often with tacit support or indifference from federal, state, and local law enforcement authorities. As *No Fascist USA!* demonstrates, the police and feds appeared to devote more energy and resources to surveilling and prosecuting anti-Klan activists than to corralling the Klan itself.

Members of the John Brown organization understood this all too well and, like their namesake, recognized that the resurgence of white terrorism was not a regional problem but a national one. Lest we forget, John Brown originally planned to initiate a war against slavery by dispatching guerrilla armies to raid plantations in Virginia and retreat to the hills, freeing slaves and causing havoc until the system was no longer profitable. He assumed that once an armed attack began, enslaved people would join the revolt. But by 1857–58, the U.S. Supreme Court's ruling on Dred Scott convinced Brown to strike the *federal* arsenal at Harpers Ferry instead. Why? Because the Dred Scott decision proved to Brown that while slaveholders were morally accountable for holding human beings in bondage, it was the federal government that sanctioned and sustained the institution of slavery. Slavery was a national crime, and the federal government was slavery's prime source of authority and protection. We tend to remember one line from Chief Justice Roger Taney's majority opinion: that Black people "had no rights which the white man was bound to respect." But John Brown and his crew understood that what was at stake extended beyond Black citizenship. The ruling effectively rendered the Missouri Compromise unconstitutional, opening the door to make slavery legal *everywhere in the United States.* The majority ruled that Congress could not prohibit slavery in the territories because it never had the power to govern territories, and that denying the right to own slaves violated the Fifth Amendment to the U.S. Constitution, which declared that no person can be deprived of "life, liberty, or *property* without due process of law." John Brown now understood the task ahead as a struggle to remake the country. So in 1858, in preparation for the raid on Harpers Ferry, he drafted "A Declaration of Liberty by the Representatives of the Slave Population of the United States of America" and what he called a "Provisional Constitution and Ordinance for the People of the United States." Its preamble called slavery "a most barbarous, unprovoked, and unjustifiable war of one portion of its citizens upon another portion, the only conditions of which are perpetual imprisonment and hopeless servitude or absolute extermination," and it declared the newly created body a provisional government committed to the destruction of slavery.

While the prevailing consensus has deemed John Brown's raid a failure, the attempt, more than any other event, provoked Southern secession and launched the Civil War, which ultimately ended chattel slavery. It terrified members of the white planter class who never imagined that a direct attack on slavery would involve so many white men—thus giving credence to the Southern conspiracy theory that a revolution was about to take place. The raid forced many white anti-slavery sympathizers to commit to action, demonstrating that there is no moderation on the question of slavery.

The key take-away from John Brown is also the chief lesson of this book. In 1859, a ragtag army made up of sixteen white men and five black men took on the federal government and the Southern planter class in what seemed like a foolhardy attempt to free four million Black people held in bondage. They were defeated, Brown was hanged, but just two or three years later the system swiftly began to collapse. When Black folks sang "John Brown's Body," declaring that his "truth goes marching on," they recognized that even in death his militant commitment and example continued to inspire, and perhaps more importantly, that the struggle is not over. The John Brown Anti-Klan Committee members took on the Klan, Nazis, skinheads, and a variety of fascists, as well as the federal government, and prevailed. While they did not eliminate the Klan, its membership fell dramatically and the conviction rate of Klansmen slowly began to rise. Anti-Klan activists changed the discourse, compelling juries to see Klan violence for what it was—domestic terrorism. They exposed the fact that the federal government, again, did not always stand on the side of justice, which partly explains why the John Brown Anti-Klan Committee became the FBI's target.

But they also knew that the struggle wasn't over and that the task ahead was to remake the country and the world. They continued to fight—against racism, sexism, class exploitation, and state violence, on behalf of the incarcerated and HIV/AIDS victims—for justice for all people. So, as we face the latest wave of fascist violence, sometimes behind tiki torches, other times behind a badge or a body camera, rest assured that their truth goes marching on.

AUTHORS' STATEMENTS

> "Now more than ever, we must unforget the past, as
> the very survival of ourselves and humanity depends
> on it—from an honest unforgetting of the long his-
> tory that has led us to this point, to a revaluation of
> our immediate past."
>
> —Roxanne Dunbar-Ortiz

"We have to do better." The words kept falling out of my
mouth. I was sitting on the curb waiting for my friend to arrive.
"We have to do better." I wasn't cold, but I was shaking. Earlier that day I had seen someone stabbed, and I was still in shock.
It was the summer of 2016, during the final heated months
of Donald Trump's first presidential campaign, when white
supremacists stabbed at least five people in Sacramento, California, less than a mile from where I was born. Months earlier, the Traditionalist Worker's Party and the Golden State
Skinheads—two white supremacist organizations—had been
awarded a permit to demonstrate at the grounds of the state
Capitol. Their goal was to unite their organizations and create a mass coalition to support Donald Trump and defend the
white race. This was before Charlottesville, but here too the
FBI tracked the rally and later framed the white supremacists
as victims.[7] It seemed like white nationalists were escalating
their violent actions on a weekly basis.

I grew up drinking root beer and practicing kickflips on
skateboards with my friends on the same Capitol grounds
where the white supremacists staged their rally, an event that
represented the exact opposite of all I held dear. And yet, my
decision to go to the rally wasn't clear cut. I felt critical of how

much attention went to street confrontations with white supremacists, and how little went to those who are doing the long-haul work of organizing to create a world where everyone has safety, dignity, and belonging. Slogans like "Nazis get out!" felt insufficient, and at times just as misguided as incitement to "punch a Nazi." Yet I also felt frustrated that, in my five years as an anti-racist political education trainer with commitments to build broad anti-racist movements that can win, we had very few strategies ready to confront white supremacy in the flesh. Ignoring the rally seemed like the worst option. Conflicted as I was, I chose to go because I had a group of reliable friends who were committed to keeping people safe and unwilling to concede public space to those seeking to advance a white supremacist agenda.

On the morning of June 26, 2016, approximately three hundred people arrived at the rally site early with banners bearing slogans such as "Smash Racism" and "From Olympia to Atlanta Antifa Fights Back." One hundred or more cops in full riot gear were there early, too. Hours passed without a sign of the white supremacists. As we waited, people around me passed out free food and water, while others walked the large perimeter looking for signs of the white supremacists. Then the call came. "They're here! We need people *here*!" Many of us ran to a strategic spot in attempt to create a human barrier that might prevent the white supremacists from reaching the steps of the Capitol. Within minutes the stabbings began.

Witnessing the violence filled my body with visceral, hot rage. But when a knife-wielding white supremacist stood at attention for chants of "*Sieg Heil,*" I froze. A large group of counter-protesters quickly surrounded the man and began to beat him. Horse-mounted police intervened, ushering the white supremacists into the shelter of the Capitol building, a protective maneuver that had not been offered to victims, just moments before, when the white supremacists stabbed five people.

Later that night, reflecting on all that had happened, I realized we had to do better. The next day I began contacting people who had confronted the Ku Klux Klan in the 1970s and 1980s. I needed to know what they had learned while opposing organized racism and supporting social movements that were fighting for self-determination. I reached out to my dear friend James Tracy and asked him to help make sense of this history. What lessons did they learn, and how might we apply those insights and strategies today? Asking and answering those questions together led us to write this book.

—Hilary Moore
Berlin, August 2019

I first met members of the John Brown Anti-Klan Committee in the spring of 1989, when I was a teenager in Vallejo, California. At the time, several white supremacist organizations announced that they would stage an "Aryan Woodstock" white power concert in the unincorporated land between blue-collar Vallejo and Napa's wine country. In the lead-up to the concert, I talked to a woman from the Committee who was distributing copies of the group's newspaper, *No KKK!, No Fascist USA!*. I asked her what it was all about, and in the next five minutes she effortlessly connected a critique of U.S. imperialism, advocacy for the Black Liberation struggle, and an invitation for me to join others protesting the concert.

None of these subjects was a hard sell for me. The crop of racist skinheads that had long been a part of the area were a source of annoyance at the Punk and New Wave shows my friends and I would attend. My father, a Vietnam Veteran, had unintentionally turned me into an anti-imperialist once he was able to tell me what he had witnessed in the Army. Black Liberation? I was down for that. I had worked as a janitor at an art gallery in town with a former member of the Black Panther Party who introduced me to the Panthers' Ten-Point Program and shared back-in-the day stories with me as we mopped floors.

To most of my friends, adherents of the Gospel According to the Dead Kennedys, white supremacy never made any sense. Two of my friends actually joined fascist organizations during this time. Nevertheless, when I met the woman from the John Brown group, I felt the need to declare that it seemed like the entire San Francisco activist scene only cared about Vallejo, a distressed Navy town, when the Nazi skinheads came around. Much to her credit, she actually engaged me in a serious discussion about how the far right functioned as a barrier to solving the everyday problems we faced, and thus why the right needed to be curtailed at every corner. I was convinced enough to attend a few community meetings and demonstrations. As a nerdy kid, however, I was not brave enough to attend the final rally where anti-fascists overwhelmingly outnumbered the white supremacists.

The John Brown Anti-Klan Committee was just one part of a larger movement that valiantly mobilized against the rise of racist organizations during the 1980s. I've always respected their willingness to go to the mat to oppose the reactionary and violent elements of the far right. As a result of studying them with Hilary Moore, I came to admire how the abolitionist spirit of John Brown and Harriet Tubman were honored in their organizing. At other points, I scratched my head at some the choices the organization made.

I imagine that it must have been difficult initially for the John Brown group's former members and allies to trust our requests for interviews. However, every one of them graciously shared with us their memories, analysis, politics, and sometimes their regrets as well. Most expressed that they were sharing their stories in the hope that the next generation of activists might learn from their history. I am extremely grateful to all of them for this leap of faith. As an author, I'm aware that writing history grants a great power to determine emphasis and set forth an analysis. I hope we have proven up to the task.

Since 1989, I've come to recognize the ways that racism doesn't need skinheads and Klansmen to wreak havoc and terrorize communities. It has always been alive and well in the everyday, mundane life of the United States—in planning codes, redlining, the educational system, the justice system, policing, prisons. Unlike the 1980s, there exists today a higher level of public consciousness about white supremacy, patriarchy, and power thanks to social movements like Black Lives Matter as well as sustained efforts by public intellectuals like Angela Y. Davis, bell hooks, Robin D. G. Kelley, Mumia Abu-Jamal, Keeanga-Yamahtta Taylor, and Ruth Wilson Gilmore who infuse historical understanding, political resistance, and social vision with insurgent optimism.

In the 1980s, the John Brown Anti-Klan Committee was a militant grassroots force that envisioned an entirely different state of affairs than the one we live in now—one where struggle, organizing, and education succeed in abolishing white supremacy, fascism, and the violent legacies of settler colonialism. Then, as now, it is a future worth fighting for.

—James Tracy
Oakland, August 2019

PAST AS PROLOGUE

"For one, when a white man comes to me and tells me how liberal he is, the first thing I want to know, is he a nonviolent liberal, or the other kind. I don't go for any nonviolent white liberals. If you are for me and my problems—when I say me, I mean us, our people—then you have to be willing to do as old John Brown did. And if you're not of the John Brown school of liberals, we'll get you later—later."

—Malcolm X, 1965

On August 12, 2017, tiki torches blazed across Linda Evans's television set, illuminating crowds of white nationalists gathered in Charlottesville, Virginia, for a "Unite the Right" rally. She was seeing the last moments of what began as a demonstration against city's plans to expel the statue of Robert E. Lee from a local park. Charlottesville had recently changed the park's name from "Lee Park" to "Emancipation Park." This was one incident in a long series of battles over Confederate statues in public places.[8] Outraged over the pending removal, five hundred white nationalists, many clean-cut and well-coiffed, in polo shirts and khakis, marched through the town with torches angrily chanting, "*You will not replace us! Jews will not replace us!*"

As with many others, Evans's first response to the events in Charlottesville was emotional: she felt terrified and outraged by the reality that mobs of aggressive white men were in the streets. The scene was all too familiar for Linda. In 1980, she was one of the core members of the John Brown Anti-Klan Committee, an organization that formed, in part, to fight the resurgence of the Ku Klux Klan and an assortment of other racist organizations. The events in Charlottesville, for Linda, prompted flashbacks to those frightening times. "Fire at night is what got to me the most, for them to be allowed to march like that."[9] During every effort Linda had been part of in opposing the Klan, she had witnessed authorities *protect* white supremacists, including one occasion in Austin, Texas, when racist white Marines shot at an effigy of a Black community leader. "It was just so clear," said Evans, "that what we're seeing today is a continuation, consolidation, and normalization of the white supremacy we were fighting back then."

No Fascist USA! is the story of the John Brown Anti-Klan Committee, a national network of white activists who took up the cause of combatting an emboldened white supremacist movement. That movement, energized by a friendly face in the White House—Ronald Reagan—successfully rolled back key gains of the New Deal and Civil Rights eras, and unleashed a new wave of racist violence in the United States. From 1977 to 1992, the Committee established more than a dozen chapters nationwide. Its mission was to counter the advance of the far right and to support a host of revolutionary groups, particularly those organized by Black and Brown revolutionaries.

This history provides a glimpse into the challenges that anti-Klan activists faced in an era before the internet made instantaneous critique and flash organizing possible. Despite the different political contexts, many of the strategic questions that anti-racist organizers faced then are equally relevant today: Are there ways of confronting racists and fascists that do not provide them with new opportunities to spread their message? How are alliances and solidarity best strengthened given the shifting and complex relationships between primarily white organizations and organizations of color? How do activists prepare for possibilities of violence and self-defense against groups that always seem eager for bloody battles? Can forces within the state be trusted to be allies in the fight against white supremacy?

Grounded in the idea that white supremacy must be countered and abolished, members of John Brown mounted fierce responses to the Ku Klux Klan when they rallied in the 1970s and 1980s. In their 1980 publication The Dividing Line of the 80's: Take a Stand Against the Klan, the Committee described the threat:

> The Klan, in Tupelo, Mississippi, elsewhere in the South, in northern cities, in prisons and the armed forces, is in open, armed conflict with the Black Liberation Struggle. The Klan, along with I.N.S., has become the border control of the Mexican/U.S. border; it is one of the major armed forces against Mexicano/Chicano peoples.[10]

In addition to tracking the Klan's activities, the Committee sought to expose connections between racist groups and law enforcement authorities. Ahmed Obafemi, a Black Nationalist activist, coined the name of what would become John Brown's well-known campaign, "Blue by Day, White by Night." Here, they discussed the role of police and prisons, and the names of Klan members who were working in law enforcement agencies or held government positions, giving them access to official influence and power. "In 1976," read *The Dividing Line*, "Earl Schoonmaker, the head reading teacher at Eastern (N.Y.) State Prison, was exposed as the Grand Dragon of the Independent Northern Klan. A Klavern of at least 35 was forced out into the open by the struggle of Black and Latino incarcerated people."[11] Given their dedication to outing state authorities' ties to white supremacist groups, the Committee refrained from requesting police protection while protesting the Klan, and did not lobby local governments to "Ban the Klan." This also

The Dividing Line of the 80's:

TAKE A STAND AGAINST THE KLAN

a pamphlet on the fight
against white supremacy
by the John Brown
Anti-Klan Committee

rested on their belief that the state organizes its power through white supremacy. In other words, the role of the police in U.S. society often functions in a manner that is similar to the role of the Klan.

A key part of the Committee's political analysis was to examine how the state contributed to the far right's resurgence, and how they worked in an interlocking fashion. *The Dividing Line*, for example, described instances in which state authorities and elected officials directly financed violent far-right organizations ("J.B. Stoner, chairman of the National States Rights Party, under the direction of the Birmingham Police, led a bombing of a Birmingham church in 1958 and was paid $2,000 by police"), supported the Klan in its organizing efforts ("U.S. Senator Robert Byrd was a high-ranking Klan recruiting organizer"), and engaged in violent crimes ("Rowe [an FBI agent in the Klan], with the explicit approval of the FBI, participated in the murder of four black children in the bombing of a Birmingham church, the murder of Viola Liuzzo [a white civil rights worker], and Leroy Moton [a Black man]"). Building on this history, the Committee also linked the threat posed to society by the Klan with the threat posed by the state, particularly the impunity with which it covertly targeted, monitored, and disrupted political groups.[12]

John Brown Anti-Klan Committee co-founder Susan Rosenberg described what set them apart from many of their anti-Klan colleagues of the day. "We believed that the KKK was not the 'lunatic fringe' of the racist movement but rather the vanguard of an enormous popular current of white racist sentiment. And we believed that without an active anti-racist movement to both oppose the racists and support Black-led efforts, we could not have a radical or progressive movement in the United States."[13]

A distinguishing characteristic of the John Brown group was its alignment with organizations fighting for self-determination. When Imari Obadele, a leader within the Republic of New Afrika, wrote that the "biggest threat comes from the white civilian armies, the Ku Klux Klan and those other semi-official forces who for one hundred years have done the dirty work of military oppression in the South,"[14] the Committee refined its role, declaring:

> The John Brown Anti-Klan Committee is a national organization that fights the racist violence of the KKK and Nazis, and their underlying cause, the system of white supremacy. We take our name from John Brown, the 19th Century white abolitionist who gave his life fighting against slavery and white supremacy. In the spirit of John Brown, we fight racism, build solidarity with the Black Liberation Movement, and support all struggles for human rights and self-determination.[15]

How to mobilize white people to fulfill that task was the central tactical question that animated the group. In the process, they encouraged white people to assume risks usually expected of people of color, including the risk of physical harm and ostracism. The group insisted that it was white people's responsibility to *get in the way of* the threats posed by white supremacists. This approach was intended to undermine the age-old norms of white silence, complicity, and active participation in racialized intimidation, coercion, and violence. In this sense, the Committee continued the work of the white civil rights organizers who had traveled to the South just two decades before. But the Committee's members differed from these predecessors because they did not view nonviolence as the only strategic option against white supremacy. They also diverged from much of the previous era's radical optimism by rejecting the idea that long-lasting change would come from either a reformed political system or a unifying conversion to a socialist system.

Following cues set by their allies, Republic of New Afrika, they envisioned that political liberation would involve the revolutionary dissolution of the United States and the subsequent formation of distinct "New Boundaries." This sentiment was in the ether at the time, reverberating in anti-imperialist struggles and supported by the larger cultural milieu of resistance around the world. Many adherents of this view supported a "New Afrika" being formed from the Southern slavocracy states with a Black majority: Georgia, Louisiana, South Carolina, Alabama, and Mississippi. The persistence of such calls was, in part, a reaction to several conditions. One was the intensification of racist terror—including the mysterious murders of two dozen Black children in Atlanta, and the general uptick in the killings of Black people across the United States during the period.[16]

The group also embraced the principle of *leadership from the oppressed*. This meant following the political lead of those most targeted by white supremacists and those who organized to counter them. For the John Brown group, supporting the strategies of those on the frontlines of the fight was part and parcel of the work of combatting racism. Its members made swift and bold moves to address these issues, conscious of their advantages as white people.

THE KLAN REINVENTS ITSELF

The Committee's work was sharpened by the Klan's campaign to rebrand itself. In 1865, the Klan forged an image of itself as protector of the lost Confederacy, a role practiced through violent opposition to the post-war period of social, economic, and government reorganization in the United States known as the Reconstruction Era. From 1863 to 1877, Black communities mobilized to win U.S. citizenship (13th Amendment), protection under the law (14th Amendment), voting rights (15th Amendment), and the right to hold political office. In response to the sudden emergence of Black citizenship, rights, and political power, the Klan formed, and used terrorist violence such as floggings, mutilations, lynchings, shootings, and arson, all in an effort to regain white control of state and federal governments.[17] Of the 265 Black politicians elected to office during this period, thirty-five were murdered by the Klan and other white supremacist organizations.[18] Most of these atrocities, which traumatized Black people throughout the country, were largely tolerated by state authorities and federal officials, as that effort reconsolidated state power through white people.[19]

Once state-sponsored racial segregation was codified in the 1896 Supreme Court decision of *Plessy v. Ferguson*, the Klan went into a lull, only to rekindle through a wave of suspicion and antipathy toward immigrants after World War I. Here, the Klan's violent intolerance widened from Black people to "aliens, idlers, union leaders . . . Asians, immigrants, bootleggers, dope, graft, night clubs, road houses, violation of the sabbath, sex, pre- and extra-marital escapades and scandalous behavior."[20] This "Second Wave" of the Klan was the largest, with the organization swelling to somewhere between four to six million members in the United States during the 1920s. Hiring a public relations team, the Klan became a normalized feature of American life, with a semi-professional baseball team, 150 newspapers, and two radio stations. It achieved significant influence in U.S. political life with sixteen senators, eleven state governors, sixty members of Congress, and numerous state municipal elections running openly as Klansmen.[21] In fact, the Klan had become such a deeply embedded feature of U.S. politics that a proposal made at the 1924 Democratic National Convention to oppose the Klan *lost* by one vote.[22]

Few images capture the Klan at its peak better than photographs taken on August 8, 1925, showing 40,000 Klansmen marching down Pennsylvania Avenue in Washington, D.C., demanding stricter laws against immigrants, even though a draconian one had been passed just a year prior.[23] Klan Grand Wizard H.W. Evans, who led the march, had relocated the

KKK Parade, Washington D.C., August 8, 1925. Photograph by Herbert A. French. *Library of Congress Prints and Photographs Division.*

national offices to Washington two years prior in order to have a greater influence on Congress.

In the 1960s, the so-called "Third Wave" of the Klan worked hard to deploy the trope that they were not *against* Black people, but rather *for* white people, white heritage, and white rights.[24] This rebranding allowed the Klan to advance allegations of "reverse racism"—that gains made by Black people would come at the expense of white people. As a result of this view, the Klan in this period pushed the idea that if Black people had a National Association for the Advancement of *Colored* People looking after their interests, then white people should have a National Association for the Advancement of *White* People looking after *their* interests. The Klan made few actual amendments to its original platform. It adapted its communications strategy in an attempt to remain appealing to whites in

DEATH TO THE KLAN!

NEWSLETTER OF THE JOHN BROWN ANTI-KLAN COMMITTEE
P.O. Box 406, Stuyvesant Station
New York, NY 10009

25¢

Vol.1 No.3   **Jan./Feb. 1980**

The Ku Klux Klan: "UP SOUTH"

When Black people refer to the North as "up South," they are pointing to the true nature of white supremacy in the US: not a regional defect of the South, but the daily reality faced everywhere by Black people.

Today, in the face of heightening struggle by the Black nation for land, independence and freedom, US imperialism is promoting the Klan as a prime way to mobilize every sector of the white oppressor nation to fight the advances of the Black liberation struggle.

Youth learns to shoot at 47-acre Klan youth camp near Birmingham. "We want to make them racists," Klansman says.

The Klan originated in the South but moved North when Black people were forced off the land in the South and into the Northern urban centers. The massive growth of the Klan in New York State in the early 20's, for example, followed the forced migration of thousands of Black people into New York and other Northern areas after World War I.

Black people are fighting for human rights and liberation in every part of this country. A major part of the Black liberation struggle is the struggle for human rights being waged in every major urban center in the country. Northern cities have become a focus in the Klan's reactionary campaign to mobilize white people to fight for white supremacy and empire.

Three key aspects of the Klan's national strategy for organizing in the North are: organizing white youth particularly in high schools, to build the armed forces of white supremacy; functioning within the state apparatus as cops and prison guards, and building mass support for killer cops and police terror against Third World people; and building a broad

continued on page

the transformed cultural context of the post–Civil Rights era. It was also the era when the Klan and similar organizations concentrated on infiltrating the military as a method of building power. In Vietnam, Klan-affiliated soldiers burned crosses to celebrate the assassination of Martin Luther King Jr. In

1979, heavily armed Klan members held a recruiting rally outside an Army base in Virginia Beach.[25]

PART OF THE MOVEMENT

The John Brown Anti-Klan Committee used its regular newspaper, *Death to the Klan!*, to connect people and communities fighting racism. This helped to develop momentum and links that contributed to the decentralized Anti-Racist Action networks from 1987 to the early 2000s. From beginning to end, the Committee emphasized the importance of maintaining strong alliances with people who had gone to prison for their political actions. They did so by helping them maintain active connections to social movements.

We began writing this book at a time when racist and fascist networks are once again more visible and on the rise at home and abroad. In order to find effective strategies to out-organize the proponents of white supremacy, it is important to understand the historical forces at play and how they echo through time. The Committee was one of many anti-Klan organizations in motion during the 1980s. Their militant stand called into question many of the assumptions held by others equally committed to the abolition of racism and fascism in the United States. Rather than focusing on the personalities of individual racists, they saw white supremacy as the common element in all the various political, social, legal, and cultural legacies of settler-colonialism. Their 1980 Principles of Unity outlined their beliefs in this regard:

> The Klan and organized white supremacy are a major way the US has always oppressed Third World people within its borders. White supremacy has been a part of every counter-insurgency terror plan that the US has developed. The struggle to free the land of the Black nation has been a fierce life-and-death struggle of Black people for 400 years. The Black nation will

win its freedom. The freeing of the land will shake the very foundations of US society; the freeing of the land will defeat white supremacy.[26]

While there are plenty of parallels with our contemporary situation, there are some key differences. Many members of today's far right are media savvy and far more capable than their predecessors of assuming a kind of mainstream respectability. The tools of the internet and social media allow much broader platforms than ever before. On the surface, battles over the removal of Confederate symbols, like those that animated Charlottesville, can seem trivial. However, such incidents are often skillfully exploited as "breakout moments" where white nationalists attempt to energize their networks and propagate their messages to new constituencies. In Charlottesville, one person told reporters, "We are simply just white people that love our heritage, our culture, and our European identity."[27] The conflicts playing out today over flags, names, symbols, and historical markers are clearly part of deeper social struggles over competing narratives of U.S. history, their meanings, and their implications for the future.

Today's far-right networks include many middle-class and wealthy participants, and their coalitions are complex. Neo-Nazi groups (Traditionalist Workers Party, Vanguard America, National Socialist Movement), followers of web-based far-right platforms (The Daily Stormer, National Policy Institute, Nationalist Front), white supremacist groups (Ku Klux Klan, Fraternal Order of Alt-Knights, Identity Evropa), and various armed militia groups (Oath Keepers, 3 Percenters, Virginia Minutemen Militia, Light Foot Militia)[28] are often able to subordinate their differences in the interest of building a unified movement.

Today's anti-racist and anti-fascist organizers face the same challenges as their political ancestors in terms of building and maintaining diverse coalitions. Typically, those willing to confront white supremacists in the streets include students, clergy, and local community members. In Charlottesville, national organizations such as the broad, chapter-based Showing Up for Racial Justice, and Redneck Revolt, which advocates armed self-defense, worked to find common ground on the frontlines. Strategies to confront white nationalists are mixed. For instance, some groups in Charlottesville were determined to remain nonviolent under any circumstance, and sang songs like "This Little Light of Mine" to counter white nationalists' chants of the "Our Blood, Our Soil!"[29] Others came prepared to defend themselves in the event that they or other counter-protesters were attacked, and arrived equipped with face-masks, first-aid plans, and shields.

The confrontations in Charlottesville ripped open many of the tensions simmering just under the surface of the anti-racist coalitions. Internet pundits and media commentators suggested that the violence could have been avoided had counter-protesters remained peaceful or chosen to not directly confront the racists. Professor and theologian Cornel West, a well-known adherent of nonviolence who was present in Charlottesville, had a very different take: "Those twenty of us who were standing, many of them clergy, we would have been crushed like cockroaches if it were not for the anarchists and the anti-fascists who approached, over 300, 350 anti-fascists. We just had twenty. And we're singing 'This Little light of Mine,' you know what I mean?"[30]

The role of the police comes into question. In Charlottesville, the police stationed around the corner did nothing to prevent white nationalists from using sticks to severely beat DeAndre Harris, a twenty-year-old Black man, in a parking garage. As the police "stood to the side and did not try to prevent" skirmishes, a white supremacist drove his car into a crowd of anti-fascists, injuring nineteen people and killing Heather Heyer. [31] President Donald Trump weighed in on the violence by saying, "I think there is blame on both sides."

In addition to the president, plenty of news outlets were also unwilling to pick sides. Adam Johnson, an analyst with the nonprofit watchdog group Fairness and Accuracy in Reporting, studied six national newspapers—the *Wall Street Journal*, *New York Times*, *USA Today*, *Los Angeles Times*, *San Jose Mercury News*, and *Washington Post*—in the month following Charlottesville. According to Johnson's report, these papers "published 28 op-eds or editorials condemning the anti-fascist movement known as antifa, or calling on politicians to do so, and 27 condemning neo-Nazis and white supremacists, or calling on politicians—namely Donald Trump—to do so."[32] Johnson's study concluded that while most "both sides" columns added a qualifier clarifying that there was no moral equivalency between antifa and neo-Nazis, this framing could not help but imply that there was. And a few explicitly argued, yes, anti-fascism was just as bad as fascism.[33]

When alt-right leaders spread racist messages at college campuses nationwide, those who opposed them often argued bitterly against each other over tactics and strategy. What role should militancy play when confronting the far right? Should those who espouse a rhetoric of racial subjugation and genocide be given platforms to spread their views and enlist new recruits? To what degree are the state and commercial media complicit in spreading the messages of the far right?

These are old questions that harken back to another time when the far right was on the march in the United States—the 1980s. Then, as now, far-right aggression was emboldened by a friend in the Oval Office. And during Reagan's time, the Klan was not the only racist organization on the scene either. The Aryan Nation's recruitment efforts targeted those influenced by Christian Identity teachings and the view that a race war was imminent. The White Aryan Resistance cleverly operated within youth culture in a concerted effort to expand its ranks with young people. The National Association for the Advancement of White People used a polite middle-class veneer in an attempt to make notions of white supremacy appear more approachable. The era leading up to Reagan's election saw increased collaboration between traditional patriotic racist organizations such as the Klan, and neo-Nazi groups advocating armed revolution against the U.S. government. This resulted in the "Nazification of the Klan," the formation of the "United Racist Front," and increased outbreaks of violence such as the Greensboro massacre that took place on November 3, 1979.

Fascist movements have played a role in U.S. politics since the 1930s. In *Right Wing Populism in America*, Chip Berlet and Matthew N. Lyons describe fascist activities as building "national, racial, or cultural unity and collective rebirth while seeking to purge imagined enemies."[34] While most fascist organizations have not had the direct access to state power that other right-wing groups have historically enjoyed, they still have played a pivotal role in influencing U.S. politics. Even when such organizations have been in a lull, their fascist tactics, cultural cues, and ideology have been able to influence forces across the political spectrum, including dominant discourses.

The call to uphold the rights of white people was notably popularized by Klansman David Duke in the attempt to rebrand the Klan's image in the late 1970s. In his revival of the National Association for the Advancement of White People, Duke gave the Klan's agenda a new face. He described his group as "primarily a white rights lobby organization, a racialist movement, mainly middle-class people."[35] This preceded the U.S. Supreme Court's decision in *Regents of the University of California v. Bakke*, which codified a precedent for "reverse racism."[36] This marked a shift toward retrenchment in the courts, and created alliance-building opportunities between street-based reactionaries and mainstream politicians.

Today's white supremacist networks build upon the rhetorical foundation laid by Duke. A 2017 report by Daniel Kreiss and Kelsey Mason in the *Washington Post* argued that the right reinforces racial affiliation as a basis for political power. Inequality, in the white nationalist imagination, has little to do with economics or the distribution of rights and resources. As Duke did, today's far right argues that white pride does not equal white supremacy. This allows proponents to sideline discussions of structural inequalities and trumpet the idea that people naturally prefer the company of their own group. Kreiss and Mason argue that, despite the fact that, "the alt-right seemingly eschews white supremacist language, at least in some public forums, to broaden the movement's appeal, its racially pure vision of a white America is as racist, exclusionary and anti-democratic as that of the segregationist 'authoritarian enclaves' of the Jim Crow era."[37]

CONTESTED HISTORIES

No Fascist USA! is a collection of stories from the underexplored history of anti-fascist activity in the United States. The book follows the formation of the John Brown Anti-Klan Committee, its dedication to movements for self-determination, and its confrontations with organized white supremacy in the streets and within the state. Chapter One traces the deep shifts in the political terrain of the radical left in the United States from the 1960s to the 1980s. It begins in New York with political prisoner support networks and the John Brown Book Club, and examines the impact of Black Liberation Army member Assata Shakur's escape from prison and the Greensboro massacre. Chapter Two explains how Reagan's election gave the green light for racist vigilante mobilizations and raised the stakes in the politics of confrontation for the Committee and groups across the country. Chapter Three maps the Committee's place in relationship to the larger anti-Klan movement. Chapter Four explores the evolution of the organization's approach by examining the deployment of cultural politics from both the left and right. Chapter Five traces the paths that key activists took after the dissolution of the Committee. Chapter Six offers lessons for continuing the fight against organized and structural white supremacy today.

Narratives about any part of dissident political history of the United States will always be contested. This is especially the case when such narratives affirm efforts to sabotage white supremacy or to confront empire, or do not conform to fixed notions of nonviolence. There are many worthy books about the political family from which the Committee sprung. The best of the bunch tend to avoid the one-dimensional portrayals of activists either as sainted revolutionaries or as misguided and dangerous insurgents. We have attempted to live up to their examples. If any insight on this history is to be successful, it must explore the real-world motivations, politics, assessments, and context of the people it examines. This has pushed us to rely on interviews with veterans of the Committee and to grapple with their contributions and failures. Any direct quote from a member or their associates represents the viewpoint of the speaker, not that of all of the former members. It also caused us to examine the gaps between what activist organizations like the John Brown Anti-Klan Committee thought would come of their actions and what eventually transpired. We walked away from our long conversations with them in awe of their courage, appreciative of their theoretical work, and sometimes perplexed by their strategic choices.

Researching this history was surprisingly easy in terms of gathering archival materials. Those involved wrote extensively and debated publicly, making their case in published statements, graphic flyers, and booklets. Many of the people we interviewed who were in the Committee, or close to it, have continued to organize.

The materials we used to research this history all have strengths and biases. We studied the Committee's own newspapers to understand its positions, campaigns, and organizational evolution. We conducted more than four dozen interviews, many with former Committee members, some with those who worked with them, and some with those who were critical of the group's approach. We examined commercial newspaper coverage of major events to which the Committee was responding. We read declassified FBI documents, including accounts from undercover agents. We scoured toolkits generated by a variety of organizations within the anti-Klan movement of time.

Throughout this book, we have attempted to define words and terminology close to the way radical activists in the 1970s and 1980s did. The meanings of words change over time as they are tested through debate and social struggle. No one definition of any of these terms was ever universally accepted. We define white supremacy as a system that delivers economic and social advantages to white people at the expense of people of color. This system is multi-layered and includes practices and advantages delivered to those who do not personally subscribe to ideas of racial superiority. The particular type of white supremacy discussed in this book is that propagated by the far right—those who actively organize and promote racial subjugation. While those of the far right always keep the option of violence on the table, they also incorporate other tactics, electoral and otherwise, to advance their agenda. Conversely, anti-racism is shorthand for the political project of undermining or eliminating both individual racism and systemic white supremacy. Dr. Ruth Wilson Gilmore's description of racism is particularly useful in expanding the endgame of systemic white supremacy: "Racism, specifically, is the state-sanctioned or extralegal production and exploitation of group-differentiated vulnerability to premature death."[38]

Any definition of fascism is bound to be incomplete. A good start is offered by Matthew N. Lyons: "Fascism is a revolutionary form of right-wing populism, inspired by a totalitarian vision of collective rebirth, that challenges capitalist political and cultural power while promoting economic and social hierarchy."[39] We add that the social hierarchy mentioned here typically includes politics that embrace the genocide and/or intolerance of groups based on their ethnicity or religious background. In academic circles, the racial aspect of fascism is often debated, with some positing that fascism doesn't need to be racist in order to be fascist. That debate can be held elsewhere. For the purposes of this study, we could not find a single fascist organization active in the United States during the 1980s that did not embrace genocide and expulsion. We also point to the value of understanding fascism adjectivally, rather than as a noun, to help understand its adaptive nature. In other words, an arguably democratic government may display fascistic behavior without being considered a totalitarian government.

The 1980s also saw what the Committee described as the "Nazification of the Klan"—a process by which sectors of the white supremacist movement jettisoned notions of working within the United States system and committed themselves to the overthrow of the government. In this book, the terms racism and fascism can seem to be used interchangeably, especially when taken from a movement publication or in a direct quote from a participant.

Throughout, we hear activists refer to "the state" and denounce "state violence." We think of the state as the sum total of the dominant legal, social, and cultural institutions. By this definition, state violence is violence carried out or implicitly sanctioned by these institutions. As we will read, the concept of state violence is often complicated by implicit or explicit collaboration with or tolerance of non-state violence. For example, the line between state and non-state racists is easily blurred when law enforcement does little to protect communities of colors from Klan-like organizations, or when elected officials appear to signal tolerance of such actors.

Closely related to this is the concept of imperialism, the process of a nation or state extending domination over another. As we will explore, fighting imperialism was a core part of the John Brown Anti-Klan Committee's ethical and political mission. The group believed that descendants of colonized people living within the United States belonged to distinct nations within nations. This meant that national liberation and self-determination were the main solutions to imperialism here and abroad. Self-determination in the traditional sense refers to the right of a people to determine their own future and allegiances free of outside interference from a colonial or occupying force. During the time period covered in this book, it also describes the right of oppressed people (or nations) to separate from the larger governments and establish new sovereign nations.

Given the clear rise of white nationalism today, parallels to the resurgence of organized racism experienced during the Reagan years are chilling. We hope that readers with anti-racist commitments will draw their own conclusions after looking at the projects and perspectives of those who were willing to lay on the line almost everything—even their own freedom—in the service of abolishing white supremacy.

ONE

ONE LONG REIGN OF TERROR

"Settle your quarrels, come together, understand the reality of our situation, understand that fascism is already here, that people are already dying who could be saved, that generations more will live poor, butchered half-lives if you fail to act. Do what must be done, discover your humanity and your love in revolution."

—George Jackson

Harsh endings punctuated 1977. Elvis Presley performed his last concert, then died unceremoniously from drug-induced cardiac failure on his bathroom floor. Apartheid activist and political leader in South Africa Steve Biko was killed in police custody, a death attributed to massive brain injury. And world-renowned Brazilian soccer star Pelé played his final game. Abrupt beginnings and fantastic distractions filled the holes. Jimmy Carter was inaugurated as the thirty-ninth president of the United States. *Rocky* won the Academy Award for best picture. The Atari 2600 gaming system made its debut. And legendary English punk band The Clash released its self-titled first album. While the coy hijinks and serial misunderstandings of Suzanne Summer and John Ritter in the sitcom *Three's Company* enveloped American pop culture, a lesser known dramatic saga was unfolding.

On June 1, 1977, Khali Siwatu-Hodari, a Black man incarcerated at the Eastern Correctional Facility in Napanoch, New

York, wrote an open letter to plea for support. The Ku Klux Klan was infiltrating prisons in the region, with large numbers of Klansmen holding jobs as guards and prison teachers.

An Open Letter:

On behalf of myself and the men at Eastern Correctional Facility, and all prisoners throughout the state of New York, I issue this open letter as an appeal for support. I am calling on all individuals and groups, and on the press, to support and join our fight against the Ku Klux Klan and other forms of organized racism in New York State. The Klan is a growing force in this country, as well as in the prisons, and it will take a concerted, conscious effort to expose and root it out.

For years we have waged a struggle against the Klan, even while as many as 60 members and sympathizers patrolled outside our cells. We thought we were alone. But now it is clear that the Klan is recruiting from Buffalo to New York City, in the high schools of Ulster and Sullivan Counties, through civic associations, and school boards, in government and openly boasting about their racism in the press.

A massive offensive must be mounted.

Historically, the Klan has operated in secrecy. Two years ago, men at Eastern broke the clandestine organizing of guards and teachers in the prison by exposing none other than the Grand Dragon of the state, Earl Schoonmaker, who was passing out white supremacist literature among white prisoners. State authorities have done little to rid us of this degenerate element, thereby condoning Klan violence against the prisoners. The Klan has used the publicity generated by our exposure to promote its new "nonviolent" image and initiate new recruitment campaigns, continuing to preach its vicious hatred of Black and other Third World peoples.

State authorities use the Klan's new image to justify their inaction. In the meantime, Klan organizing in this very prison and others is on the rise and reported in detail in newspapers and magazines. The Inspector General has investigated our charges, and a report is now being suppressed by the state government. We can no longer rely at all on the state of New York to carry out even the most minimal defense of our rights.

Therefore, we have taken two courses of action. First of all, we have initiated two federal lawsuits against the Klan, charging harassment and abuse of Black and other Third World prisoners. These suits charge guards as well as officials and give us the power to force the state to reveal what we prisoners already know about the Klan. These suits will be heard in Federal Court in New York City and must be supported. Secondly, we have worked on compiling this press packet, with the aid of outside supporters, to bring the word to the public in as much detail as possible.

We ask that you show your solidarity with our struggle against the Klan by coming out to support the suits this summer, and by using this material to continue to investigate Klan activity all over the state. You, the concerned people and press, are our only hope of broadening the campaign we began here in the prisons three years ago. We will continue to fight the Klan in every way possible here, but the power of a united force, fighting inside and outside against the Klan is our hope of a total victory.

Unite to Smash the Klan!

Khali
Khali Siwatu-Hodari
(nee Frank Abney)

Siwatu-Hodari's letter coincided with a resurgence of the Klan that followed a long period of decline after peaking out in the 1920s.[40] Far from being solely a Southern problem, the Klan wreaked havoc across the United States, including in the Northeast. Building slowly, the Klan infiltrated police departments, prisons, and the military. For incarcerated people, this led to a constant state of siege, harassment, intimidation, and violence.[41] In 1974, a brutal beating of an incarcerated Puerto Rican man at Napanoch, New York, led others incarcerated to establish the first chapter of the National Association for the Advancement of Colored People (NAACP) behind bars.

Prison guards' harassment of the incarcerated surged along with increased efforts to sever connections to their outside support. A white woman named Nancy Loori gave up her position as director of volunteer services at Napanoch after receiving death threats. People on the inside contacted outside supporters, alerting them that Klan members were employed by the New York State Department of Corrections. The Klansmen were attempting to prevent incarcerated Black people from utilizing recently established educational programs. Later in 1977, the New York *Daily News* conducted an investigation into allegations that the Klan staged a rally on land owned by a correctional officer. But this was not exactly breaking news. Since 1974, and consistently throughout the rest of the decade, the New York *Daily News* exposed not only extensive Klan infiltration and recruitment efforts within Napanoch prison, but incidents in which such infiltrators attacked incarcerated Black people, including firebombing their cells. Reporter Brian Kates observed the growth of the Klan in the North: "Nowhere has their influence been greater than in prisons. In New York alone, Klan units have gained a stronghold among both guards and incarcerated people at correctional facilities in Napanoch, Walkill, and Attica."[42]

Shortly before Siwatu-Hodari sent his letter, another major incident publicly revealed the Klan's activity within state institutions. This time, Klan activity was exposed inside California's Marine Corps Base Camp Pendleton. It was well known that the Klan had a chapter operating on the base. Numerous active-duty white Marines wore KKK symbols, posted threatening flyers in common areas, and carried large knives in order to intimidate Black Marines.[43] It was only when long-simmering racial tensions erupted into violence that the situation became news. Although an investigation uncovered that a group of sixteen Klan members on the base were armed with a .357 magnum revolver, clubs, knives, and KKK paraphernalia, it was thirteen Black Marines who were charged with assault after barging into a room and attacking those inside thought to be holding a Klan meeting. The actual KKK meeting was being held in the room next door.

Witnesses testified that Marine Klan members regularly distributed recruiting materials and emblazoned the words "nigger sticker" on their knives. The American Civil Liberties Union represented the Klan in court, prompting the resignation of thirty-five people. Finally, the Marines arrested and transferred one Klan member, Corporal Daniel Bailey, in a last-ditch effort to quell the racial tensions. The events at Camp Pendleton intensified anxieties that the Klan, and other white supremacist groups, were infiltrating the armed forces in preparation for an impending race war.[44] This incident contributed to the sense that the Klan, while increasingly marketing itself as a nonviolent cultural institution, was still a paramilitary vigilante group that was allowed to operate within the shadow of state institutions.

Around this time, Judy Gumbo and Stew Albert, two veteran activists living in upstate New York, received Khali Siwatu-Hodari's letter. Working to bring young white radicals into support organizing for incarcerated people, Judy used her position as a professor at State University New York at New Paltz to build contacts. Together with formerly incarcerated people who were now students, they formed the Inside-Outside

Prison Coalition, a campus-based group that leveraged university resources to support people incarcerated for their political actions. The group produced flyers about the plight of political prisoners, organized fundraisers, and screened films about state surveillance, the targeting of activist groups, and the rebellion at Attica State Prison. They also visited incarcerated people during frequent trips to Naponach and other New York state prisons. New Paltz students on parole were the first to introduce outside activists to Siwatu-Hodari, a member of the Black Panther Party and president of the NAACP chapter in the Napanoch prison. These connections were instrumental in creating the conditions for the founding of the John Brown Anti-Klan Committee. For instance, Bob Boyle, originally from New York City, was an early member of the Inside-Outside Prison Coalition. He was studying at New Paltz and worked on political prisoner cases through the National Lawyers Guild.

Prison support work in upstate New York began mingling more intentionally with the work in New York City. It wasn't long before Boyle connected with Lisa Roth, a New Yorker who had worked in the Student Nonviolent Coordinating Committee at her high school and later the Students for a Democratic Society. Roth helped form the group Friends of Assata and Sundiata,[45] which was at the forefront of radical organizing. She recalled how, at this time in the late 1970s, the movement was forced to grapple with the realities of imprisoned comrades. "By the early to mid-seventies many former members of the Black Panther Party were in prison throughout New York. So many of us who got our start doing anti-racist support work for the Black Panthers ended up doing support work for incarcerated people."

Even the most committed activists had trouble understanding the implications of Siwatu-Hodari's letter. Could staff throughout the New York prison system be members of the Ku Klux Klan? They were skeptical. Roth admitted, "Our initial response was that the prisoners meant that the guards were really, really racist. They couldn't possibly mean that they were members of the Klan. But they struggled with us and urged us to research the situation." Siwatu-Hodari's letter made clear that prison support activities such as running errands for people inside were not an adequate response to the threats posed by the Klan. "We were pushed to respond," remarked Pam Fadem, a founding member of the Committee, "The Klan was burning crosses *in* the prisons, beating people. We were pushed to respond by Black leadership."

The support network in New York City was taking off around the same time. To explore how best to respond to the fact that so many leaders were imprisoned, Pam Fadem, Lisa Roth, and Alan Berkman formed the John Brown Book Club, a study group that met in Roth's living room. The commingling of the Inside Outside Coalition and the Book Club gave rise to the official formation of the John Brown Anti-Klan Committee.

"Our main strategy was to bring white people into contact with the Black revolution and allow them to be changed by it the way we had been," explained Laura Whitehorn, who joined the group after it formed. All of the founding members had participated in the early Civil Rights and Black Power movements through organizations such as the Congress of Racial Equality and the Student Nonviolent Coordinating Committee. The group decided to bring these threads together—political prisoner support, anti-Klan work, and rigorous study of liberation movements. The choice of John Brown as a namesake struck a defiant pose. For them, it signaled that the era's liberal white agenda fell far short of the work that needed to be done to abolish white supremacy.

Throughout the history of the Black Freedom movement, the reliability of white allies was constantly tested. An early emblematic rift was the controversy at the 1964 Democratic National Convention in Atlantic City, New Jersey. Civil Rights organizer Fannie Lou Hamer brought sixty Mississippi

Fannie Lou Hamer, Mississippi Freedom Democratic Party delegate, at the Democratic National Convention, Atlantic City, New Jersey, August 1964. Photograph by Warren K. Leffler. *Library of Congress Prints and Photographs Division.*

Freedom Democratic Party (MFDP) activists to contest the seating of their state's Jim Crow delegates to the convention. The all-white Credential Committee yielded a mere two at-large, non-voting seats while keeping sixty-eight other old-guard delegates in their positions.[46]

This drove home a sense that the government, established political parties, and many white allies would be unreliable—and if pushed, hostile—to the goals of Black Freedom movement. The MFDP refused the deal and walked away.[47] Writing from solitary confinement in 1963, Martin Luther King Jr. expressed his frustration with moderate white clergy who denounced his nonviolent direct-action tactics. King wrote: "I must confess that over the past few years I have been gravely disappointed with the white moderate. I have almost reached the regrettable conclusion that the Negro's great stumbling block in his stride toward freedom is not the White Citizen's Councilor or the Ku Klux Klanner, but the white moderate."[48]

In this context, adopting the name John Brown intended to indicate the lengths the group was willing to go to in order to abolish white supremacy. In 1859, Brown led a group of twenty-one people in a raid on Harpers Ferry federal arsenal in Virginia. Brown's goal was to seize weapons and catalyze an abolitionist war against white enslavers. The U.S. Marines, led by soon-to-be Confederate commander Robert E. Lee, defeated Brown's militia. In his last speech before being executed, Brown appeared to be at peace with his decisions: "Now, if it is deemed necessary that I should forfeit my life for the furtherance of the ends of justice, and mingle my blood further with the blood of my children and with the blood of millions in this slave country whose rights are disregarded by wicked, cruel, and unjust enactments, I submit; so, let it be done!"[49]

John Brown, circa 1859. Reproduction of daguerreotype attributed to Martin M. Lawrence. *Library of Congress Prints and Photographs Division.*

Harpers Ferry was the culmination of Brown's lifelong commitment to end racialized slavery in the United States. A decade prior, he had helped Black people in Massachusetts form a self-defense organization to counter the 1850 Fugitive Slave Law. When the fate of Kansas as a free or slave state was undecided, Brown's small group of guerrillas attacked and killed many pro-slavery settlers. There were some who reached the conclusion, as Brown did, that only principled militancy could undo white supremacy. Yet there were others who believed that a more peaceful legal fight was a better way to end slavery and place the nation on a road to greater equality.[50]

In the long arc of racial justice organizing, people have held many views about John Brown. Black activists in the Student Nonviolent Coordinating Committee initially cautioned white people who traveled to the South to avoid emulating Brown and adhere instead to collective decision-making as part of a group. In contrast, Malcolm X held up Brown as exactly the type of white person the movement needed: "If a white man wants to be your ally, what does he think of John Brown? You know what John Brown did? He went to war. He was a white man who went to war against white people to help free slaves."[51]

In their first act as the John Brown Anti-Klan Committee, members discovered that Klan leader Janice Schoonmaker was serving on a local board of education and that there was a Klan Youth Corps campaign to recruit in East Coast high schools. The Committee's research involved connecting names of active Klan members to towns, and identifying what, if any, roles they played within public institutions. Once they had a scoop, they looked for ways to publicly expose Klan members. As Whitehorn described it, "We had a list of names of the Klan guards in the different prisons. We made posters with their names with the intention of going to the small towns they lived in in upstate New York to expose them." Members regularly drove the two hours between Napanoch and New York City in order to gather information.

The group's early research culminated in the publication of their first pamphlet. In it, they publicized thirty-five prison guards that incarcerated people exposed as active members or sympathizers of the Klan. Digging deeper, members of the group traveled to Albany to locate the incorporation papers of the New York Klan. They printed these papers, exposing the Grand Dragon of the New York Klan, Earl Schoonmaker (married to Janice), had been a prison teacher and the head of the Napanoch chapter of the New York State Correctional Officers & Police Benevolent Association.[52] Following complaints from a white female prison employee who alleged that she was threatened and harassed for showing sympathy to incarcerated Black people, Schoonmaker had been investigated, and in December 1974, he was suspended from his job. In 1975, the NAACP filed a lawsuit against the prison, but this did very little to tangibly improve prison conditions. Despite the disciplinary action and widespread attention in the press, including coverage in the *New York Times*, violence continued at the prison. Activists behind bars were often placed in solitary confinement, assaulted, and harassed.

The Committee worked to publicize the demands of incarcerated people to immediately remove Klansmen from their jobs at Napanoch. During the summer of 1977, incarcerated people took over a cellblock to protest Klan-instigated brutality, a rodent-infested mess hall, and the use of rotten eggs in their food. Court records showed that about fifty incarcerated people overwhelmed several corrections officers and took thirteen hostages. Felix Castro, the imprisoned leader of the Latinos Unidos organization, was credited with negotiating the return of prison staff and later faced charges of instigating the uprising.[53] When news broke that Klansmen were planning cross burnings in the local Klan unit, or "Klavern," at Pine Bush, New York, the group decided to investigate Schoonmaker more closely. To get more information about his role, Whitehorn agreed to go to Schoonmaker's house posing as a journalist. She wore a wig. "I sat in his house asking him questions, ready for him to reveal something we could use, but it was nothing that surprising," she recalled. "He hated Black people, Jews, and the Catholics." On multiple occasions, Laura Whitehorn, Terry Bisson, Lisa Roth, Nancy Ryan, and Afeni Shakur all piled into Laura's van, driving two hours north to attend the deposition.

Incarcerated people at Napanoch continued to demand that Klansmen working at the prison be fired. John Brown members met with them regularly, as they were increasingly concerned about the threats they faced for challenging the white supremacists. Here they learned that prison guards associated with the Klan had received clearance by the administration, and several had received promotions. Some guards maintained their jobs and retaliated against activists on the inside with intimidation tactics and harassment. One guard wore his Klan robe inside the prison and burned a paper cross in front of the cells of the incarcerated Black men.

At this point, the John Brown crew decided that bringing more people into the fight was needed, to increase prison support work and fight white supremacists in prisons. They also focused on educating people about the connections between police brutality at home and the role of empire in suppressing populations in Third World countries. Their first pamphlet, *Smash the Klan!*, opened with the letter from Siwatu-Hodari and outlined important details of the pending case against the prison. It also offered fact sheets and contact information for getting involved. The pamphlet stated:

> We have known about Earl Schoonmaker's Klan affiliation for 3 years. We have had lists of violent acts against prisoners at Napanoch and other prisoners. These are not unrelated to the atrocities which have characterized the Klan's 100 years of racist terror. Exposure of the Klan's whole history and strategy is a responsibility that must be shared by all honest forces in this country.

With this tangible anti-Klan material, the group made its initial attempts at conducting public outreach in white communities. First, members went to supermarkets. "It wasn't particularly strategic, but that is where we thought we would find white people we could talk to," remembered Boyle. In addition to free Smash the Klan! pamphlets, they offered "Death to the Klan!" T-shirts for $3.50, and buttons for 60 cents.

Never taking an official position on the role of white working people, they often completely missed the opportunity

Smash

Earl Schoonmaker Jr. (without a hood), the Grand Dragon of the Independent Northern Klans, Inc., New York state's largest KKK order, stands with wife and other top-ranking members at Pine Bush, N. Y.

"The Schoonmakers are some of the really great people of our time. They're not afraid to stand up for what they believe in is right. The liberals would give the country over to the niggers and the Jews who control the businesses and the news media. Earl won't do that and neither will we. We're gonna keep it where it belongs—with the white people."
—a New York State Klansman
quoted in Gallery, March '75

the Klan

John Brown Anti-Klan Committee, Box 411 Times Plaza Station, Brooklyn, N.Y. 11217

to organize around labor and economics. When shoppers stopped by their table in Brooklyn, members tried out conversations with white people who weren't already part of the movement. Bob recalled talking to a working-class white woman when she approached the table.

"She had three crying children, she was carrying her stuff, maybe she was a single mother, maybe not. And here I am going to law school and telling her that she is privileged and if she didn't support Black Liberation, something was wrong. This was the line. We couldn't talk to this woman from where she was coming from, that she worked all week and was dealing with the kids and had to do her shopping, was probably living in a three-story walk-up. It wasn't getting anywhere."

While the concept of "white privilege" had yet to be popularized, the Committee continued an open-ended analysis that had already gone through several iterations throughout the decades. W.E.B. Du Bois never used the term but theorized in 1935 that white workers received positive psychological wages based on their skin color. These invisible wages created a diabolical bargain in which white workers gained the illusion of superiority and lost just about everything else in terms of wages, power, and the possibility of their own emancipation. In a sense, his description of the politics of whiteness was the opposite of subsequent understandings of privilege. Depending on their politics, theorists have emphasized the individualistic aspects of the idea or the structural causes. The basis of the theory is simple. People of color in the United States are excluded from economic, social, and political access that whites provide for one another. The interlocking system that upholds this inequity is led by elites with the near full participation of less privileged white people, who also get limited access to power. The process of chronic exclusion involves a violence against equality, fairness, justice, and freedom. This violence lies at the core of white supremacy and its legacy from the era of settler-colonialism through to the current period.

In the 1960s and 1970s, Theodore Allen developed these ideas to assert that there was no scientific basis for the category of the white race, and that it was invented as a method of class control. He formed this thesis after meticulously searching through pre-colonial records in Virginia and finding no mention of "white" until after Bacon's Rebellion in 1676. The rebellion united Black and white laborers against a colonial regime that was seen as coddling indigenous raids on settler colonies. Fearful of what might come after, Allen documented the use of whiteness to confer material and social advantages—privileges—on whites in order to sabotage potential Black-white alliances. Allen described privilege as a "poison bait" that would never allow for working-class power.[54] Cedric Robinson forever changed this debate in the early 1980s with his seminal work *Black Marxism: The Making of the Black Radical Tradition*. He argued that the roots of racism reach far back into Europe's history, where the "tendency of European civilization through capitalism was thus not to homogenize but to differentiate—to exaggerate regional, subcultural, and dialectical differences into 'racial' ones."[55] This meant that not only was racism a tool of capitalist elites, but capitalism and racism were inextricably interwoven.

Post–World War II policy changes sharpened the ways that material advantages were distributed toward white workers. The white sections of the low-wage working class shrank, while poverty among Black and Brown workers expanded. Policy after policy, from the subsidization of suburbs to the disinvestment of cities, reinforced this dynamic. New Deal labor policy purposely excluded labor protections for farm and domestic workers. Mainstream labor organizations raised few objections to the parts of the New Deal that jettisoned workers of color. In this context, two of the most influential, yet divergent formulations of white skin privilege emerged.

In the mid to late 1980s, feminist writer Peggy McIntosh emphasized the day-to-day advantages of privilege through her famous writings on "the invisible package of unearned assets" that white people can count on "cashing in each day." "White privilege," wrote McIntosh, "is like an invisible weightless backpack of special provisions, maps, passports, codebooks, visas, clothes, tools and blank checks."[56] Author J. Sakai put forward that, as a whole, working-class white people could never truly be revolutionary due to unbreakable attachments to empire and settler-colonialism. He further argued that the white members of the working-class were not part of the proletariat at all, thanks to their status as settlers, and that the citizenship and labor struggles of groups who later would become white was "nothing more nor less than a push to join the oppressor nation, to enlist in the ranks of the Empire."[57] Sakai's distinction reverberated through the Committee, for they saw white privilege as the means that the state uses to organize its support base.

The events in New York prisons made it clear that Jim Crow wore a different face outside of Southern states. New York was simply "Up South," as Malcolm X had described. The normalization of increased Klan activity was rampant. In a blow to the people incarcerated at Napanoch, the New York High Court ruled in April 1977 that prison guards were allowed to join the Ku Klux Klan. Months later, members of the NAACP and Latinos Unidos took over a wing of Napanoch, taking eleven hostages. A grand jury returned indictments against ten of the men involved. The men were then quickly transferred to other facilities, hampering further organizing.[58]

With legal channels shutting down, it seemed to many

anti-racist organizers that the "massive offensive" Siwatu-Hodari urged against the Klan was the only option left on the table. The newly minted John Brown Anti-Klan Committee was more than happy to oblige.

BEGINNING FROM AN AFTERMATH

In the late 1970s, radical optimism was on the ropes. Only a decade before, it seemed that "The Movement" might somehow redeem the violent history of white supremacy and settler-colonialism in the United States. The right's reaction against the gains of the Black Freedom movement was defined with a wave of conservative politicians winning office. A rancid bouquet of white supremacist ballot-box organizations bloomed, ready to follow the right's electoral gains with violence in the streets. Many activists remained in the fray. International solidarity work turned toward opposing intervention in Central America and apartheid in South Africa. Domestic organizers stared down bulldozers leveling low-income communities. The Committee's founders confronted the stark reality of old friends behind bars and the ongoing wars between law enforcement and Black organizers, radicals, and revolutionaries.

The movement against the Vietnam War and U.S. imperialism shaped the politics of many members of the organization. The war, and the compulsory draft of civilian men, had drawn hundreds of thousands of young people into the anti-war movement. For some, avoiding military service was simply a matter of self-preservation. Others began to see the war as part of a larger system of oppression that reinforced white supremacy, capitalism, and U.S. militarism. This analysis saw Black, Indigenous, and Latino people[59] living within the United States as internally colonized communities, and imperialism as the main target for radical organizing. The people who came to the Committee were addressing the same questions that were first asked of them in their student years: What is the role of white people in dismantling white supremacy? Is racism a permanent feature of the U.S. American experience? How does fascism harness racism in the United States? How can both be abolished?

These questions remerged as part of the unfinished business of the 1960s, particularly the factional fights that rippled through the U.S. left, and that ultimately ended the Students for a Democratic Society (SDS). Many of the original members of the Committee had been members of SDS. Emerging in 1959 from the remains of the progressive Socialist League for Industrial Democracy, the organization started with great optimism about the redeemability of U.S. institutions. Its inaugural "Port Huron Statement," written in 1962, identified racism, militarism, and nationalism as the key evils holding back progress. Foreshadowing a later cultural turn towards anti-imperialism, it critiqued exploitation of Third World countries by Western capitalists. Working in projects such as "Friends of Student Nonviolent Coordinating Committee," members regularly delivered white volunteers to support voter registration, nonviolent direct action, and Freedom Schools in the South. Some actions drew the connections to many concerns of the era. The 1968 student occupation of Columbia University, for example, linked military research and the college's gentrification of Harlem.[60]

White students' complicated relationship with the Black Freedom movement mirrored the larger one between the era's white and Black radicals. Throughout the 1960s, questions of when violence and insurrection might be called for were always under discussion. These questions became more urgent as thousands of young people drafted to fight in Vietnam were killed in battle, injured, tortured, or held as prisoners of war. It seemed that "the system" would, as John F. Kennedy warned, "make peaceful revolution impossible and make violent revolution inevitable."[61]

The Black Freedom movement began to demand more of its white supporters. In 1966, the Student Nonviolent

Coordinating Committee asked white activists to leave the group and to focus on organizing against racism in their communities.[62] In fits and starts, the "organize your own" experiment had already begun a few years earlier. Attempts at doing this created the Economic Research and Action Projects of the Students for a Democratic Society, which experimented with community organizing in impoverished communities. It was an attempt to build an "interracial movement of the poor." Ironically, only one such project, Jobs or Income Now Community Union, gained traction, situated itself in a low-income white community, and made an honest go of heading off reactionary politics there. The rest fell short. Other New Left groups, such as the Sojourner Truth Organization, embraced workplace organizing and sent organizers into factories to address the politics of white privilege within the working class.[63]

Protests at the Democratic National Convention in Chicago placed the violence of a Northern city in the national spotlight and peeled back illusions that the Democratic Party could be easily reformed. Multiple factional fights within its ranks ultimately ended the group. The faction that formed the Weather Underground was based on the idea that white youth could challenge the oppressor nation and align with the revolution of Black people. This set of politics abandoned the left's traditional emphasis on class struggle and promoted the idea that national liberation movements would be the vehicle for revolution in their time. Central to this understanding was the idea that colonies existed internally and externally. For example, Black people living within the United States were colonized as surely as those living under European rule in Africa. SDS was anti-imperialist and committed to organizing through militancy. The murder of Fred Hampton was an important turning point for the Weather Underground organization, eventually leading it to embrace a path of underground armed struggle. Inspired by the writings of Che Guevara and a cornucopia of successful anti-colonial uprisings overseas, the

Weather Underground embraced Foco theory—strategies for armed insurgency and guerrilla warfare.

Their particular interpretation held that clandestine group structures taking "exemplary action" could replace mass organizations, and that acts of militancy and property damage against symbols of oppression could incite mass rebellion. Over the next five years, the group claimed responsibility for dozens of bombings. The Weather Underground's template for action was to target a symbol of U.S. power and to publicly associate the act as a counterattack against government repression. Among their targets were the U.S. Capitol, the Pentagon, the U.S. Justice Department, a Long Island Courthouse, the New York Police Department, banks, and police cars. The only human casualties of their operations were three of their own members: Diana Oughton, Terry Robbins, and Teddy Gold were killed when a bomb they were constructing in a New York townhouse accidentally detonated.

From 1969 to 1975, the Weather Underground published communiqués, a volume of revolutionary women's poetry titled *Sing a Battle Song*, and a detailed exposition of their political ideology titled *Prairie Fire: The Politics of Revolutionary Anti-Imperialism*. The group's statements warmly embraced revolutionary movements across the globe and upheld them as the basis of change. They were pessimistic about building a strategy around economic class, especially one that relied on participation from its white section. Weather Underground members saw revolutionary potential in "Third World peoples in the U.S., and also women, youth and members of the armed forces." It was an outlook that would be adopted by many organizations long after the Weather Underground's eventual demise.[64]

The United States was in a position of overwhelming power after World War II, and in post-war restructuring, the U.S. supported imperial European forces in regaining access to their previous colonies, such as France's rule over Vietnam. The United States also fought to prevent Vietnam from becoming an independent state capable of influencing other Asian countries, including Japan and Indonesia, and thus restructuring the balance of regional power.[65] When John F. Kennedy escalated the war, it became clear that Vietnam would not be an obedient colony.

The standard liberal account of the Vietnam War has been that the United States tried to save South Vietnam from the threat of communism, and despite a valiant effort, was not able to see it through, and thus retreated. A right-wing account, on the other hand, has been that the U.S. military was stabbed in the back by American society and politicians, and if there had been more time and resources, the United States would have won. Polls conducted in 1975 by the Chicago Council of Foreign Affairs indicated that two-thirds of the U.S. population believed the war was fundamentally wrong and immoral, and not a mistake the U.S. government happened to make. Television played a significant role in popular disproval, bringing the violence of the U.S. government into the homes of average Americans. Within this vast tilt toward condemnation, many in the radical left saw the Vietnamese resistance, led by a diplomat turned revolutionary, Ho Chi Minh, as a living model for fighting imperial powers such as France and the United States. In fact, the struggle of Vietnam seemed to indicate that it was, at least in some ways, possible for a small country to pull out of the transnational economic system.

Decolonization efforts in developing countries provided both inspiration and a road map for action. European countries were being shown the door from occupied territories on an annual basis. In the year 1960 alone, more than a dozen African nations—including Cameroon, Senegal, Togo, Mali, Madagascar, Congo/Kinshasa, Congo/Brazzaville, Somalia, Benin, Burkina Faso, Ivory Coast, Niger, Gabon, Chad, Nigeria, Mauritania—gained independence from European empires. In 1962, the same year the Port Huron Statement was signed, many young people in the United States were gaining political consciousness through the Civil Rights movement. The Algerian struggle for self-determination successfully liberated the country from France. In 1974, Angola and Mozambique won independence from Portuguese rule. The following year, the Portuguese were ejected from Cape Verde and Guinea-Bissau. In Latin America, revolutions by socialist and national liberation forces, such as the Sandinistas in Nicaragua, were beginning to emerge. At the same time, U.S. interventions, often violent and covert, increasingly destabilized the region.

In 1976, the Weathermen initiated the Hard Times Conference in an attempt to consolidate different radical strands of the movement. If unity was the goal, then Hard Times failed. The Prairie Fire Organizing Committee criticized what they believed to be an effort to submerge anti-imperialism and racism into class-only politics and challenged the conference leadership to explicitly embrace women's struggles. This perspective was shared by the members of the John Brown Book Club who were in attendance. A year later, at a conference, Prairie Fire finally split in two, with the May 19th Communist Organization (named after the joint birthdays of Ho Chi Minh and Malcolm X) organizing on the East Coast. Both organizations would eventually promote John Brown Anti-Klan Committee chapters across the country.

"There really was a sense that the movements from the 1960s and 1970s had failed," recalled Laura Whitehorn. One of the ways activists adapted to this massive political shift in the late '70s was to double down on their commitment to movements for self-determination. The concept of self-determination was rooted in Malcolm X's assessment, following his return from Mecca, that liberation for Black people in the United States involved forming a separate nation.[66] For Committee members, it was national liberation struggles that animated their political imagination. As China Brotsky, a member of the San Francisco chapter of the Committee, explained: "National liberation movements were setting the world on fire, at the very moment we were formulating our politics—between American Indian Movement, and Puerto Ricans, the FALN in New York, the Panthers, and Vietnamese, Cambodians, Chicano, and Mozambique. For us, it was completely normal and logical."

"It was a very ideology-driven movement," Whitehorn said. "Because there was such a premium on nonviolence during the 1960s, there was a particular struggle over the role of armed self-defense." The question as to what kinds of actions bring about change and revolution has long shaped struggles against capitalism and white supremacy. Following the U.S. defeat in Vietnam, Nixon's humiliating resignation, and the revelations of the Church Committee, the legitimacy of U.S. power was considerably undermined. For radicals and revolutionaries on the left, these events offered rich opportunities to educate, organize, and catalyze transformational change.

During the 1970s, Black organizing in the United States was both mainstreamed and radicalized. This was the decade of the "first Black mayor." The Reverend Jesse Jackson's People United to Save Humanity coalition combined traditional issue-based organizing with pressure on the Democratic Party to expand Civil Rights–era policies. Meanwhile, the Republic of New Afrika (RNA) and the Black Liberation Army (BLA), two organizations from the 1960s, remained in the revolutionary camp through the 1970s. While Black political organizations had long been the subject of U.S. government surveillance and infiltration operations, those articulating political self-determination were targeted the most. Adapting to government and police disruption programs, including the possibility of assassination, became a defining feature for Black political groups during this period.

The FBI targeted both nonviolent and militant organizations through its counterintelligence program, COINTELPRO. While few of the prominent groups of the period escaped scrutiny, FBI director J. Edgar Hoover made it clear that the destruction of Black organizations was the primary goal of his campaign. His memo in March 1968 outlined the major objectives of the agency: preventing coalitions between Black groups, sabotaging the rise of a "black messiah," neutralizing "troublemakers," and discrediting their organizations in the eyes of white liberals.[67] The fourth goal of the program demonstrated this logic in softer tactics:

> Prevent militant black national groups and leaders from gaining respectability, by discrediting them to three separate segments of the community. The goal of discrediting black nationalists must be handled tactically in three ways. You must discredit and individuals to, first, the responsible Negro community. Second, they must be discredited to the white community, both the responsible community and "liberals" who have vestiges of sympathy for militant black nationalist simply because they are Negroes. Third, these groups must be discredited in the eyes of Negro radicals, the followers of the movement. This last area requires entirely different tactics from the first two. Publicity about violent tendencies and radical statements merely enhance black nationalists to the last group; it adds "respectability" in a different way.[68]

In concert with police across the country, the federal authorities carried out this agenda with precision. Quietly working to exacerbate political and personal divisions within and among movement organizations, domestic counterintelligence operations included everything from traditional surveillance to assassination.[69]

The individuals who would later form the original chapter of the John Brown Anti-Klan Committee were attempting to find new footing in the wake of the political turbulence experienced during the period. Supporting the activists and organizers who landed behind bars seemed essential. Daily support included tasks such as legal research and media pressure on prisons. Memories of Black revolutionary George Jackson's death in California, and the slaughter that came at Attica State Prison after incarcerated people organized a rebellion against inhuman living conditions, loomed large in the minds of activists.[70] Legal aid groups such as the Midnight Special Collective and the National Lawyers Guild collected status reports about prison conditions and ongoing cases, as well as tips on how to exercise one's rights behind bars.

Communication between incarcerated people and activist networks was critical and often stifled. People on the outside focused on finding ways to outmaneuver the isolating structures of prison. During this period, courtroom battles were at the forefront of resistance to oppressive prison conditions, and support from radical Black organizations was instrumental in galvanizing social support and political pressure. For example, the 1969 Panther 21 case was critical in establishing a template for subsequent support campaigns. Outside allies of imprisoned radicals publicized the case, packed the courtroom in support of defendants, and covertly coordinated communication between incarcerated people. When the New York City Police Department charged twenty-one members of the Harlem Black Panther Party with 156 counts of "conspiracy" to kill several police officers and destroy numerous buildings, the holes in the case were quickly revealed under immense public support for those being tried. The prosecution's case rested largely on the testimony of undercover agents who had infiltrated the groups over many months. Afeni Shakur, one of two women charged, reflected on the impact of outside solidarity on the outcome of the trial: "People thought we were good people . . . they had faith in us enough to come to the trial every day for eight months. So, the jury understood that."[71] In 1971, the jury took only forty-five minutes to acquit the defendants, pointing to the lack of physical evidence. The support infrastructure activists developed in1969, and the lessons learned there, were modified and applied during subsequent conspiracy cases.

The Black Liberation Army and the Republic of New Afrika greatly shaped the growing resistance to official repression at that time and were seen as a threat by the U.S. government. Formed in 1968 in Detroit, the RNA helped to set the tone and tenor of Black Nationalism far beyond its own membership. Founded by Richard and Milton Henry, who changed their names to Imari and Gaidi Obadele, the organization melded anti-colonial socialist thought with a return to African traditions and spiritual practices.

The RNA emerged following the dissolution of the Detroit-based Malcolm X Society. Its founding cabinet included Richard and Mo Williams, Betty Shabazz, and H. Rap Brown. Peeling away from calls for interracial integration, they held that Black people living in the United States constituted their own distinct nation. They called for monetary reparations for the generations of atrocities perpetrated by white enslavers, and they envisioned a nation established from territories belonging to the former slave states of Louisiana, Alabama, Georgia, and South Carolina, where a second Reconstruction could begin. This call for a separate nation contrasted with many organizations of the New Left, although it echoed demands of the socialist left of the 1930s.[72] The Republic of New Afrika's slogan to "Free the Land" was influenced by Malcolm X, who, speaking in Berkeley in 1963, endorsed the idea of an independent Black nation.

Emerging in 1970, the Black Liberation Army's initial members included many former Panthers, most of whom were also Panther 21 defendants. At that point, the national Black Panther Party was in the middle of an intense split over numerous issues, including its relationship to armed struggle. The subject of revolution was always a source of tension within the Panthers. In 1966, images of Panthers openly carrying rifles into the California State House became iconic and obscured their work at setting up what they called "survival programs" that offered free breakfasts for children, literacy classes, health clinics, and popular education. Their cultural work, including the printing of regular weekly newspapers and working with brilliant musicians such as Nina Simone, fostered an unprecedented culture of resistance. Co-founder Huey Newton wrote about the necessity of armed struggle, yet the Panthers had to remain a civilian organization in order to organize openly. In another reality, the civilian Panthers and the underground Black Liberation Army might have pursued a dual strategy, but internal divisions closed off this option. The Panther 21 trial and the expulsion of Eldridge Cleaver from the Party cemented the split. The BLA moved toward Black independence without excluding armed struggle against the U.S. government. Their strategies wagered that armed struggle could catalyze an uprising, and rejected the electoral tactics of the West Coast Black Panther founders.[73]

Assata Shakur became the Black Liberation Army's most well-known member. Shakur was born JoAnne Deborah Byron in New York, in 1947. At three years of age, she moved with her mother and grandparents to Wilmington, North Carolina. With frequent trips between New York and Wilmington, Shakur saw the condition of Black people in big Northern cities and small Southern cities, which informed her college studies and attraction to Black Nationalist groups. She joined the Black Panther Party in Harlem in 1970, and the Black Liberation Army shortly thereafter. From 1971 until 1973, Shakur and the BLA were accused of a series of bank robberies, holdups, and shoot-outs with the police. In all these cases, she was acquitted or charges were dropped.[74]

In 1973, a confrontation between BLA members and police on the New Jersey Turnpike left BLA member Zyad Shakur and State Trooper Werner Foerster dead. Ballistic records suggest that Assata Shakur never fired a weapon during the showdown. Yet she and Sundiata Acoli, another BLA member, were later charged with murder. Shot with her hands in the air, Assata was arrested on the turnpike while Sundiata hid in the woods for a day before later being arrested. Their arrests caused ripples throughout the radical counterculture. She was held in a men's prison in unforgiving conditions, housed with white supremacists, and denied visitors. It was a moment, seemingly frozen in time, that would have great consequences. A 1973 poem penned by a collective of women in the Weather Underground voices how Shakur's saga captured the revolutionary imagination. [75]

> Although we had never seen one another
>   I wondered how you liked to spend those moments
>   when freedom meant
>   you knew
>   they didn't know.
> And during those last months
>   when they hunted you hard
> I was an invisible supporter,
>   working on another front.
> Knowing of those tearing apart times
>   when the days are like the flashes
>   of a strobe light.
> And the earth turns with a racing rhythm
>   running the guerrilla
>   through the changes of a normal lifetime
>   in a single month.
>
> And when you were captured, sister,
>   I wept
>   for all of us.

These events, and their connection to the centuries-long continuum of Black resistance, greatly influenced the formation and politics of the Committee. The question of what it means for white revolutionaries in the United States to support Black Freedom movements and Indigenous sovereignty goes back to the first slave revolts and Native uprisings on the continent. In this regard, the politics of anti-imperialism, and the influence of imprisoned radicals, evolved and further defined these questions during the 1970s. The emergence of political activists such as Bobby Seale, Angela Davis, and Martin Sostre in prison shaped the political priorities of those on the outside. Imprisoned revolutionaries also contributed to an immense body of books and pamphlets that defined the political goals of the movement.[76] Whitehorn stressed this point, "I don't think people today understand just how much people in prison influenced and created the ideology of the anti-imperialist, anti-racist movement on the outside. This is how it started. The nationalist movement had been attacked by the state."

FINDING FOOTING

In the fall of 1977, just months after the first chapter was formed, Laura Whitehorn left Boston to move back home to Brooklyn. In Massachusetts she had taken part in the "Battle of Boston" that erupted around the busing crisis. In 1974, two decades after the *Brown v. the Board of Education* decision, federal courts ruled that Boston's policy of segregated schools was a form of illegal discrimination. Over the next few years, racist protesters violently confronted Black youth and their families in a last-ditch effort to maintain racial segregation. When white supremacist gangs attacked Black homes with bats, Molotov cocktails, and spray paint, Whitehorn and others asked what they needed. It was then that they organized to defend the families.[77] "I moved to New York because I had a hard time finding other white people who saw anti-racist work as support for national liberation, not only a response to divisions in the working-class. That makes a big difference. I saw it as the priority, not just another thing to do in the context of other work," explained Whitehorn.

Back in New York, she reconnected with old comrades who had just rented a post office box in Brooklyn and began to establish the first chapter of the John Brown Anti-Klan Committee. Brooklyn was in the midst of a spike in racist violence, fueled in part by changing neighborhood demographics and a sharp decline in manufacturing jobs. The Committee held its own regular community defense actions, keeping overnight vigil in front of Black homes that had received threats. "We were literally staying up all night on certain blocks to prevent people from driving by and throwing Molotov cocktails at homes, burning them out," said Pam Fadem.

The chapter attracted new members, and during this period Debbie Siedman, Mark Dewan, Natalee Rosenthal, Nancy Ryan, and Terry Bisson joined. A controversy at City University of New York (CUNY) followed the U.S. Supreme Court's decision allowing affirmative action. One of the early campaigns was what they called Operation Snowflake. In 1970, the college adopted an "open admissions" policy to increase higher education access to "academically underprepared" students. This coded language actually called for a demographic shift from a 95 percent white student population "to one third white, one third black, one fifth Hispanic, and ten percent Oriental."[78] Faculty groups complained that the effort would dilute academic standards, which created a momentum within the institution to shut down open admissions. "Officials argue that the essential change at City College has not been that it is now dealing with underprepared students—only 11 percent of freshmen entering in 1970 got diplomas four years later—but that the 'Harvard of the proletariat' has become a 'multi-ethnic' institution for the first time."[79] When Committee members leafleted on campus in 1978 they met student organizations such as the Arab Student Association and Black and Puerto Rican Student Community. These groups had a history of supporting the Black Panther Party and the Young Lords, as well as demands for separate ethnic studies schools serving students from developing countries.

The group's reach expanded as the Committee teamed up with the Moncada Library. Founded in 1978, the Library took its name taken from the barracks that launched the Cuban Revolution. The Library opened at 434 Fifth Avenue in Brooklyn's Park Slope. Started by members of the May 19th Communist Organization, the Library served as the gathering place for revolutionaries to debate a path forward for a movement in transition. It was here that the Committee members chose to have a regular, local, and place-based presence, even as chapters grew in other regions. They created political education events to connect local anti-racist campaigns with movements to decolonize. They also offered Spanish-language courses as an act of solidarity with Puerto Rican activists who were organizing for independence. "By learning Spanish at the Moncada Library, people can learn about the content of the Puerto Rican liberation struggle and the culture of resistance of the Puerto Rican people, and other Latin Peoples. This can be an important tool in fighting white supremacy and a contribution to building solidarity," read a Committee flyer from that period.

The Brooklyn-based chapter produced newsletters featuring event listings, book reviews, analysis of the ongoing police brutality in New York, and suggestions for supporting people incarcerated for political reasons. The group hosted movie nights every Sunday at the Library. Among the films they screened were *Black's Britannica*, about the Black liberation struggle in Britain; *Lucia*, about the role of Cuban women in revolution; *My Country Occupied*, about a woman joining the Guatemalan resistance; and *Generations of Resistance*, about the tactics of resistance to South African apartheid.

The Moncada Library also worked with the Committee to respond to the Klan's recruitment of youth in the region. "It is fascism, not democracy, that is being defended when a 17-year-old youth becomes the Grand Dragon of the KKK in New Jersey and is applauded and joined by many white youth," read a statement published by the Committee and the library. The

Learn Spanish at the Moncada Library

The struggles of Third World nations for their language are a central part of the struggle against genocide, to preserve their nation's culture, and part of the struggle for liberation. This is why the Puerto Rican independence movement has fought to preserve and defend the Spanish language, both here and in Puerto Rico. Puerto Rican people in the U.S. demand bilingual education and fight for their culture as basic human rights and as key to the fight against genocide and for national liberation.

The Moncada Library has offered Spanish classes for the past year in solidarity with the Puerto Rican struggle for independence and socialism, and to provide people in the community an opportunity to learn Spanish in a progressive context.

By learning Spanish at the Moncada Library, people can learn about the content of the Puerto Rican liberation struggle and the culture of resistance of the Puerto Rican people, and other Latin American peoples. This can be an important tool in fighting white supremacy and a contribution to building solidarity.

Classes are scientific and enjoyable, and taught by an experienced teacher. People who have had difficulty learning Spanish before will be able to learn the language in these classes.

classes begin Sunday, Sept. 28

beginners & intermediate classes available

tuition: $40 for 8 weeks

To reserve a place in the class, or for more information, call or visit:

MONCADA LIBRARY, 434 Fifth Avenue (between 8th & 9th Street), Park Slope, Brooklyn

Telephone: 499-2767   By train: F to Fourth Avenue, RR to Ninth Street

Hours: Tuesdays and Thursdays, 3-7 PM; Saturdays, 1-5 PM; Sundays, 6-9 PM

impact of raising awareness among youth about racist groups would be seen four years later when school districts responded with anti-Klan educational books for students. The National Education Association published *Violence: The Ku Klux Klan and the Struggle for Equality* in order to help public school teachers build anti-Klan curriculum in the classroom.[80]

In spring of 1979, the library started the Young People's

Program, which sponsored young Black and Puerto Rican teenagers to create murals reflecting how they saw their political and cultural life. Mary Patten, an artist and community activist at the library, collaborated with local store owners in Park Slope to host the murals. In response to the national crisis posed by police violence against youth of color—including the killing of twenty-eight Black children over a two-year period in Atlanta—the Moncada Library organized an after-school program for youth to get together to talk about the threat of police violence in their lives. Each day focused on a theme, from the events in Atlanta to the Klan in schools, to drugs, to racist teachers.

A surge of police violence against Black and Latino people in New York in the 1970s underscored the idea that New York City was simply "Up South." Following a familiar script, nearly all of the incidents started with routine interactions with law enforcement and ended with an unarmed Black or Latino person getting shot, often in the back. This included a Black small-business owner in the Crown Heights neighborhood, an eighteen-year-old Black man in the Bronx, a nine-year-old Black child, and a twenty-nine-year-old Puerto Rican man shot twenty-one times by English-speaking police officers.

Members of the Committee felt pressed to draw connections between police killings and the rise of white vigilante violence. "We didn't use the phrase *state power* all that much," recalled Whitehorn, but through increasing demonstrations against the police, the Committee created campaigns with catchy names like "Blue by Day, White by Night" and "PBA is the KKK!" From the group's point of view, the Police Benevolent Association and the New York Police Department at times shared membership with organizations such as the Klan, and even more pointedly, took actions that mirrored the program of the Klan. It wasn't simply a matter of formal violence from organized racists and the New York Police Department that concerned them. The group would demonstrate in front of stores and street corners where Black people were attacked by groups of white people, but their commitment to defense extended much further. "I was walking my dog in Park Slope late one night, and I saw a Black man being backed down the middle of the street by a crowd of white guys carrying garbage cans, sticks, and bats," Fadem recalled. She asked a passerby to hold her dog's leash while she stood between the man and the crowd, screaming at them to leave their intended victim alone. Because of this, a few other people joined her, and the man was able to escape, which redirected the violence to Fadem and others who attempted to defuse the situation. It was an individual decision guided by what would become a hallmark of the organization's politics: White people had the responsibility to assume the risks that Black people experienced every day.

Fadem recalled a Black woman approaching their outreach table at a Brooklyn supermarket. She asked her, "Why are you doing this? You're white." After shuffling through an assortment of possible responses she simply said, "Because we don't want our children to have to grow up this way."

Throughout the thirteen-year arc of the organization, the chapters of the Committee were most often based in major U.S. cities such as New York, Boston, Washington, Houston, Austin, Chicago, San Francisco, and Los Angeles, but they emerged in less metropolitan places as well, including New Paltz, New York, Bowling Green, Kentucky, and Meriden, Connecticut. While some chapters were more robust than others, they often emerged in response to Black and Brown organizing against police brutality, racist vigilantism, and government counterintelligence operations. For instance, in 1978, three Black women, two of whom were students at Hampshire College in Amherst, Massachusetts, were badly beaten after a conflict with a liquor store clerk. When they were detained without bail and denied medical attention, Hampshire students organized and protests erupted, including boycotts of local schools and shopping malls as well as a mass march to the local municipal building. When the World Women's Task Force on

Hampshire campus organized a "community review board" to assess the role of racism in recent conflicts with the police, they reached out to the local chapter of the John Brown Anti-Klan Committee seeking help organizing protests and community speak-outs. Other chapters started in proximity to prisons in upstate New York, generating local community support for political prisoners.

In these early years, Committee members learned quickly that supporting Black and Brown liberation struggles resulted in a particular kind of backlash. While doing community outreach in Meriden, Connecticut, Roth recalled, "I remember we had an open meeting where Klan members came. They didn't do anything during the meeting but spy on us. We didn't have a plan about what to do if they came, which was stupid. But the way we figured out who they were [was that] after the meeting two of the guys [who attended] were trying to run us off the road and driving too close for an hour." At times, backlash from white supremacist groups led to physical attacks on Committee members when they went tabling.

State surveillance wasn't a surprise either, but it still presented the group with a confusing, steep learning curve. During the period of the Committee's founding, some members built support for the class-action lawsuit that May 19th member Judy Clark led against the FBI for COINTELPRO. This was one case in a series that exposed the reach of the counterintelligence program of that era. *Clark et al. v. the United States of America* sought $100 million dollars in compensation for damages, and charged President Richard Nixon, the FBI, the U.S. Postal Service, the Justice Department, and the New York Telephone Company with "illegal wiretapping, break-ins, and mail tampering." Whitehorn later joined the Committee for the Suit Against Government Misconduct, which was led by Mutulu and Afeni Shakur. She remembered, "Mutulu said to us, you know, no one cares when the FBI does this to Black people. Fred Hampton was murdered, and his family can't even get

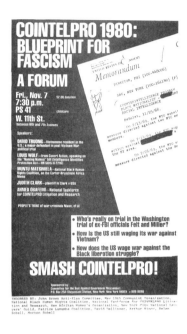

COINTELPRO 1980: BLUEPRINT FOR FASCISM

A FORUM

Fri., Nov. 7
7:30 p.m.
PS 41
W. 11th St.
between 6th and 7th Avenues

$2.00 donation

childcare

Speakers:

DAVID TRUONG—*Vietnamese resident in the U.S., a major defendant in post-Vietnam War political trial*

LOUIS WOLF—*from Covert Action, speaking on the "Naming Names" Bill (Intelligence Identities Protection Act—HR 5615, S 2216)*

MUNTU MATSIMELA—*National Black Human Rights Coalition, on the Carter-Brzezinski Africa Memo*

JUDITH CLARK—*plaintiff in Clark v USA*

AHMED OBAFEMI—*National Taskforce for COINTELPRO Litigation and Research*

PEOPLE'S TRIAL of war criminals Nixon, et al

- Who's really on trial in the Washington trial of ex-FBI officials Felt and Miller?
- How is the US still waging its war against Vietnam?
- How does the US wage war against the Black liberation struggle?

SMASH COINTELPRO!

Sponsored by:
Committee for the Suit Against Government Misconduct
P.O. Box 254 Stuyvesant Station, New York, New York 10023 • 989 8890

ENDORSED BY: John Brown Anti-Klan Committee, New 19th Communist Organization, National Black Human Rights Coalition, National Taskforce for COINTELPRO Litigation and Research, New Afrikan Women's Organization, New York City National Lawyers' Guild, Patrice Lumumba Coalition, David Dellinger, Arthur Kinoy, Helen Sobell, Morton Sobell

damages in court. But then they do it white people, and white women, and it's going to get attention and money." This would shape how members thought about their role fighting racism and repression. "It was very clear: [We] white people [would] use our privilege to better position Third World people in their fight for justice," continued Whitehorn. Their efforts to do this did not go unnoticed. In the summer of 1978, Judy Clark and Mululu Shakur spoke about the suit—colloquially called the "Grey Suit," because L. Patrick Grey was head of the FBI at the time—at an event at Columbia University's Teachers College. "The event was packed. The tickets sold out, we had posters for sale. It was very public," remembered Whitehorn with a tone of surprise in her words. "We were driving home on Broadway to go into Brooklyn when we saw a lot of fire engines on 98th Street. It turned out there was a fire in Judy Clark's apartment. Her apartment burned down the night of the event." Whitehorn described being one of the first people to enter the smoldering apartment the next morning. "There was a table in the living room at the front of the apartment where we did all the flyer-making and collating. On top of this burnt table, there was a pristine poster for this event. It was like saying, *We did this*." The point was driven home again when friends down the street came home a few days later. "One night they started to walk up the stairs and realized the stairs have wet, grey paint on them. At the top of the stairs was a paint can that said, 'Battleship Grey,' which was [the FBI head's] nickname."[81]

THE FRONTLINE OF TEXAS

During that period, Klan chapters across Texas were targeting organizations in communities of color in anticipation of an "imminent race war." They were also calling for attacks on immigrants along the U.S.-Mexico border. In response, chapters of the Committee formed in Austin and Houston in 1978. One core organizer of these chapters was Linda Evans. Before she moved to Texas, the tensions surrounding the collapse of the Students for a Democratic Society (SDS) had helped shaped her life. This led her to Texas in search of new ways to build a movement. Evans was born in May 1947 in Fort Dodge, Iowa, a small town with an economy based on gypsum mining and farming. Her father worked as a partner in a local construction firm and her mother as a schoolteacher. In 1965, she left home to attend Michigan State University. Putting her studies on hold in 1967 to organize against the Vietnam War, Evans quickly became an SDS-Weatherman organizer in Michigan and Ohio.

In 1970, Evans was released from Cook County Jail after serving a sentence stemming from the "Days of Rage" protests that rocked Chicago in October 1969. In a 72-hour street uprising, insurrectionary protesters smashed windows and attacked property in an effort to "bring the war home." The Weather Underground considered the action a victory that proved there were white people who were willing to fight the police to bring down the system. They had hoped that such actions would inspire masses of the student movement to do the same. For example, leading up to the Days of Rage, the group took up a series of bizarre actions in Flint, Michigan, and Pittsburgh. In Pittsburgh, they demonstrated at a local high school, running around the campus yelling "jailbreak" and distributing pamphlets against the war.[82] A Weather Underground communiqué claimed victory: "Our actions showed the Vietnamese that there were masses of young people in this country facing the same enemy that they faced. We showed that white people would no longer sit by passively while black communities were being invaded by occupation troops every day."[83]

Several dozen protesters were arrested during the Days of Rage, but only Evans and Judy Clark were convicted. Evans recalled that it was the male-dominated debates within SDS that pushed her toward militancy. "I wanted to be in the streets, wherever the action was. I was definitely part of the Action Faction. At that point, women weren't looked upon as intellectual leaders, either. I fit right in. I got some respect that way. But as far as being pressed to develop myself as a leader in the movement no, no, no forget it."[84]

In June of 1969, Evans traveled to Hanoi, Vietnam, as part of an anti-war delegation that secured the release of two U.S. airmen captured by the Vietcong. Her delegation included author Grace Paley, SDS leader Rennie Davis, and James Johnson, a U.S. Army private who had refused to deploy to Vietnam in the famous Fort Hood 3 case. The visit cemented Evans's commitment to radical anti-imperialist politics. She was moved deeply by the ways that the Vietnamese people welcomed citizens of a country responsible for bombing them daily. The delegation was treated like official U.S. emissaries. Meetings would always begin with tea and Vietnamese cookies served by the highest-ranking officer in the room. This humility, Evans believed, symbolized the humility of a people and the Vietcong's political project. The Vietnamese didn't prescribe the ways for North Americans to organize. They were steadfast in their insistence that activists within the "belly of the beast" had a unique role in ending U.S. aggression across the globe.

By the time of her release, most of her friends had joined armed underground groups. To the FBI, this made Evans a valuable surveillance target. Agents constantly approached her, curious as to the whereabouts of her comrades. "I didn't know who to trust," said Evans. Looking for a new direction, she met with activists from Austin, Texas. Falling in with a group of radical women who lived on a commune outside of town, Evans learned how to play guitar and formed a band. It was through this scene that Evans met Trella Laughlin, a Southerner who would become one of her closest friends and a central part of the Committee's Austin chapter.

Trella Laughlin was born in Jackson, Mississippi, in 1937—a time when the antebellum South was still referenced fondly by politicians and social aristocrats. She graduated from Central High School in its last year as a racially segregated, all-white institution. Laughlin's parents were typical members of the local White Citizens' Council. As members of the owning class, they saw themselves as protectors of a moral order. Compared to the Ku Klux Klan, the White Citizens' Council offered a "much nicer way to be racist," Laughlin insisted. The Council was more public in its presence and covert in its politics than the KKK. Through pressuring local governments to prosecute civil rights activists and appealing to insurance agencies to cancel policies held by movement-friendly churches, the Council used its access to institutional power to uphold racial inequality and violence.[85]

Growing up white within the owning class in Jackson meant particular things in the 1940s. For Laughlin, it meant running around at the big parties her parents hosted while the adults had conversations about the natural gas industry. It meant being raised by a Black nanny who Laughlin felt was more of a parent to her than her biological mother. It also meant beginning to push back on the social niceties—being pleasant, quiet, accommodating—expected of Southern white women.

Laughlin attended segregated schools, and just before she graduated in 1954, Jim Crow laws took their first real hit when the U.S. Supreme Court ruled that segregating schools was unconstitutional. A full fifty-eight years before this, the landmark *Plessy v. Ferguson* ruling of 1896 had established the practice of "separate, but equal." The case provided justification for stripping Black people of their power and dignity by considerably constraining access to public schools, libraries, pools, restrooms, water fountains, banks, and restaurants. Laughlin witnessed her community enraged by the prospect of a desegregated future: "It felt like things just hit a wall. Now that the law said it was illegal, people talked about keeping things the way they were with or without the law." By 1956, the White Citizens' Council boasted 253 chapters across thirty states.[86] Their 60,000 members sought to challenge, or at least slow down, the consequences of the *Brown v. Board of Education* decision. Their goal was to maintain the "natural rights" of racial segregation while maintaining "states' rights" to internally regulate public health, morals, marriage, education, peace, and order.

During this time, politicians began to manipulate growing levels of white economic anxiety in an attempt to channel it into antipathy for the emerging Civil Rights movement. This would later be a central component in the Republican Party's "Southern Strategy." Such strategy involved "dog whistle" tactics in which phrases like "law and order" were used as code, understood one way publicly and another way among white supremacists. The White Citizens' Council was emblematic of how class anxiety was aggressively racialized. Considered the sophisticated alternative to the Klan, it used its leverage with institutions to further a white supremacist agenda that involved committing economic sabotage, creating social pressures, and fixing elections. Many leaders within the Klan worked closely with the White Citizens' Council to determine what issues and regions could be won over to their agenda. "My parents didn't want to be seen as supporting the Ku Klux Klan, although they gave money to them," recalled Laughlin. "Often, they would say things like, 'I don't support violence, but Martin Luther King Jr. had it coming.'"

At seventeen years old, Laughlin knew she had to leave Jackson. She would find the words for it later, but she needed to see her hometown from the outside, and the Deep South felt too volatile for her to stay. After many years, Laughlin made her way to Arkansas to find land for a lesbian commune. The dream of living off the grid of patriarchy was a short-lived one, but she met Linda Evans in the process. Arkansas rice growers were contaminating land and drinkable water with the same chemical herbicide unleashed on the Vietnamese: Agent Orange. The women raised funds for and won a court injunction against the spraying. However, the local sheriff refused to serve it unless the group floated a bond to protect the farmer from losses incurred. Evans left and tried apple-picking in Missouri with migrant workers before returning to Austin.[87]

In Austin, Evans volunteered with a variety of causes such as anti-apartheid education and solidarity work against U.S. intervention in Latin America. In conversations with Betty Ann Duke, a Texas-born activist, the two started to recognize a disconnect between their international priorities and the local issues impacting Austin's Black and Chicano communities. At the suggestion of the Austin Brown Berets and the Black Citizens Task Force, Duke and Evans founded Women Against Boat Racism. Every year, white North Austin clubs organized speedboat races along the river next to low-income neighborhoods of color in East Austin. Residents would complain about noise, traffic, and an overall influx of wealthy people haphazardly using the riverbank space. One year, a small girl was struck and killed by a speedboat.

Women Against Boat Racism worked with the Brown Berets and Black Citizens' Taskforce to organize a local boycott of the races. The collective founded the Red Women's Press and set up a print shop on West 12th Street, enabling them to make a living and produce posters for the movement. They acquired a federal grant to hire women from the Brown Berets, a militant portion of the Chicano Movement organized in response to migration policy, police brutality, and land grabs across Texas, New Mexico, Arizona, Colorado, and California.

The Austin chapter of the Brown Berets officially formed in 1973 in response to police beatings of Latino people, including Gilberto Rivera, who was attacked while leaving a fundraising event for the Mexican American Youth Organization, which was starting a political party, Raza Unida.

At the time, increasing racial tensions were deepened by a spate of police violence in communities of color. Among the most notorious incidents was the 1979 case of Gril Couch, a Black man who was killed by two white police officers in plainclothes after an argument over a boom box. In response, Austin's left began a campaign to establish a Citizens Police Review Board. Evans recalled, "We stopped being Women Against Boat Racism and started being John Brown Anti-Klan Committee as a conscious effort to become part of the movement against white supremacy." Jackie Starnes and Leslie McCulloch joined Duke and Evans in the efforts. The New York chapter decided to send Pam Fadem to Austin to help get the chapter off the ground.

The Committee began working closely with the Black Citizens Task Force (BCTF), a membership-based organization in Austin's Black community. The BCTF was founded by John Warfield, a Black scholar from Michigan who started the African American Studies department at the University of Texas. He used university resources to build bridges among radicals, community members, and intellectuals. Warfield envisioned an organization not confined to electoral politics but, rather, dedicated to organizing for Black self-determination through local campaigns. He recruited three longtime Austin organizers: Anthony Spears, a veteran of the Austin Black Panther Party Chapter; Dorothy Nell Turner; and Velma Roberts, who had founded the Freedom School for Black Students when the court ordered Black children to be bused to white schools. At the time Warfield came to town, Roberts also served on the board of the National Welfare Rights Organization.

The politics of the Task Force changed over time. "John

was very clear: BCTF had a statement of political principle that resonated with Malcolm X's analysis of land and self-determination," explained Susan Richardson, a Task Force organizer who attended high school in Austin. Richardson described how the early rhetoric of self-determination was aspirational. Over the years, the ideas influenced their newspaper, *Grassroots Struggle*, and political education meetings but did not necessarily translate into their organizing work. As Richardson put it, "We had relationships with some people within Republic of New Afrika, but the nationalist strategy was never the guts of Black Citizens Task Force."

The Task Force organized campaigns that focused on reforms, such as the Black Voter Action Project. "It worked for some time," recalled Richardson. "Austin was still trying to get a critical mass of Black elected officials. You have to keep in mind that, in 1972, Austin had its first Black city council person. So we have a united front to create a generation of Black elected officials, especially in the South. We were trying to grab as much state power as possible."

The role of the Task Force was to keep the heat on local government. "We kept the spotlight on who was getting hired," Richardson described. Representation wasn't just about elected officials. "Dorothy (Turner) was always real clear that if Black people were paying tax dollars, the city should be hiring Black workers. End of story. People needed work, especially those just getting out of prison. The Task Force helped them get jobs." They won several key real estate battles that created Black community centers, such as the Arthur B. Dewitty Center in East Austin, which served as a headquarters for their employment access campaigns. The Task Force also used university resources to create a series of film screenings and community discussions to "do some serious consciousness raising around South Africa and police shootings in Austin."

With the agenda to build power within the Black community, Warfield saw the Task Force as an instrument for circulating radical ideas, identifying the community's basic needs, and lobbying local government to better meet those needs. Warfield encouraged radical Black students coming to Austin to work with the Task Force. "The point of your getting this education is so that you go back into the community and help make fundamental change," said Richardson.

The Black Citizens' Task Force also attracted University of Texas students like Izielen Agbon and Amilcar Shabazz, who would later join the Republic of New Africa. They were studying Frantz Fanon, Eldridge Cleaver, and the Black diaspora, putting their studies to use by facilitating monthly community political education meetings and producing a newsletter. Richardson stated that they "wanted to give people a sense of theory, so they could be hopeful on that long road." This was in response to the common perception at the time that the Black Freedom movement had not succeeded. "We wanted to emphasize that movements move in ebbs and flows. Just because a mass movement had subsided doesn't mean the work was over. The work in between big moments is still the work. You're going to struggle until the day you drop. And the big theories hold that perspective, and oppose becoming demoralized."

Richardson admitted that even though the organization worked with a wide spectrum of groups, including those that were reformist and revolutionary, the Task Force maintained its focus: "It was fine working with radical whites, but we were always going to be grounded in our community." She continued, "Yes, the Black Citizens Task Force was about fighting white supremacy, but if you talked to Dorothy and Velma, they were much more worried about the white liberals than about the Klan. Because you knew what the Klan was. The white people sitting in power wouldn't give them jobs. It was more important to them to educate people around the less obvious forms of white supremacy, asking questions like *Why we can't get jobs? Why can't we get services in our community?*"

With the proliferation of the Klan in Texas and the South

in general, the Austin chapter of the John Brown Anti-Klan Committee focused on disruption. "Whatever the Klan did, we were there. We were there to make sure they did not go on un-opposed," declared Laughlin. The Klan used an array of tac-tics to build their base and exert influence, from staging formal rallies displaying members in full robes, to conducting recruit-ment campaigns in high schools, to producing and airing public access TV shows. The John Brown crew was bent on disrupting every attempt the Klan made, and saw these as opportunities to bolster resistance by white people to white supremacy.

In 1981, two hundred miles southeast of Houston, the small town of Galveston Bay saw a series of attacks by the Klan against Vietnamese fishermen. Between 1975 and 1983, the ar-ea's refugee population rose to 100,000 as a result of the Viet-nam War and the U.S. resettlement program in Texas.[88] Many of the white fishermen in Galveston felt threatened by the eco-nomic competition, which made way for racist attacks such as boat burning and sniper fire on Vietnamese boating crews. The Klan was brought into the conflict when white fishermen held a rally against the Vietnamese community. This was followed by a Klan "boat parade" in which armed Klansmen motored around the bay with burning crosses. The Klan also burned an effigy of a Vietnamese person, and later torched a boat belong-ing to a Vietnamese fisherman.[89]

The John Brown Anti-Klan Committee openly disrupted a number of these Klan gatherings. "About ten of us would go out. We had our little signs out and would start marching. A huge bunch of Klan members came, probably about fifty. They marched around us and they knew our names. I was scared shitless, but we kept marching, because you cannot let fear stop you," Laughlin recounted.

In 1980 the Grand Dragon (state president) of the Texas Klan, Louis Beam, was arrested for conducting paramilitary training in a national park. His trial on misdemeanor tres-passing charges was heavily covered by local media. In his testimony, Beam openly divulged that he had pictures of Adolf Hitler on display in his home next to those of his close family. Evans and another Committee member approached him using the pretense that they were University of Texas Social Movement students, angry that they were being required to study only left-wing movements by biased instructors. The group also started a door-to-door campaign to expose the fact that Klansmen had infiltrated a local Boy Scout troop in an attempt to initiate young boys into paramilitary training. The Committee campaigned with the Black Citizens Task Force to demand that the Texas legislature investigate and that the Boy Scouts revoke the charter of the infiltrated troop. Commenting at a public hearing, BCTF's Velma Roberts saw this as sign of an impending race war. "I'm not going to be murdered by a Klansman. We will teach each other not only to defend, but to attack."[90] A Klan spokesman concurred, explaining that the training was in preparation for what they thought would be a communist overthrow of the government, or a race war.[91]

It wasn't too long before a postcard arrived at Linda Evans's house with a picture of a coffin with the words "John Brown Anti-Klan Committee" written on it. Other members' houses and cars were attacked with rocks. It was not uncommon for Committee members such as Betty Ann Duke to regularly wear bulletproof vests. Laughlin remembered the anxiety that came with confronting the Klan. "It was a real education, especially if you're a nice owning-class white girl, to learn what length the cops, the FBI, and the Klan will go to mess with you." Members of the Austin chapter had their cars broken into, their action plans stolen, and their cars' brake lines cut.

The stakes felt high. "We wanted to destroy the Klan," Evans stated. Making a choice that would later bring serious consequences, Evans began doing underground support work while still a public activist. Among other things, she was later convicted of creating false IDs for comrades planning clandestine actions against the U.S. government.

Then, as now, cable television was a major tool for far-right culture and recruitment. In response to this and the influential far-right series, *Race and Reason*, hosted by White Aryan Resistance head Tom Metzger, in 1980 the Austin chapter of the Committee launched their own program, *Let The People Speak!* Hosted by Trella Laughlin, the show promoted anti-racist politics and interviewed many members of the Black Citizen's Task Force. The show was aired on Austin's public cable access station. With episodes called "Racism Isn't on the Rise, It Never Fell," and "Klan Murderers," the show gained popularity in cities, particularly San Francisco and Washington. *Let the People Speak* quickly became a vehicle for the Black Citizens Task Force to educate the public about their campaigns and resistance to white supremacy. Laughlin used equipment from a videography class she taught at Austin Community College to help set up a BCTF television show, *Liberation*, which aired twice a week. As she recalled, "I got more of an education spending my days with the fine people in the Black Citizens Task Force than anything ever offered at school."

Working together, the Task Force, the Brown Berets, and the Committee formed a trio. They made their first public appearance while pressuring the Texas State Legislature to investigate "survival camps" where young boys in the Explorer Scouts were trained to spot "illegal aliens" at the Mexican border and Civil Air Patrol cadets were "taught by Klansmen to kill with rifles, knives, and wire thongs" in preparation for the coming race war.[92] As a result of their organizing, they received threatening phone calls and postcards with pictures of white men holding rifles and the message, "There's one in the chamber with your name on it."

An incident at Decker Lake, just fourteen miles outside Austin, escalated the sense of crisis. Police stumbled upon white nationalists shooting an effigy that had Task Force leader Dorothy Turner's name on it. Pipe bombs found in a gunman's trunk never resulted in any charges, and the district attorney told the Task Force members that their hands were tied. The police told Turner that the shooters were mostly young military men on furlough, so there was no cause for alarm. "Here you are exercising your free speech rights to organize to try and change things," said Task Force member Amilcar Shabazz. "You're not hurting anybody or calling for anybody to be hurt. And here comes all of this organized opposition, meant to intimidate and surveil you. It necessitates a certain kind of vigilance."

The Task Force was looking for white people who would "actively problematize white nationalism and white supremacy," according to Shabazz. At that time, there had been incidents of police violence against people of color that had sparked broad community outrage. One incident involved thirteen off-duty police officers from Houston who got inebriated at a barbeque and then raided a low-income housing unit in East Austin, the Della Apartment Hotel. The intoxicated police officers senselessly attacked and terrorized numerous Black residents of the hotel. Another incident involved an interdepartmental memo targeting Rastafarians, classifying them as members of a cult. The Committee joined the Task Force doing door-to-door outreach and increased turnout at city council meetings where these incidents were being confronted and debated.

Meanwhile, Laughlin was hearing more and more about the paramilitary activity of the Klan across Texas. Their armed training camps were talked about openly in Houston. A small chapter of the Committee formed in Houston and was quick to hold public demonstrations denouncing these camps. Among other things, they wrote editorials titled "Help Stop the Klan Organizing Drive," which were published in local newspapers. They invited local residents to help build a movement, as they put it, "in solidarity with the New Afrikan Independence Movement that will contribute to the defeat of the Klan." Laughlin remembered, "The Klan march[ed] constantly. In Houston,

San Antonio, Waco, Dallas, Austin. That was their plan. They were very orderly about it."

The Committee's confrontational approach and uncensored messaging set it apart from other groups. JBAKC members saw the Klan working to organize white people from all classes, and they committed themselves to doing the same, but in solidarity with the rights and dignity of people of color. They used provocative slogans such as "Death to the Klan" to be clear about their intentions. "We didn't hold back!" Laughlin admitted. "We were a bit self-righteous too." Leafleting had proved frustrating because, as Laughlin recalled, "We knew we'd be spit on. It happened all the time, and once you're spit on, you start to think of getting your message out in other ways." They sought to disrupt the narrative that joining the Klan was a community activity and highlighted the consequences of white supremacy in the greater Austin community.

In Austin, the Republic of New Afrika provided the larger framework for radical groups to collaborate, including the predominantly white May 19th Communist Organization. On the local level, it was understood that they would work with liberation struggles located in their particular area. In Austin, Evans and Duke held leadership positions, and Laughlin described the Committee's decision-making process as "trickle down." Evans and Duke would meet with the leadership of the Task Force and Brown Berets to discuss their shared campaigns, while also coordinating a larger anti-imperialist strategy. Afterwards, they would report back to the rest of the chapter to develop tactics together. "It made sense at the time. It was about being effective. There was a bunch of us who hadn't worked through our own white supremacy. It would be insulting to impose that on Black leaders like Chokwe Lumumba, who had to deal with that shit too often," asserted Laughlin. This would later shift as some people in leadership positions left the organization and began joining armed underground groups.

Even though they shared some members, the May 19th Communist Organization and the John Brown group played distinct roles. May 19th members worked more closely with the Republic of New Afrika and other national liberation organizations, and intended to ratchet up direct confrontations with white supremacists. Austin's John Brown chapter sought to build a public, mass-based movement to openly challenge structures of racism. Laughlin recalled the moment when Evans announced to the Austin chapter that she was joining the May 19th group. "She got more serious. It really meant she was joining the higher tier of sophisticated communists. The John Brown Anti-Klan Committee wasn't necessarily communist, although we did a lot of study of the issues we were up against."

In fact, the strategic framework from the Republic of New Afrika included a lot of rigorous study. Izielen Agbon and Amilcar Shabazz would hold regular political education sessions for the Task Force and other Austin-based radical organizations as a form of revolutionary training. "Oh, it was so intense! I remember staying up until five in the morning learning about the history of imperialism," exclaimed Laughlin. Even though she had gone through some academic higher education, her experience studying within the movement was much more rigorous and relevant. "It was one of the ways we came together, connecting to these ideas. You could feel the stakes, and people's lives were part of what we were discussing."

This organizational structure created a contradictory dynamic in the Committee. The Austin chapter found that wanting to work under the leadership of other revolutionary groups was much easier than actually doing it. Committee leadership expected local chapters to take cues from anti-imperialist organizations. Yet in Austin the Task Force was pragmatically closer to traditional reform-oriented civil rights organizations than it was to revolution-oriented Black nationalist groups such as the Republic of New Afrika that were calling for the overthrow of the U.S. government and the establishment a separate Black nation in the South. This tension was never resolved. Instead, it was left to people's individual responses. Evans described her personal disdain for reform work. "We were revolutionaries [and] didn't worry about winning reforms, [or building] programmatic unity. Sectarianism didn't allow us to even listen to what people benefiting from reforms had to say."

THE DIVIDING LINE

As the 1970s came to an end, two dramatic events occurring three hundred miles and just one day apart became stark previews of the racial fault lines that would soon define the Reagan era and cast long shadows over the future of the John Brown project. The first took place on Friday, November 2, 1979, when members of the Black Liberation Army broke Assata Shakur out of the Clinton Correctional Facility in New Jersey. Shakur's escape succeeded due to a mix of military-style extraction and good luck. Sekou Odinga, Mtayari Sundiata, Winston Patterson, and Silvia Baraldini, posing as visitors with fake names and addresses, were able to sneak in with guns that they then used to take two guards hostage in the visiting hall. From there, they walked Shakur out to a getaway car.[93]

Following her breakout, the FBI and local New York Police Department conducted raids on suspected safe houses in Manhattan and Somerset, New Jersey. The latter became a focus, and the FBI plastered wanted posters throughout neighborhoods. In response, members of the New York John Brown crew distributed "Assata Shakur Is Welcome Here" posters to cover up the wanted signs. Around this time, there were a number of cross burnings in Somerset, an area known to have aided Assata Shakur before her arrest and on the day after her escape. Akinyele Umoja, a leader in the New Afrikan People's Organization, remembers the chaos of the times: "The FBI's hunt for Assata enabled them to harass many political groups and reassert themselves in the Black community. Many women who looked like Assata were harassed following her escape."

Intense police surveillance, harassment, and raids continued until Assata publicly surfaced in Cuba five years later. The second dramatic event happened one day after Assata's prison break. On November 3, 1979, in Greensboro, North Carolina, thirty-five armed members of the United Racist Front, an umbrella organization newly formed for members of the Ku Klux Klan and the American Nazi Party, drove to the site of an anti-Klan demonstration that was part of a campaign to support Black textile workers. They parked their cars, pulled shotguns, pistols, and rifles from their trunks, walked up to the multiracial crowd, and shot more than twenty rounds of ammunition at protesters for eighty-eight seconds. They killed five anti-Klan protesters and wounded ten more. They then drove away without a sign of police pursuit.

The Greensboro Police Department declared that the Communist Workers' Party, the organization many of the dead belonged to, was responsible for the shooting, citing provocation. Overnight, the incident was transformed from a "massacre" by the Klan to a "shootout" between two extremist organizations. The Greensboro Police Department officially reported that antagonism between the two was the reason people were killed.[94] The killings also exposed sharp differences in politics between the Klan's opponents. Other anti-racist groups castigated the Communist Workers' Party for staging the demonstration at a Black housing project, which placed the community at risk.

It was later revealed that the FBI and the Bureau of Alcohol, Tobacco, and Firearms were fully aware of the Klan and Nazi plan to attack those gathering at the rally. The police also had an informant working inside the Klan who had participated in bringing the two groups together in the United Racist Front. Historian Catherine Fosl, who was then a student influenced by the National Anti-Klan Network, described a sense of the impending threat: "You had to think twice about going to [an anti-Klan] rally in a way that you didn't have to think twice about going to an anti-war rally or civil rights rally or feminist rally."

A third defining event happened just two days later. On Monday, November 5, 1979, New Yorkers poured into the streets for the Tenth Annual Black Solidarity Day. The National Black Human Rights Coalition called for a general strike, plastering posters across Harlem declaring, "Don't Work, Don't Buy, Boycott Big Business—General Strike!" Business as usual was disrupted when around 1,500 Black people and their supporters marched from Harlem to the United Nations Plaza, a five-mile route that covered more than half the length of Manhattan Island.

Protesters held signs that read "Republic of New Afrika: Free the Land," "Death to the Klan," "Black People Charge Genocide," and "Human Rights is the Right to Self Determination." During the six years Assata Shakur had been imprisoned, she had become a kind of symbol of the times; for the FBI, she was the soul of the Black Liberation Army that they had finally captured. For activists worldwide, her escape symbolized a hope for resistance against the legacies of colonialism, white supremacy, and oppression of Indigenous communities and people of color. Black Solidarity Day was an ideal occasion to publicly celebrate Shakur's escape to freedom by reading a statement she had recently written:

> November 1979 and crosses burn the face of America. November 1979 and hundreds of Ku Klux Klan members march all over the country carrying clubs, chains and machine guns. 1979—black families are fire bombed. 1979—over 40% of black youth are unemployed. 1979 and a white policeman shoots a handcuffed black man in the head and is acquitted. 1979—and five policemen shoot a Puerto Rican man armed only with a pair of scissors 24 times. 1979—and Philadelphia, the 4th largest city in the country

is sued by the Justice Department for systematically condoning and encouraging widespread police brutality, especially against Black and Puerto Ricans.[95]

In three brief pages, Shakur described the atrocities of the prison system and its role in controlling Black people and revolutionaries.

The network of support built around Assata and Sundiata Acoli of the Black Liberation Army was extensive and robust. Groups such as Friends of Assata and Sundiata worked diligently to build community support networks. "We were asked to build support for Assata," recalled Whitehorn. Because several Committee members were also part of Friends of Assata and Sundiata, including Lisa Roth, solidarity work continued alongside anti-Klan work. "We didn't know what was going to happen, but when she was liberated, we could see how important all that work was," continued Whitehorn.

During that time, the Committee's New York chapter focused on amplifying support for Assata Shakur. The Madame Binh Graphics Collective, with members of the Republic of New Afrika, created and printed one thousand of the famous "Assata Shakur Is Welcome Here" posters. The Committee distributed these posters, including copies of Assata's statement, throughout New York City and New Brunswick, New Jersey. People in Harlem began putting the posters in store windows, which elicited a crackdown from police. Around this time, the Committee began printing the newspaper *Death to the Klan!*, which it also distributed in the Assata support efforts.[96] The first issue, released in November 1979, featured the headline "Assata Shakur Escapes!" and an article assessing the new stage of Black Liberation that had begun.

"Racist organizing was everywhere," said Fadem, describing the feeling of crisis and desperation felt by activists at the beginning of the 1980s. "It was Nazi punks, it was new racist organizations, it didn't matter where it was. We were being pushed." So the John Brown Anti-Klan Committee pushed back. Its members began building a national network to confront and expose the Klan and similar white supremacist organizations that formed the underbelly of the Reagan years.

TWO

ROOTS, RADICALS, AND REAGAN

"The real danger today comes from the people in high places, from the halls of Congress to the boardrooms of our big corporations, who are telling the white people that if their taxes are eating up their paychecks, it's not because of our bloated military budget, but because of government programs that benefit black people; those people in high places who are telling white people that if young whites are unemployed it's because blacks are getting all the jobs. Our problem is the people in power who are creating a scapegoat mentality. That, that is what is creating the climate in which the Klan can grow in this country and that is what is creating the danger of a fascist movement in the 1980s in America."

—Anne Braden, 1979

Ten days after Assata Shakur was arrested Ronald Reagan announced his bid for President of the United States. Reagan's election in 1980 was a game changer. The political terrain had suddenly shifted to the hard right, and a surge of white supremacist activity was immediately apparent. In response, an explosion of networking against white power groups began coalescing into a nationwide movement. This explosion brought the John Brown Anti-Klan Committee into contact with a diverse array of anti-racist groups. Throughout Reagan's first term, the organization's chapters struggled with the tensions that came with maintaining a radical orientation while positioning themselves within a big tent where groups with a wide range of approaches could forge strategic alliances.

Reagan's election also signaled to groups on the far right that they could operate with greater impunity. Reagan's presidential campaign, like Trump's decades later, deftly manipulated racist resentment and antipathy. In 1980, at the Neshoba County fairgrounds in Mississippi, the Great Communicator used racial codes, hushed tones, and subtle signals that energized white supremacists. The fairgrounds were just a few miles from the site where, in 1964, students and Freedom Summer volunteers James Chaney, Andrew Goodman, and Michael Schwerner were murdered by members of the local White Knights of the Ku Klux Klan with the collusion of the local sheriff's office and police department. Reagan made no mention of this history in his speech. Instead, he focused on "states' rights." His voice boomed over the crowd:

> I believe in states' rights; I believe in people doing as much as they can for themselves at the community level and at the private level. And I believe that we've distorted the balance of our government today by giving powers that were never intended in the constitution to that federal establishment. And if I do get the job I'm looking for, I'm going to devote myself to trying to reorder those priorities and to restore to the states and local communities those functions which properly belong there.[97]

By focusing on protecting "states' rights," he played a segregationist card used to suggest subordinating federally mandated school and housing integration to Jim Crow–era laws.

The Gipper's election marked a crushing defeat over Democratic president Jimmy Carter and signaled a break with the old Franklin Delano Roosevelt–style politics known for bipartisan efforts to create social welfare programs and increase government jobs in a booming post–World War II economy. The inauguration of neoliberal British Prime Minister Margaret Thatcher served as an assist in what would become hard times for the left-leaning counterculture of the 1970s. Reagan was a two-term conservative governor and B-rate Hollywood actor who achieved notoriety on the left for trying to get Angela Y. Davis fired from her teaching position at UCLA in 1969, and for ordering the use of bayonets against Berkeley anti-war protesters. His core priorities were cutting taxes for the rich, reducing regulations on corporate power, and attacking communism everywhere.

In 1962, Reagan had flipped from being a Democrat to a Republican, effectively marrying his anti-communist passion with Barry Goldwater's monumentally racist campaign for president.[98] By endorsing Goldwater, Reagan signed onto a style of racially paranoid politics, appealing to the fears of Southern white conservatives. This would have lasting effects in the decades to come, including the growth of the religious right.

The impacts of these shifts were significant and far-reaching. Organizer and author Suzanne Pharr has described this era as the emergence of "modern domination politics" by which the privileged few seek to control the lives of the many. "Very few predicted how fast right-wing ideology would move into the mainstream or recognized this political force for the steamroller it was."[99] This steamroller came in the form of the New Right Coalition composed of socially conservative Christians, business elites, and a reactionary low-income white population willing to vote against its own economic interests in order to remain aligned on other fronts, including law enforcement focus against Blacks and Latinos. The New Right began mobilizing against such issues such as abortion, welfare, equal rights protection, affirmative action, multiculturalism, drugs, crime, and most forms of taxation. This coalition advanced by articulating a sense of national political identity that was rooted in white cultural codes and evangelical Christian networks. The New Right perpetuated the Old Right's hard anti-communist doctrine and militancy, and adapted it to the changing times. The New Right also benefited from rising popular anxieties about economic instability and the perceived decline of U.S. power under Jimmy Carter. The political climate of precarity and fear this created reverberated along racial lines. Emmet Burns, regional director for the NAACP of Virginia, Maryland, and the District of Columbia, described this time period: "With the federal deficit what it is, with the conservative climate in our government what it is, some people are going to be looking for reasons why things are the way they are. They're going to be looking for scapegoats and I feel I am a scapegoat. I can't wash away my blackness."[100]

Reagan was an electoral project of the New Right. His attack on big government on behalf of big business, disdain for anything communist, and cavalier sensibilities were a window of opportunity for the New Right to advance aggressively. And although some neoconservative sectors became disillusioned with Reagan once he took office, the New Right agenda continued to move the nation's political and cultural center in conservative directions. These conditions fostered a significant increase in vigilante incidents and coalition building among networks of white supremacists and fascists.

Reagan skillfully bridged class divides among white people by harnessing their racial anxieties and economic uncertainties. His patrician style resonated with people turned off by Black empowerment and the anti-authoritarian challenges posed to the status quo by the social movements and youth counterculture of the 1970s. Most notably, many Reagan supporters believed that the gains won by civil rights groups took something away from white people, and that immigrants and people of color were the cause of their precarity. This view was aggressively advanced by the Klan in the 1970s and later found its way into federal court cases through the 1978 Bakke decision upholding affirmative action.

The Klan endorsed Reagan in 1980. In an editorial in the *Knights of the Ku Klux Klan* newspaper, the Imperial Wizard of the Invisible Empire of the Ku Klux Klan, Bill Wilkinson, boasted that Reagan's platform "reads as if it were written by a Klansman," and promised to march in Reagan's inaugural parade.[101] Reagan, like Trump later, took his sweet time before rebuking the endorsement, using silence to send a message.[102]

While Reagan had no direct affiliation with the Klan, he kept quiet about the crisis of racist violence in America, including atrocities such as the murders of Black children in Atlanta and the Greensboro Massacre. This was a kind of signaling that encouraged more right-wing attacks. Author and scholar Manning Marable called Reagan's election the final "green light largely responsible for unleashing racist terror."[103] "The Reagan administration is turning out to be a boon for the Klan," said Sam Royer, Grand Dragon of the KKK in Maryland in 1982.[104]

The Klan was just one of many organizations active in the Reagan-era resurgence of white supremacy. Just as important was David Duke's National Association for the Advancement of White People. Duke's organization, as its name implied, attempted to frame white supremacist politics in terms of rights-based legal reasoning used by the Civil Rights movement. The White Aryan Resistance, started by California Klan leader Tom Metzger, reached far beyond the Klan's traditional base toward younger recruits. Other active groups included the American Front, a revived Posse Comitatus, Aryan Nations, the Order, Church of Jesus Christ–Christian, and the National Alliance.

In the John Brown Anti-Klan Committee's worldview, the growth of the far right during the Reagan years was a logical extension of the history of white supremacy in the United

States. "We thought Reagan was the worst," said Whitehorn, "but depending on how long your view of history is, he wasn't entirely a surprise either." Some on the far right forged new alliances. Some, like Aryan Nation, ventured toward declaring war on the U.S. government.[105] Others, like Tom Metzger, pursued elections as a path to power.

The John Brown Anti-Klan Committee's response was to create more chapters, form more alliances with organizations on a local level, increase its militancy, expand its assessment of the white supremacist threat, and connect efforts across the previously divided lines between May 19th on the East Coast and Prairie Fire on the West Coast. Julie Nalibov, a member in the D.C. chapter, observed, "After Greensboro and Reagan, we tried to look more at where white supremacy was at its core, even if it wasn't the Ku Klux Klan. We talked a lot more about white terror. The Klan was a metaphor as an organization." In this context, the Committee's efforts to educate the public about racism and "Klan-like" groups were significant. During this political moment, the candid acknowledgment that white supremacy existed outside the Klan was still a matter of controversy, and the group made it a point of their community outreach work.

Working at the pace of the threat they perceived, the John Brown Anti-Klan Committee rapidly expanded during Reagan's first term. What started out as a book club in New York City very quickly turned into a national chapter-based organization. Many of the founders held leadership roles and brought new members into decision-making based on variable factors and commitment. The campaigns that the original New York chapter instigated—"Stop Killer Cops!" and "Blue by Day, White By Night"—were useful banners for new chapters to align with. Often, these campaigns were the unifying messages that connected locations across very different political realities. In an attempt to let local chapters have enough autonomy to shape their own campaigns, yet have organizational coherence and accountability to the anti-imperialist strategies that held their loyalty, the Committee adopted a kind of informal level of decision-making where people's personal relationships to May 19th or Prairie Fire determined each chapter's approach and culture. In other words, the John Brown Anti-Klan Committee was a way for two separate organizations to create a network with shared points of unity and campaigns across chapters.

CONFRONTATIONS AT THE CAPITAL

In the lead-up to Reagan's inauguration, the Klan began mobilizing nationwide, particularly in and around Washington, DC. The Committee was but one of many anti-racist groups to respond, but their political militancy often put it at odds with many of the other anti-racist organizations with which it shared a common opposition to the Klan.

After Reagan's victory, the group's chapters in New York, Boston, and Washington, D.C., along with the Moncada Library in Brooklyn, organized a national day of action called "Take a Stand Against the Klan." Laura Whitehorn was sent to D.C. weeks before to help organize the event. From a small office in a church, she made phone calls to meet with various organizations to see if there was local support for an event. She remembered that international student groups—African and Palestinian—were among the most responsive. It was here that she learned that COINTELPRO had targeted even the smallest groups of Black writers and poets.

The Committee printed flyers with a picture of a two-sided coin in front of the White House. One side of the coin featured the face of Ronald Reagan, and the other a hooded Klansman. "This is not an individual question or a local issue. We cannot hope to have any effect in stopping the Klan, in Park Slope or anywhere, unless we turn our individual anger into building a mass movement that will fight alongside Black and Third World people," read the text from a Committee flyer.

On January 20, 1980, around fifty people gathered on the

steps of the U.S. Justice Department at 925 Pennsylvania Avenue. They were protesting Reagan's inauguration. "We are targeting the U.S. Justice Department as a defender of white supremacist organizations, like the Klan, and the state's complicity in acquittal after acquittal of every racist killer cop in America," said Natalee Rosenstein, a N.Y.C. Committee member, on a bullhorn during the demonstration. When the speeches ended, they began a picket line, circling the Justice Department and chanting, "New York, Miami, Tennessee, Death to White Supremacy!" and "White by Night, Blue by Day, Killer Cops Will Have to Pay!" The rally turned into a two-mile march north to the Calvary United Methodist Church, where the John Brown chapter held an anti-Klan teach-in.

To the surprise of Whitehorn and Rosenstein, about five hundred people showed up to the teach-in. Multulu Shakur had helped them frame the event, focusing on international state-sponsored, white supremacist organizing. Rosenstein started by describing lessons she learned as a white person involved in anti-imperialist struggles. She spoke about the role violence plays and how important it is for anti-racist struggles to remain public, especially in the face of challenges that come when confronting the Klan. During the teach-in, Rosenstein described what she saw as the way out of the emerging Reagan era: "We as white people have to work collectively and build organizations. We have to forge ourselves into a disciplined movement with a leadership accountable to the forces leading the fight against the Klan."

Another speaker was Camille Bell, mother of Yusef Bell, one of many Black children murdered in Atlanta. Ms. Bell argued for people to go into their own communities to stop white supremacy. Other speakers included Muntu Matsimela of the National Black Human Rights Coalition; Ahmed Obafemi, the East Coast VP of the Provisional Government of Republic of New Africa; Serge Mukendi from the Congolese National Liberation Front; Said Hamad of the Palestinian Liberation Organization; and Jimmy Garret and Loretta Ross of the Yuland Ward Memorial Fund.

Following the protests of the inaugural parade, the John Brown Anti-Klan Committee called more members to the D.C. area. Julie Nalibov was among those who answered and moved to Washington. Julie was part of a new wave of Committee members who were expanding the capacity of the organization. These younger members were selected by the Committee's leadership, mentored intensively, sent reading materials, and slowly brought into decision-making roles. Julie was twenty-three and looking for a change, so asked where she could be most useful. The organization's leadership pointed to the small, tight-knit Washington chapter where everyone lived together. One of the Washington members wanted to move to New York City, so a location swap was coordinated.

Once she settled in, Julie focused on John Brown Anti-Klan Committee work during the day and supported herself with a waitress gig at night. "It was a big city, and I liked how many issues were intersecting," Nalibov recalled. With 70 percent of the population comprised of Black residents, the "Stop Killer Cops" campaign she had supported in New York City was already a familiar one in Washington. One thing she was not prepared for, however, was the more overt display of racism. She came from a progressive liberal home that connected their politics to their Jewish faith. In D.C., she saw "swastikas flown openly and proudly" for the first time in her life.

Nalibov had previously encountered open racism only through images and stories about the Vietnam War and apartheid in South Africa. "I grew up knowing racism was bad, but like a lot of white students at the time, I didn't know what to do about it." She recounted that Black students at Hampshire College, where she had studied, were fed up with white students' cluelessness about not knowing what to do. She became a leader in the movement to divest from apartheid South Africa, where she learned that for a white person, to be anti-racist meant you had to take action. It took some years, however, for her to figure out what this meant domestically. Julie came to the conclusion that challenging white supremacy in the United States meant taking on the institutions that most threatened Black communities at the time: the police and the Klan.

Political life in the Washington region was divided by the Potomac River, separating Maryland from Virginia. Just across the waterway was Arlington, a middle-class white suburb. In 1958, George Lincoln Rockwell, a former WWII veteran, declared Arlington the home of the American Nazi Party. He openly shared that Arlington's appeal was that he could win financial and social support from white people there. Convinced that any publicity a hate group received only served their agenda, progressive forces in Washington attempted to "quarantine" such groups by keeping them out of the media. By 1983, however, it was clear that over twenty-five years, the quarantine strategy had no lasting effect. The American Nazi Party headquarters was prolific in the publishing and sale of anti-Jewish, anti-Black, and anti-Communist literature. Its members also regularly picketed Jewish-owned establishments such as the local pizza place, Mario's Pizza. Nazi flags openly flew above the National Socialist bookstore in Arlington, and became an attraction for tourists.

During that period, the Committee aimed to expose the connections between fascist ideologies, organizations, and members, and sought to confront the activity and recruitment efforts of white supremacist groups. The Ku Klux Klan called itself "the Invisible Empire," and this quality of invisibility, according to the Committee, contributed to its ability to survive and spread. "We try to expose Klan leaders. They mostly operate in a clandestine way, and when we can expose them and show them for what they are, it takes away some of their ability to organize," Christine Rico, a D.C. chapter member, told reporters.[106]

In addition to carrying out investigative work, the D.C. chapter sought to directly disrupt the established normalization of the Nazi and Klan presence in Virginia and Washington. The Committee gathered local phone books and made calls to Nazi members' homes and workplaces to confirm their contact information. "It was kind of bold and a little crazy," admitted Nalibov. They produced flyers that said, "All progressive white people: Don't let these terrorists organize in your community!" The flyers incorporated pictures of Klansmen at a local recruitment drive, their rank within the Klan, the addresses and phone numbers of where they worked, and an invitation to the Montgomery County Courthouse for a public demonstration against white supremacists' recruitment on February 21, 1983. The Washington chapter passed out flyers and spoke to newspapers demanding that Marc Gobleck, an employee at the county-level Department of Transportation, be fired for serving as a recruiting officer in the local Klan.

During autumn of 1983, a rebranded American Nazi Party organization called the New Order petitioned the Yorktown

High School Board of Education to use the school facilities for the "White Pride Day" festival they had scheduled for the same day as national "Black Solidarity Day." Using school spaces was a common recruitment tool of the Klan, and a tactic that the Nazi Party attempted to emulate. The principal of Yorktown High, however, denied the Nazis' request. Previously, the Nazi group had held its annual White Pride Day at local hotels, but the fascist group knew the fight they were picking. Matt Koel, the leader of the New Order, told newspapers that he wanted to "test the County's willingness to abide by the court's ruling."[107] Shortly thereafter, Arlington County school officials granted permission.

In 1973, the Fourth Circuit Federal Court of Appeals had declared that "simple political beliefs are not a basis for denying the [use] of facilities made available for all."[108] This decision and others like it were commonplace rulings upholding the First Amendment. In fact, the 1973 ruling had overturned an Arlington County law banning the Nazi Party from using the high school as a meeting location in 1970. Given this history, the Washington chapter of the John Brown Anti-Klan Committee was not surprised that the Nazi Party was using the tactic of petitioning for the use of public schools to wade into the controversy. As Nalibov said, "We had seen this so many times before, how hate groups organize around the First Amendment." Indeed, this strategy was often the first line of defense for white supremacist organizations to employ. She continued, "Of course, our position was, is it really freedom of speech, if that speech incites violence and threatens the lives of people of color?"

As news about the possibility of Nazis renting the school gym spread, phone calls from concerned parents poured into the school board, prompting the principal and the Parent Teachers Association to explore other legal measures to prevent the New Order from using the gymnasium. Yet, despite the initial rejection, Arlington's school officials eventually announced they were "bound by law" to rent their public facilities to the Nazi group. Considering the obvious provocation involved in scheduling a White Pride event on Black Solidarity Day, community members then reached out to the local chapter of the NAACP to get involved. In the absence of a strong response, people in Arlington turned to the Anti-Defamation League, which suggested they take a "quarantine" approach. This meant granting the proposal quietly and working with the local media to block out White Pride Day from press coverage, keeping local impact contained and national coverage at a minimum. The NAACP and Anti-Defamation League were hands-off on the local level. With mounting public pressure, the local John Brown Committee jumped into the fray.

School officials sided with the Anti-Defamation League after giving up on the possibility of using legal rebuttals to prevent the Nazis from using the school to stage a white supremacy event. In response, concerned parents and teachers promised to collaborate on developing curriculum about Nazi Germany for the upcoming school year. School officials organized a parallel event off school grounds where community members could go on the night of the New Order's gathering to discuss the impacts of Nazism. This seemed to quell tension in the community, but only for a short time. Soon, it came out that students were receiving anti-Semitic flyers on campus and that the school board had received another request: The New Order proposed to shorten the length of their festival in exchange for time in the classroom with high school students to talk about race relations in the United States. In response, the John Brown Anti-Klan Committee decided to gather the people who were outraged and frustrated by the negotiations. "We didn't think we could stop the Nazi gathering, but we thought that if we could talk to the students and support the ones who didn't want the gathering, we would at least show a loud voice of opposition," explained Nalibov.

Two weeks before the Nazi gathering, Julie Nalibov and

Susan Bisgyer, a friend of the Washington chapter, went to Yorktown High after school let out. Being just five years older than a graduating senior, Julie felt that she could easily connect to the high school students. It was typical for students to hang out after school, talk, and smoke before moving on with their day. "We first found the kids smoking cigarettes. We made some assumptions that they wouldn't appreciate the principal's 'hands tied' approach, and so we talked to them about the gathering," said Julie.

Julie and Susan hung out with the students and talked with them about what it meant for Nazis to have the right to access public spaces, and which communities have the choice to ignore Klan activity and which do not. They told the students about the Klan rally in Washington that had been shut down just ten months prior by the "Labor/Black Mobilization to Stop the Klan in Washington." There, 5,000 anti-Klan protesters, led by a coalition of Black union groups, had blocked off downtown Washington, where the Klan planned a march. It was touted as a successful test of protecting public space from hate groups in a Black-majority city. The three dozen Klansmen that showed up, did so late and in normal clothes, and were escorted by police to Lafayette Park for a question and answer session with media. This was when the news coverage switched gears and focused on the tear gas being used on the anti-Klan demonstrators, who were throwing rocks at the Klansmen guarded behind the police line. The event received a lot of mainstream coverage, mostly critical of the tactics used by anti-Klan demonstrators. Despite mainstream depictions of overreaction, including coverage in the *New York Times*, the John Brown Anti-Klan Committee claimed it as a victory for anti-Klan efforts across the country.[109]

The students at Yorktown High had already heard about the rally in Washington. Julie and Susan passed out "Death to the Klan" flyers to students who told them they were appalled that Nazis were using their school, and showed interested in organizing against it. School security was high, which meant that Nalibov and Bisgyer's outreach to students wasn't welcome. "We were willingly walking off campus," Nalibov recounted, "but they arrested us for trespassing. It was ridiculous, but we decided to make it a publicity thing—that the Klan had First Amendment right to be on campus but not us."

A local print shop offered to print their "Death to the Klan" flyers for free. With those in hand, explained Nalibov, "We went around to every possible group—Black churches, synagogues, Jewish groups," and as a result received extensive coverage for being arrested. Opposition to the New Order from political groups inside and outside Arlington grew. In response, the police notified the principal that they would deploy twenty additional officers to "keep the peace" while the New Order invited the local Klan chapter to join their White Pride festival.

Some criticized the Committee for bringing too much attention to a fringe organization like the Nazis. In particular, the Committee received considerable pressure from the Anti-Defamation League, a conservative law organization that had suggested school officials "stay away from the meeting in order to cut down on the amount of publicity the New Order gains from the gathering." But the reputation of the Committee, publicized by the police department, had impact as well. The principal, feeling the pressure of the conflict, sent a letter to parents of students:

> Dear Parents,
> As you know, I did everything in my power to prevent the New Order, American Nazi Party, from meeting at Yorktown High School. Legally, however, my hands were tied, and the New Order will be renting the room at Yorktown, Saturday November 5th, from 7-10p. This will be a private meeting with approximately 20-25 members. As principal, I feel I should inform you that a left extremist group, the

John Brown Society,* has been trying to involve students in a counter demonstration that evening. This group has a history of violence and I urge you to ensure that your son or daughter stays away from Yorktown that night because we fear for safety of anyone involved.

Meanwhile, some of the Jewish students with whom Nalibov and Bisgyer had met became more vocal about the matter. Beth Sorkowitz, a Yorktown senior and student representative on the school board, expressed her anger at community leaders, wondering, "Where are our Jewish leaders?" She called for action from Jewish students, criticizing community leaders who were "too busy handing out plaques at lunches" to take on the Nazis in their midst.[110]

A few days before the gathering, a school board meeting was flooded with residents from Arlington and surrounding counties. Five people, including three Holocaust survivors, signed up for the five ten-minute speaking slots. After the first speaker, the board turned off the microphone and used the rest of the time to discuss an unrelated teacher evaluation report, effectively silencing community voices on the matter.

The day before the Nazis were scheduled to come to Yorktown High, the John Brown Anti-Klan Committee called for a press conference outside the school to clarify the story of the event. Nalibov was questioned about the group's militancy and what they planned to do while the Nazis were in the school. Her first response was to describe the Klan's long history of terrorism against Black people in the United States. In addition, she clarified, "We don't intend to prevent the Nazis from entering the building. We don't think we can do that." The local newspapers reported only that the John Brown Anti-Klan Committee "promises nonviolence."

The day of the gathering was cold, rainy, and fraught with tension. The anti-Klan demonstration started two hours before "White Pride Day" began. Reporters with cameras and curious onlookers gathered to see what would happen. Approximately one hundred anti-Klan protesters arrived, and, despite the warnings from the principal, groups of students from Yorktown High showed up too. A silence came over the crowd as two hundred police arrived, lights flashing, to escort two buses full of Nazis and Klansmen onto school grounds. Once the buses were parked at the entrance, the anti-Klan groups broke into yells: "Cops and Klan Go Hand in Hand!" and "We Don't Want You Here!"

Nalibov remembered how quickly things escalated. "We don't know who, but some people started throwing things—like bottles and pieces of fruit—at Nazis as they got off the bus. Then someone hit the police chief in the head with a rock. So, they started grabbing us." It became clear that some of the onlookers were undercover police poised to extract anyone that seemed to be leading anti-Klan activity. Nalibov was grabbed by police, and Committee member Sandra Roland tried to pull the officer off her, but she too was tackled by a plainclothes cop. Nalibov recalled when fear set in: "They were going to detain us inside the school building. I was terrified. We would be away from cameras, away from [the] crowd, inside the building with eighty Nazis and Klansmen and cops."

Nalibov and Roland were threatened with felony charges of assault on a police officer and inciting a riot. Many news stations had showed up to cover the rally, and the D.C. chapter later tried to subpoena them for their video footage in Nalibov's defense. Local Quakers testified on Nalibov's behalf, confirming that she was holding a bullhorn, which contradicted the charge of throwing rocks. Nalibov explained, "My bail was $10,000. Sandra got community service and had to wash police cars. It's on my record, but it was a suspended sentence. I was banned from Arlington County for a year, which was fine with me."

The D.C. chapter would continue to organize two years after the events at Yorktown High School. Around this time, chapter members started to question the effectiveness of organization's approach—in particular, how holding a militant political line, in their case, was often at odds with building a mass movement. Their message was potent, but unable to reach beyond their current organizational partnerships in any long-term way. Nalibov admitted, "I was young. I was surrounded by anti-imperialist activists, which was important to me. But it was waitressing that showed me I didn't even know how to talk to normal people, even people who were more generally anti-racist." It seemed that aspects of the organizational culture in the Committee—a self-righteousness underpinning the militancy—was stifling their campaigns. In the early 1980s, the John Brown Anti-Klan Committee was still young. It would take a few more years for these early reflections to influence their decisions.

UP SOUTH IN NEW ENGLAND

In 1980, the Klan was growing. Scotland, Connecticut, made national news when the Klan staged its first rally there in fifty years, marking a staunch effort to unite white supremacist groups across the region. The subsequent series of Klan rallies that took place in Connecticut, with the slogan "Rebels and Yankees get together for the coming race war," both galvanized and splintered anti-Klan organizing.[111]

Scotland is a small town about thirty-five miles west of Hartford. With a population of around 1,000, it is an unassuming place that people more often drive through than visit, unless they stop to explore Civil War history or the local Antique Tool Museum. "It was the perfect place for the Klan to build its base," recalled Terry Bisson, an early member of the John Brown Committee from eastern Kentucky. The Klan held rallies at the Electric Bolt factory as part of a recruitment effort targeting white people who felt economic anxiety. As Bisson explained, "Connecticut was known for manufacturing defense weapons since the Cold War, and a lot of that industry was on the decline."

In September 1980, news broke that a Scotland resident had rented his farm to the Klan for a meeting. Residents shared with reporters a certain level of shock and dismay, but no one indicated that they would be taking action. Comments ranged from "I think it's a shame the rally has to happen" to "I think we should just ignore it." Other news reports captured voices of support. For example, a handful of young white men from the local mill and factory told the press that the Klan's message was compelling. "We have to stand up for what we are," one Klan sympathizer declared.[112] Their support echoed the Klan's blunt messaging of "white rights"—that after nineteen years of affirmative action for Black Americans, white Americans also deserved jobs, housing, land, and more political power.

While discord stirred among residents of the region, everyone galvanized by the rally who didn't live in Scotland seemed focused on the potential for violence. A federal judge banned concealed weapons for the weekend, enabling checkpoints and car searches. The police department anticipated clashes between the Klan and anti-Klan protesters, which spurred them to spend hundreds of thousands of dollars to bulk up security at the event. Imperial Wizard Bill Wilkinson of Louisiana and Grand Dragon Jim Locke of Pennsylvania flew in to lead the cross burning and appoint a new Grand Dragon for Connecticut. "We don't want any trouble," said Locke, while mounting a "White Christians Only" sign outside the farm gate. He proclaimed, "The Klan is for law and order."[113]

The rally took place on September 13, 1980. There were two hundred state troopers, forty-five Klansmen, one hundred Klan supporters, and one hundred anti-Klan protesters.[114] White reporters were the only outside observers allowed into the ceremony. Their articles recounted stories of economic hardship and the Klan as a place of belonging. When journalists covered the anti-Klan protesters, they referred to groups spitting "anti-Klan venom" and Communist messages. Nine anti-Klan marchers were arrested, and the resounding takeaway was that those opposing the Klan were as prone to violence as the Klan.

The rally in Scotland foreshadowed growing differences among anti-Klan groups. A group's tactics for how best to stop the Klan were based on that group's assessment of the Klan and the potential threat it posed. Was the Klan a symbolic fringe group, a nonviolent organization for law and order, a terrorist organization, or something else? Each group answered those questions differently, and as a result, their tactics for countering the Klan ranged from face-to-face confrontations to ignoring the Klan and holding alternative events such as prayer circles for peace. For anti-Klan organizers, the question of who controlled narratives about race relations mattered, because such narratives shaped whether the John Brown Anti-Klan Committee's efforts were seen as welcome resistance or unwelcome provocation. Oftentimes, when a community was not already organized to confront the Klan, pre-existing tensions within a community were exacerbated by anti-Klan efforts, making the politics of forming a united front much more complicated.

During the five years following the Scotland rally, Klan organizing accelerated in Connecticut. Klansmen recruited at high schools, organized youth corps military training camps, and held a series of rallies in Meriden, Scotland, Windham, and East Windsor, as well as in Vermont. The biggest confrontation came in 1981, when the Klan organized a rally in support of a white police officer who had shot and killed a twenty-four-year-old Black man. On February 24, 1981, Keith Rakestrau and his two brothers, Gary and Rodney, were at the Meriden Square shopping mall, just twenty miles south of Hartford. News reports allege that the brothers were shoplifting, which spurred a chase by a security guard into the mall's parking lot. Gene Hale, the husband of the security guard, was waiting in the parking lot to pick up his wife from work when the Rakestrau brothers ran into him. Hale was a white off-duty police officer and a former U.S. Army investigator. He wrestled one of the brothers to the ground and, after scuffling for some time, shot into the car that Keith was driving. Hale alleged that Keith was attempting to run him over. The gunfire killed Keith instantly.

In the following days, organizations such as the Inner City Exchange and the NAACP made public statements demanding Hale be suspended or fired. They organized a series of vigils and public gatherings to honor Rakestrau and demanded justice, but the police chief only temporarily demoted Hale to office detail during the department's investigation. Controversy over the killing continued for weeks. Tensions peaked when Louisiana Grand Wizard Bill Wilkinson, moving on a "Connecticut is ready for recruitment" strategy, announced the Klan would hold a rally on March 21 to demonstrate public support for Hale. Meanwhile, the FBI confirmed it would take over the investigation of the incident.

On March 21, 1981, about forty Klansmen and sympathizers marched from a war memorial to the steps of City Hall holding signs that read, "Support Your Local Police Officer." Approximately one hundred anti-Klan demonstrators clashed with marchers, throwing rocks and glass bottles, injuring twenty-one people.[115] The incident became known as the most violent demonstration against the Klan in Connecticut's history. Even though anti-Klan chants drowned out the speeches, the police provided a protective escort for Klan members to City Hall.[116]

The controversy spurred a range of anti-Klan efforts. In 1981, the statewide Connecticut Educational Association developed an "educational counter-offensive" with tool kits for teachers and readings lists of interracial children's books. Liberal organizations believed that the rise of the far right under Reagan was simply unfortunate detritus from an era the country would soon leave behind. For example, the National Education Association, the Connecticut Education Association, and the Council of Interracial Books for Children combined their resources to design lesson plans for teachers in a tool kit called "Violence, the Ku Klux Klan, and the Struggle for Equality." Aiming at early education for children, they developed this toolkit with the assumption that the more people understood the origins and role of the Klan, the less likely the Klan could be understood as a conventional civic organization. Other education-based groups, such the Southern Student Activist Network, took it a step further and organized a series of lectures featuring recent victims of Klan violence, explicitly connecting to the nationwide anti-Klan campaign.

The Progressive Labor Party and its spin-off organization, the International Committee on Anti-Racism (INCAR), sustained a presence in Connecticut's anti-racist efforts throughout the early 1980s. Notably, INCAR brought together students and factory workers with the intention of building a Communist Party dedicated to solidarity with an international working class. In 1982, the Anti-Racist Coalition of Connecticut (ARCC), composed of churches, labor unions, and community groups around Meriden, formed in response to the Klan rallies. They worked to pass the state's first "hate crime" law, by which the frequency of racially motivated crimes as determined by local police departments would be analyzed.

Campaigns to create laws that gave police more power were not in alignment with the radical organizations the John Brown Anti-Klan Committee took cues from. The Committee was steadfast in holding some political positions. "We never let go of the fact the Klan should not exist," recalled Lisa Roth. When groups were looking to manage, quell, or subdue the emboldened racist right, the John Brown Anti-Klan Committee would produce literature challenging whether First Amendment protections should extend to organizations with violent histories like the Klan's. A John Brown outreach flyer read:

The Ku Klux Klan has no right to march. The Klan is a right-wing armed organization dedicated to the violent subjugation of all Black people. Armed fascists have no right to parade through the streets organizing for genocide and war. The fact that the US government promotes, protects, and builds the

Klan, and many white people defend the Klan, is not about "free speech," but white supremacy. The Klan is being built today to defend an empire in crisis. US imperialism needs the Klan to organize white people to total loyalty to the system, and to attack the just struggles of Black (New Afrikan) and other Third World people for human rights and liberation. From Miami to Georgia to Washington D.C. Black people have stopped the Klan from marching on their cities. Anti-racist white people can follow their example and do the same. All progressive people have a right and responsibility to stop the Klan. The Klan has no right to march or even exist.

The flyer had pictures of seven KKK organizers then working in Connecticut, Boston, Brooklyn, and Maryland. It included their names, their phone numbers, and information about their organizational roles. At the bottom, the flyers summarized the John Brown Anti-Klan Committee's political position: "Death to the Klan! Fight White Supremacy! Support Black People's Right to Self-Defense! Land and Independence for New Afrika—the Black Nation!"

In March 1983, Lisa Roth, Terry Bisson, Julie Nalibov, Laura Whitehorn, and Russell Neufeld made frequent trips to Meriden for city council meetings deliberating on a permit for a white supremacist rally on April 30. "We were trying to get them to pass a resolution. We said they could set a standard and declare it illegal for a terrorist organization to be in public space." The local John Brown Anti-Klan Committee knew that their appeal would not sway the city council. They intended to raise the issue in ways never before discussed in this local community forum. They knew they were not popular with the city council, but they also knew that by being vocal in council meetings, they'd attract new supporters.

This was a double-edged position to take. "We were seen

as outside agitators, we were seen negatively," which limited the reach of the message, said Bisson. "But looking back, we missed the chance to work with other people who at least agreed that the Klan shouldn't exist." On the day of the rally, it was apparent that the connections members had made during the council meetings were relatively successful, turning out twenty young white people to protest the Klan. Police set up barricades when they saw this group of people gathering. "We decided we were going to serve lunch to the anti-Klan protesters. We handed out pita bread sandwiches filled with gravel and frozen cans of Coca Cola. Of course, we threw them at the Klan," recounted Roth.

The Committee had mobilized a modest gathering of people—small, yet still exciting. But the fact that there was no local chapter in Meriden raised questions about their early attempts at strategy. It was common for the Klan to seek out small, mostly white towns where infrastructure was waning or where they had pockets of support. It seemed logical that the Committee would find ways to get involved in anti-Klan efforts in such places. However, its commitment to following leadership of other organizations often meant they were simultaneously focusing their efforts on issues such as gentrification and police shootings in bigger metropolitan cities. As a result, the core leadership of the John Brown Anti-Klan Committee in the Northeast was spread thin, trying to sustain momentum in tactical chapters and driving long distances to Klan-afflicted areas. "After a while, it became this routine thing. It didn't make much sense anymore," Bisson admitted.

The New York chapter began to wind down in the mid-1980s. "The Klan would announce another rally at Meriden City Hall, and we would rent cars and drive up there. The police would get paid overtime, so they were quite happy to work out their procedures. The Klan would do their thing. We would do our thing. The police would do their thing. Then everyone would go home. It didn't seem right to me; we were basically funding the car rental agency and just reacting to the Klan." Committee members were left asking themselves: *What is the best long-term strategy for confronting white supremacists?*

BURNING CROSSES IN THE CITY OF ANGELS

During this period, the Los Angeles chapter of the John Brown Anti-Klan Committee grappled with the complexities of fighting white supremacy through the court system. The main catalyst behind the L.A. work was movement veteran Michael Novick, who was part the Prairie Fire Organizing Committee. In 1982, he was dispatched from Chicago to work in Los Angeles. Growing up in Brooklyn in a working-class Polish family involved in trade unions had instilled in him a sense of what it meant to organize one's life around politics. Novick was the first in his family to go to college, and, because it was located close to home, he attended Brooklyn College. Novick had become politicized by seeing Brooklyn's "Urban Removal" programs demolish low-income neighborhoods. Novick wanted to use his role as student president to fight racism in higher education.[117] He and fellow SDS organizers supported integration efforts at the college, which aimed to diversify the 98 percent white student body. He learned quickly how racism divided movement organizers when Columbia University's SDS members supporting this campaign were violently run off campus by white students.

When Novick arrived in Los Angeles, he founded the Take a Stand Against the Klan Committee with a group of twelve people. Even though Prairie Fire Organizing Committee and May 19th were separated, both groups shared the view that they were fighting U.S. imperialism, not just the Klan, and that the fundamental force that would disrupt white supremacy would be national liberation struggles. "We want to fight as full allies of national liberation in the struggle against imperialism," read a solidarity statement written by May 19th in support of the Black Liberation Army. "As white people, we no longer want to live in this exploitative and oppressive system and that is why we must unite with a revolutionary strategy and make it our own."[118] In direct response to the growing influence of the White Aryan Resistance, a Klan offshoot founded by television repairman Tom Metzger, the Los Angeles crew decided that it would have more impact to coordinate with national efforts. To do this, the Take A Stand Against the Klan group became a chapter of the John Brown Anti-Klan Committee network.

In 1980, Metzger won the Democratic nomination for Congress in California's 43rd district with 46,361 votes. Democratic leaders had abandoned the district, because they thought it wasn't worth their time to challenge the entrenched Republican incumbent. They had scoffed at Metzger's populist campaign, which targeted working-class and middle-class white people living in the suburban and rural areas with messages about the powerlessness of "the little white guy."[119] They ignored the extensive media coverage of Metzger's speeches, interviews, and rallies, all of which focused on how white Christian culture was being degraded by Mexican immigrants, other Hispanics, Blacks, Asians, and "satanic Judaism."[120] News articles covered every moment of his campaign, often highlighting the Klan chapter he organized at the Pendleton Marine Base, or his involvement with David Duke's "Klan Border Patrol." Democratic leaders later argued that extensive media coverage was responsible for Metzger winning the Democratic nomination.

The John Brown Anti-Klan Committee in Los Angeles saw Metzger's bid for state power as anything but laughable. "Tom Metzger is an important and dangerous leader because he is able to conceive and carry out multiple strategies all at once," read a three-page spread in *No Fascist USA!*, the chapter's newspaper.[121] In the 1960s, Metzger supported the presidential bids of libertarian Barry Goldwater and segregationist George Wallace. For Metzger, those experiences were crucial opportunities for learning how to use electoral campaigns as part of long-term strategies that were not dependent upon actually winning elections. Metzger spent ten years rising in the ranks of the John Birch Society, a national far-right organization known for its anti-communist propaganda and demands for limited government. Simultaneously, Metzger built the Minutemen, a militarized survivalist group that focused on self-defense and stockpiling weapons. He also helped to form the White Brotherhood in the 1970s, where he combined forces with Ku Klux Klan leader David Duke.

After splitting with Duke in 1979, Metzger started the California Knights of the Ku Klux Klan. Although he won the Congressional district Democratic primary in 1980, he lost the general election after the Democratic chair disavowed his candidacy and instead endorsed the Republican incumbent, Clair Burgener. Undeterred, in 1982 Metzger ran for the U.S. Senate and received 80,000 votes. "Tom Metzger is surely playing a role reorganizing the clandestine, disciplined fascist armed forces. Whether this terrorist force is primarily skinheads, survivalists, or alienated white workers makes little difference. If we don't oppose them today, their targets will be oppressed and progressive people tomorrow" read an article in *Death to the Klan!*[122]

Klan activity in Sunland, California, a white suburb of Los Angeles, was becoming more visible in the 1980s. In July 1983, robed Klansmen marched with Confederate flags to honor a white police officer killed by a Black man. This was just a couple of years after Los Angeles Police Chief Daryl Gates came under scrutiny for saying, "Blacks might be more likely to die from choke holds because their arteries do not open as fast as arteries do on normal people."[123] There was little to no public response to the robed demonstration, which enabled the Klan to apply for a permit from the local fire department to hold a cross burning. They were denied on the basis that California was in a drought, and a cross burning would pose a fire hazard.[124] When the fire department promised to help them find

Counter-protesters just prior to confronting John Brown Anti-Klan Committee members in Sunland, CA. *Photo from the collection of Michael Novick.*

---

a safer site for the cross burning, the L.A. chapter of the Committee joined up with Makungu Akinyele and Akinyele Umoja, members of the New Afrikan People's Organization (NAPO) and the Center for Black Survival to stage a protest against the proposed cross burning.

At the protest, members of the Jewish Defense League (JDL) physically attacked the anti-racists. According to Novick, the JDL had an infiltrator within the Klan, yet would not share the intelligence to help mount a coordinated campaign against it. Incensed over the support that the Committee and NAPO expressed for Palestinians, the Jewish Defense League often seemed to consider all critiques of Israel to be anti-Semitic.

On December 3, 1983, twenty-five white supremacists burned three 20-foot-high crosses in Lakeview Terrace, a predominantly Black neighborhood outside Los Angeles. The burning was intended to be a unification ceremony of the local Ku Klux Klan, Aryan Nation, and White Aryan Resistance.

Members of the three organizations had negotiated with the Los Angeles Police Department prior to the burning to allow the event to happen in exchange for their arrests after the ceremony. In other words, the police department gave permission for illegal activity. When they were brought to court, Judge Sidney Cherniss told the Klan and their friends, "You're slimy, low, and scummy. I'll say it right to your faces. You have no right to be in this country. You ought to look in a mirror and realize what a terrible person you are."[125] Seconds later, he dropped all charges, explaining that the prosecution had made mistakes in the drafting of their criminal complaint.

The early 1980s presented a steep learning curve for the John Brown Anti-Klan Committee as they attempted to find footing in a shifting political terrain. The blossoming electoral strategy of far-right organizers such as David Duke and Tom Metzger seemed to confirm the Committee's accusations that the Klan's agenda was never far from finding footing in mainstream politics.

THREE

AFTER WINTER MUST COME SPRING: THE ANTI-KLAN MOVEMENT

> The ruling class will tell you that
> there is no ruling class
> as they organize their liberal supporters into
> white supremacist lynch mobs
> organize their children into
> ku klux klan gangs
> organize their police into
> killer cops
> organize their propaganda into
> a device to ossify us with angel dust
> —Jayne Cortez, "There It Is"

In 1983, organizers in the New Afrikan Independence Movement addressed anti-Klan activists, offering their assessment of what had changed since Reagan's election and what was needed from grassroots struggles. In the spring edition of *Death to the Klan!*, they wrote about the passing of "winter in America," a time from 1973 to 1978 that marked a decline in Black-led organizing. They continued:

> Since 1979, our resistance movement has been grow-
> ing. In its resurgence we have come with several im-
> provements in our style of struggle and we have also
> come with some of the old erroneous styles. One of

these is spontaneity. A great deal of political education remains to be done in this area. As had been said
before, our primary task can be put into three words:
organization, organization, and more organization.[126]

This came in response to the recent mobilizations in Boston and Washington, D.C., where diverse masses successfully
shut down planned Klan events. What was now needed, they
explained, was to usher this spontaneous "embryo" of consciousness into the long, "protracted" struggle of New Afrikan
liberation. Political education and "higher forms of organization" were the suggested tactics. The article concluded, "History is our best teacher."

This assessment served as a call to action and refined
the approach of the anti-imperialist portion of the anti-Klan
movement. Calls to "Stop the Klan!" were necessary but glar-
ingly insufficient. It seemed the driving factor of this reactionary tendency, according to the article, was often either
vengeance or desperation, two states of being that often stifled
what was seen as politically possible. Instead, the New Afrikan
Independence movement presented an impetus to anti-Klan
activists to become organizers. This meant going beyond confrontations with the Klan and intentionally inviting people
into the movement. For example, making active opportunities
for people who became politicized by protesting the Klan to
become invested in long-haul work for anti-imperialist movements. One implication of such a call was that anti-Klan organizations would have to be more open and accessible to join.
The task, however, was to achieve this without diluting the
potency of anti-imperialist politics. This clear call to reorient
and scale up reverberated through the John Brown Anti-Klan
Committee.

The years 1982 and 1983 marked an important transition
in the arc of the organization. Although uneven across chapters, the Committee as a whole transitioned from organizing

John Brown Anti-Klan Committee members counter white supremacists with the memory of Malcolm X. Photograph by Trella Laughlin.

around protest to organizing around building coalitions that could coordinate with other sectors of the anti-Klan movement. In part, this shift came from external pressures. The members adjusted their approach as the impacts of Reagan's election were becoming more known and familiar. They readied themselves as the recently formed white power movement declared war on the United States government, ratcheting up FBI investigations. Yet the most influential pressure came from the Committee's long-held relationships with the New Afrikan People's Organization and the New Afrikan Independence Movement. Ahmed Obafemi played the strongest role in pushing the May 19th Communist Organization and Prairie Fire Organizing Committee to work together on a national, coordinated level. Ramping up toward a series of grand jury trials, the FBI intensified its surveillance and harassment of May 19th. Central to the agency's investigations were the escape of Assata Shakur and the tragic 1981 robbery of a Brinks armored car in Nanuet, New York.[127] The FBI used these incidents to exceed the restraints set on them following Congressional inquiries into previous COINTELPRO excesses.

Michael Novick remembered, "They basically said, you're both working against the Klan, we need you to work together." Factional fights were mostly backgrounded. "The push from the New Afrikans helped [us] overcome a certain amount of rivalry and turf mentality," said Novick. The first national Committee conference was organized in Chicago. From there members of May 19th and Prairie Fire who took up the John Brown name reconstituted into a broader national organization with a specific emphasis on opposing white supremacy and supporting the New Afrikan Independence movement. During the conference the two organizations shared lessons from their local struggles and strategized on their new organizational approach: building broad coalitions with a revolutionary spirit.

THE KU KLUX KLAN HAS COME TO TOWN

In the summer of 1982, residents of Austin, Texas, turned on local Channel 24 to watch *Good Morning, Austin*. It was like any other Thursday, except that on this day, the Grand Dragon of the Texas Klan, Gene Fisher, and Imperial Wizard James Stanfield were on the show, describing their youth training camps and showing off their shotguns and semi-automatics. That afternoon, local radio station KLBJ hosted the same Klan members, this time inviting Austin listeners to call in and chat with the Klan. Over the next two days, the Klansmen made two more television appearances. They used this media blitz to publicize their upcoming August rally in Bastrop, Texas. "We're going to destroy Communism," they boasted, and vowed to "take action, violent if necessary" to counter those who dared to oppose them.[128] For these Klan leaders, three things were essential: deploying border patrols for "sealing" the border between the United States and Mexico, purchasing land for "survival camps" in preparation for an inevitable race war, and staging cross burnings. In response to their media blitz, the Black

Dallas Police protect Klan members. Photograph by Trella Laughlin.

Citizens Task Force newspaper ran a headline that read: "The Ku Klux Klan Has Come to Town."

In 1982, the Task Force had joined up with the Brown Berets and the East Town Lake Citizens to form the Austin Minority Coalition. Their aim was to build a united force against the problems they faced in their respective communities: police brutality, high utility rates, and gentrification.[129] The Austin Committee chapter participated in this coalition. Their efforts included driving community members to political education meetings, mobilizing white support for actions against developers' land grabs in the barrio, investigating Klan activity, and monitoring police actions in communities of color.[130] For instance, the Austin chapter was able to find phone records of frequent calls between CIA agent Charles Beckwith and local Klan leaders about land purchases in Bastrop, Texas, a half hour east of Austin, where the Klan burned a cross along with a casket inscribed with "reserved for commies."[131]

The organizations in the Austin Minority Coalition shared the belief that an active anti-racist majority could be established, and that the best way to get there would be for groups to specialize their efforts. For the Task Force, the Brown Berets, and East Town Lake Citizens, this involved building community power, addressing a community's basic needs, and engaging in self-defense. They would have to apply pressure to moderates while also confronting paramilitary formations like the Klan. The majority of elected positions in Austin were held by white people who often spoke about opposing racism but still colluded with racist local policies and practices. For example, they wouldn't take a position against the University of Texas's financial support for South African apartheid and they would implicitly condone racist police behavior by supporting lengthy misconduct investigations.[132]

In January 1983, the Klan submitted a legal request to stage a rally at the Capitol in Austin. The Austin Minority Coalition was the first community-based formation that intervened, beginning with attending a series of city council meetings. They recognized that, time and again, local governments had sanctioned Klan rallies on First Amendment grounds. During the previous year in Atlanta, the Klan, represented by the American Civil Liberties Union, had won approval in federal court to march after its request was rejected by the local government, and even won a temporary restraining order preventing the city from interfering with the march. Weeks before the city council made a decision about the Klan permit, the Austin Minority Coalition knocked on doors to spread the word and bring people to the meetings in an attempt to reframe the debate.

A series of editorials in local newspapers urged residents to stay at home and let the Klan march. Some of the editorials also accused groups that wanted to stop the Klan of being instigators who would make things worse. In response, the Brown Berets circulated a leaflet arguing that resistance to the Klan was a matter of survival for their members. "Our plan is not to infringe upon anyone's First Amendment rights, an argument used by public officials and the media to confuse the issue, but rather to expose the Klan's practice of genocide, which constitutes a criminal act according to the United Nations' Convention on War Crimes Against Humanity."[133]

By the time the Austin city council meeting took place in January, there wasn't a resident in Austin who hadn't heard about the opposition to the rally. The council room was filled to capacity with more attendees gathered outside. The mayor of Austin, Republican Carole Keeton McClellan, delivered the decision. She prefaced her comments, "Believe me when I say we abhor, deplore, and detest the Ku Klux Klan." She then motioned to grant the Klan a permit with the restrictions that no vehicles were allowed in the parade, and no rifles, shotguns, or other weapons were to be carried by any marcher.[134]

Charles Ordy, the only Black council representative, agreed to read a statement from the Black Citizens Task Force about the Klan's history of racist violence in the United States. "The freedom of speech is not absolute," read Ordy, his voice commanding the room's attention. "If a person is not allowed to scream fire in a crowded movie theater, we do not see how the KKK is allowed to propagate their racist theories and actions. The essence of the KKK's ideology is white supremacy." The Task Force's statement received cheers and applause from the people who filled the council chambers. The decision was made to grant the Klan a permit, but the attention had succeeded in escalating public momentum to oppose it. Before leaving the council room, the Black Citizens Task Force called for a human rights march that would commemorate Malcolm X's assassination on February 21, coinciding with the Klan's rally.

The Austin Minority Coalition began preparations, with each member group taking on specific tasks in coordination with the others. Their collective intention was to have an anti-Klan rally that represented a wide range of the Austin community, including different ethnic neighborhoods, youth, and university students. The Black Citizens Task Force focused on holding open meetings for members to learn more about the rally and its relationship to their ongoing campaigns against racist local policies. The Brown Berets focused on tabling and leafleting to counter the dominant media messaging to ignore the Klan. The Austin Committee used its cable television show, *Let the People Speak*, to broadcast the Coalition's messages.

Trella Laughlin recalled, "If the city was going to let them March, we wanted to make sure the only messages about the march were of anti-racist people coming together to stop them." The Committee went to schools and community centers and did door-to-door canvassing in white neighborhoods to build "widespread opposition to the Klan," said Laughlin. They wrote and distributed a pamphlet that declared: "Stopping this march . . . is an issue of stopping an organization that would deny Black and Third World people the most basic of human rights—the right to live."

Through action planning meetings, the leadership within the Austin Minority Coalition and the Austin John Brown crew formulated a clear role for anti-racists willing to put their bodies on the line. Austin chapter members conducted reconnaissance work before the rally, gathering information about where the Klan was staging and how many police were present. The group also prepared to act as a physical buffer between the Klan, police, and other Coalition members. However, debates inside the chapter churned regarding the security of the group's members during the rally, particularly in light of the increased number of death threats members received as the rally drew closer. With Linda Evans and Betty Ann Duke underground, leadership of the Austin chapter turned to Trella Laughlin. She asked the New York and Washington chapters to send ten of their members to support the march.

Some of the Committee members wanted to form a separate contingent to give strong vocal support for the revolutionary "Free the Land!" message. Others took the position that a separate presence at this particular march would be too dangerous, given the high number of Klansmen and police expected. "Some of us wanted to scatter amongst the crowd," recalled Bisson. But others wanted to play a variety of roles, from blocking the Klan's route options to providing security for the Brown Beret and Black Citizens Task Force. They decided on the latter.

On a sunny day in Austin in 1984, chanting from 2,500 anti-Klan demonstrators could be heard for blocks. From the beginning, the police presence loomed large with four hundred officers in the streets and SWAT teams positioned on rooftops. Protesters surrounded the seventy white supremacists—some in red and black Klan robes—marching alongside the KKK Boat Patrol formed in 1979 to attack Vietnamese fishermen. The police formed a perimeter around the Capitol building. A wall of riot police in green military uniforms protected the Klan members, who intended to march from the park to the State Capitol and back. The human rights march brought out a broad cross section of Austin, including professors, students, teachers, and punk rockers. People chanted, "We're fired up, won't take no more!" Banners read *"Abajo Con el Klan"* and "Reagan and the Klan Go Hand in Hand." The massive crowd fell silent when Black Citizens Task Force leader Velma Roberts took the bullhorn. "We have been discouraged by people saying we should ignore the Klan," she commanded. "We think silence is consent. And if we decide to ignore the Klan, then they come into our community and march."[135]

Terry Bisson remembered the visceral sense of being in a crowd unified against the Klan and its supporters. The goal to drown out any Klan speeches was met. The plan to block the Klan's march route, however, didn't work, and Coalition leadership had to improvise. Bisson recalled the strong sense of solidarity among the protesters throughout the day, from sharing food and water to helping each other avoid arrest. "I threw a huge bolt, almost hitting [a] Klansman in the head. I was immediately thrown to the ground by plainclothes police.

They had me down, but I was rescued by the crowd—by our people—who pulled the cop off of me, and I got away."

The Coalition assigned multiple John Brown members to roam the edges of the march route, collecting information about police and Klan activity. These members dressed in unassuming clothing and carried walkie-talkies to communicate with other organizers. Trella Laughlin remembered how things began to go wrong. "[The police] had already changed the route. And here I was, dressed up in this old lady dress, wearing this old lady hat, talking on my walkie-talkie in the car, but we couldn't get through the blockades." This meant that quite a few John Brown members were not present when the police began targeting leaders of the Brown Berets.

Things escalated when police began escorting Klan members to their cars. Pieces of pavement were broken up and hurled at their vehicles. Three lines of police stood between anti-Klan demonstrators and robed Klansmen. The police line started moving toward anti-Klan protesters and approached Brown Beret leader Paul Hernandez. Video showed a person, later identified as a plainclothes policeman, shoving Hernandez from behind and into the police line.[136] A group of ten uniformed police officers handcuffed him, threw him to the ground, and beat him with batons for two consecutive minutes. His ribs were cracked during the attack.

Eleven activists and one reporter were arrested during the rally. Legal proceedings would drag on for years, punctuated by postponements and new arrests. Three members of the Brown Berets—Paul Hernandez, Maria Limon, and Adela Mancias—were charged with "resisting arrest" despite the nationwide release of video showing Hernandez and Limon being beaten by police without provocation. Hernandez believed that he was specifically targeted due to his work helping victims of police brutality file formal complaints against cops. The Task Force supported this claim, "The A.P.D. [Austin Police Department] has been known to selectively target and brutalize

East Austin community activists and members of their family because of their political beliefs. This police brutality is usually covered up by the ineffective Internal Affairs Division of the A.P.D., whose standard procedure is to find any accused officer innocent. The officer is then encouraged to file [perjury] charges against the victim. The situation on Sat. Feb. 19th was no different."[137]

Judge Leslie Taylor came down with the decision to sentence Hernandez to thirty days in jail, while Limon and Mancias were acquitted by the same jury. In 1984, the three filed a $36 million lawsuit against the Austin Police Department and County Attorney Margaret Moore for "acting under color and pretense" of law in their arrest at the rally.[138] They lost the case, but the publicity was instrumental in Hernandez's later bid for a seat in District 51's House.

Austin Committee members Trella Laughlin, Susan Rautenberg, Marie Chauvin, Carolyn Ritter, and Jacqueline Starnes, and supporters Mike Hood and Judy Stone were also arrested at the rally. At first, charges were dropped against Chauvin, Hood, and Stone, but the three were later re-arrested. Two days before the hearing, the motions filed were allegedly lost, which delayed the trial process. Tom Williams, a local punk rocker, was arrested during a raid of a Rock Against Racism fundraiser, and when the Committee showed up to pay his bail, an additional $5,000 was added to the amount.[139]

The Austin Committee was one of the first chapters to take part in local coalitions. Even though contradictions arose while navigating leadership from different national and local organizations, the Austin chapter learned that coalition work did not compel them to dilute their politics. The members began learning from the Black Citizens Task Force about the time, the consistency, and the communication skills needed to build an organization with a membership base. They also learned that situational coalitions, in which disparate groups come together for a joint action or short-term campaign, created the opportunity to invest in another kind of community self-defense: coordinated and invested relationships. The Austin chapter was able to maintain its militancy and develop long-term alliances with other groups dedicated to fighting white supremacists and fascists.

COWBOYS OF RICHMOND

In 1983, national headlines focused on a case brought by the NAACP against the City of Richmond, California, for excessive brutality by members of its police department. Known for its ports, shipyards, and railway system, Richmond was a highly segregated industrial city just north of Berkeley. In Richmond, Chevron's oldest oil refinery and train tracks demarcated the mostly Black inner city and the Asian communities that have long called Richmond home. Inner Richmond contrasted starkly with the affluent, mostly white Richmond Hills area with its closer access to the coastline.

The Richmond Police Department had been known for its "tough" conduct, but in 1983 an actively organized white supremacist group inside the department known as "the Cowboys" was publicly exposed. The Cowboys had formed following Black rebellions in the early 1970s, around the same time that police departments were also developing SWAT teams and counterinsurgency units. Throughout 1982, forty Black Richmond residents filed multiple allegations of police brutality, harassment, and arbitrary assault. The families of Johnny Roman, twenty-five years old, and Michael Guillory, twenty-two years old—two of the five Black men killed by Richmond Police Department over a three-year period—brought a civil trial against the City of Richmond on allegations of police misconduct and death by excessive force.[140]

Prairie Fire Organizing Committee, in line with its priorities of supporting Black Liberation created the Dare to Struggle Committee Against the Klan, a precursor to the John Brown Anti-Klan Committee in the Bay Area. The situation in

Richmond called for concerted pushback. They first connected with the NAACP lawyers who were responsible for exposing police brutality in Oakland. Dare to Struggle placed the emergence of the Cowboys in a long historical continuum of white efforts to dominate and control Black people, beginning with the role of slave patrols in the era of settler-colonialism. The racist brutality of the Cowboys made this point apparent. "It was really awful," Siff recalled. "The Cowboys had created posters and shirts that compared somebody they killed to a deer. It was a game to them."

Gerber collected clippings in the daily newspaper relating to police violence and racism. "It was an enormous stack of articles. It was a jolt to me how many. That was huge in sharing with other groups and making our point concrete," said Gerber. Using the clippings in their community outreach efforts, they were able to persuasively demonstrate how a culture of white supremacy pervaded Bay Area police departments and society at large. Brotsky described how the group started a campaign to pressure the Richmond police chief—not because he was the only one in the department responsible for racism, but because going after him "would set a precedent." Dare to Struggle intended to counter the classic argument of "a few bad apples" with an evidence-based case, supported by clippings, that proved chronic, system-wide corruption.

The testimonies during pretrial hearings revealed that police officers who were members of the Cowboy group were easily identified by the cowboy-style boots and hats they often wore, and by the fact that they often worked at night for the explicitly stated reason of wanting to be in on "more action." Among the police identified as members of the Cowboys were Officers Clinton Mitchell and Michael Dudkiewicz, along with Sergeants Frank Hanratty and Dennis Browne. What's more, careful examination of the brutal shootings of Black people by white police, in addition to testimonies from Black police officers, pointed not only to an organized white supremacist group within the department, but also to a pervasively racist culture within the police department as a whole.

During the year before this case, five Black men were killed by the Richmond Police Department. Over the preceding three years, Black families looking to buy houses outside the "toxic triangle" near refineries were attacked by the Klan through numerous cross burnings, arson attacks, a car bombing, and an armed raid on a housing project. In 1981, when Black residents took to the streets to protest police brutality, they were met by robed Klan members in a "Support Your Local Police" counter-demonstration. This was also the year Tom Metzger announced that he would run as a "pro-white" candidate for the California Senate.

Brotsky, Siff, and Gerber were part of the Bay Area Prairie Fire chapter. Since 1980, they had been organizing support for Black Panther Geronimo Ji-Jaga Pratt while printing the newspaper *Arm the Spirit*, a publication of the prison abolition movement during the 1970s and 1980s. With the rise in police shootings of Black men around the region, particularly in the cities of Richmond and Concord, the Prairie Fire chapter continued its relationship with the New Afrikan Independence Movement on the West Coast. Soon, Brotsky, Siff, and Gerber formally adopted on the "Stop Killer Cops!" campaign conducted by the John Brown network. After the 1981 Brinks debacle, Prairie Fire chapters in the Bay Area, Los Angeles, and Chicago, along with the Dare to Struggle committee in San Francisco, took up the work of building support and solidarity for the people who had been arrested. That work reconnected these anti-imperialist organizations in a stronger way with people in May 19th and the John Brown Anti-Klan Committee on the East Coast. Coupled with their growing understanding of the state of the white supremacist movement, the organizations agreed that the work would be stronger if they united into one national organization, so Dare to Struggle joined the John Brown group.

Through the "Stop Killer Cops!" campaign, the Committee members began working with the NAACP lawyers and community groups that were supporting the families of the two victims, Johnny Roman and Michael Guillory. First, they shared their research and findings—particularly information about racist attacks in the area—with lawyers working on the case. The NAACP told the group that it was a regular practice for the Cowboys to abduct young Black men in Richmond and then drop them off in affluent white suburbs, such as Pittsburg, a forty-five-minute car ride away. In such places, if the victims were not able to get back quickly, they would often be harassed and detained again by local police. The Committee realized they would be well suited to apply pressure in those very same affluent neighborhoods.

They began submitting articles in local newspapers pointing to the fact that many of Richmond's police officers and key figures in the case, including Police Chief Leo Garfield and federal judge Robert Aguilar, did not live in the part of Richmond where the police had killed the men. This highlighted the contradiction that those responsible have a great deal of power in the case, could easily remove themselves, and were therefore disconnected from the daily onslaught of brutality. At the same time, Siff and Brotsky started visiting the suburban neighborhood of El Sobrante, where Police Chief Garfield lived, in order to gather information for planning a protest there.

On May 22, 1983, the group led an early morning demonstration outside Garfield's home. Eighty people gathered there and chanted, "Chief Leo, you can't hide, we charge you with genocide!" On a bullhorn, Barbara Jacobs, a Bay Area Committee member, announced their reason for being there: "He cannot return to the peace and quiet of the suburbs while he and his department are responsible for the murder and brutality of the Black community on a daily basis."[141] While in Garfield's neighborhood, the John Brown crew talked to his

5th Annual RUN AGAINST THE KLAN!

Saturday, September 10 at 9:00 A.M.

Old Boathouse, Lake Merritt, Oakland
at 14th Street & Lakeside

Sponsored by the John Brown Anti-Klan Committee
A benefit for educational work against the KKK and racist violence

5 km. and 10 km. RACES

- Course starts at Boathouse parking lot. Course is concrete, fast and flat.
- Race starts at 9:00 a.m. SHARP. Pick up race numbers race day between 7:30 and 8:30 a.m. No advance mailing of numbers.
- Awards to first, second, and third men, women and children.
- Prize awarded for most pledge money collected (see reverse)

REGISTRATION FORM

Return this form with check payable to:
John Brown Anti-Klan Committee
220 9th Street, #443 • San Francisco, CA 94103

For more information call:
415/ 431-8339

Mail registration closes:
Saturday, September 3, 1988

Late registration on race day:
($10.00) between 7:30 and
8:30 a.m.

Name _____

Address _____

City_____ State___ Zip_____

Phone_____ Sex___ Age_____

CHECK APPROPRIATE BOX

☐ Not racing but want to help on race day.
    (Free T-shirt)

☐ Not racing but want to help with a contribution.

☐ Pre-registration with T-shirt $9.00 (Under 18, $6.00)

☐ Race day T-shirt $6.00.

T-shirt size:
Circle one S M L XL

WAIVER *(must be signed)*

In consideration of the acceptance of my entry, I hereby waive all claims for damages or injuries against any of the individuals or groups affiliated with the RUN AGAINST THE KLAN including the John Brown Anti-Klan Committee and the City of Oakland. I further attest that I have full knowledge of the risk involved and have trained sufficiently to participate in this event.

_____
               (Signature)

neighbors about his lack of oversight of the Cowboys and how it was impacting the Black community in Richmond.

During this period, the Bay Area chapter began creating more opportunities for people to join in their efforts. Members started the "Run Against the Klan!" 5K run, which became an annual event. "It was much broader, in terms of who would show up, than some of the other programs we were doing," said Roth. They created radio announcements broadcast on local stations. One hit included Committee members talking about the event while running and out of breath. Over the course of five annual marathons, hundreds of people participated in the run around Oakland's Lake Merritt wearing T-shirts that had a picture of a Klansman with a sneaker print on his hood. The money raised from the marathons went toward printing, supporting other anti-Klan demonstrations, and funding speaking events with members of the New African Peoples Organization, and other activists from the Black Liberation Movement, like the Republic of New Afrika.

As community pressure was building, the federal judge hurried the case by ordering the City of Richmond and the families of Roman and Guillory to settle outside of court. Richmond's city council refused to settle out of court and rejected an initial resignation from Police Chief Garfield. The John Brown crew interpreted this as a vote of confidence for the defense and a green light for the Cowboys. However, when the trial went forth, on June 3, 1983, the judge found the Richmond Police Department guilty of "patterns and practice" of racial violence and awarded $3 million in damages to the families of Roman and Guillory. One week later, Chief Garfield turned in his resignation.

In the 1983 April issue of the newspaper *Death to the Klan!*, the Bay Area chapter argued that "nothing has fundamentally changed" in the terrain of white supremacy.[142] The Cowboys were still employed as police officers in the city of Richmond. But what *was* changing was the Committee's approach to resistance. The Bay Area group was an example, where, without compromising its politics, a chapter began working with organizations such as the NAACP that had political views and tactics very different from their own. The Committee experimented with using multiple strategies that got results, as in the small victories against police brutality in Richmond. This kind of experimentation was uneven across chapters, and at times at odds with the organization's own rhetoric, but it signaled a reckoning with vestiges of the sectarianism that the Committee was born into. In the years after the fight against the Cowboys, the Bay Area chapter started the "Just Say No to Nazis" campaign, a play on Nancy Reagan's "Just Say No to Drugs" campaign.

THE ANTI-KLAN MOVEMENT

As white supremacists grew emboldened during the first term of the Reagan administration, so did a diverse range of organizations that opposed them. National debates about the origins of racism and how to stop it were suddenly possible in new ways. As anti-Klan networks endeavored to coalesce into a united movement, political differences prevented their unity from being all-inclusive. The two main points of contention were differing views on how to deal with government culpability for white supremacy, and whether or not racist activities of white supremacists and fascists were entitled to protections by the First Amendment.

After Greensboro, there was massive growth in movement infrastructure. Some activists formed "watch groups" that focused on documenting white supremacist activity in order to augment legal interventions. At first, long-running organizations such as the NAACP and the conservative Jewish organization known as the Anti-Defamation League of B'Nai and B'rith collected information about the Klan and related groups, but in the mid-1980s, the NAACP turned its attention to how public officials responded to the Klan. In 1981, the Southern

Poverty Law Center, a legal rights organization specializing in civil rights litigation and advocacy, began working with the NAACP and the National Urban League to launch Klanwatch, a Klan monitoring project. In 1983, the Southern Poverty Law Center released the handbook *What To Do When a Hate Group Comes to Town*. Taking inspiration from the Simon Wiesenthal Center in Los Angeles, a human rights organization that specialized in researching the Holocaust, Southern Poverty Law Center started publishing *Intelligence Report*, a public report on white supremacist groups. In addition to collecting information about the activities of such groups, they took a social approach to countering white supremacists: "The important thing is removing any appearance that people are condoning [the Klan]."[143] The Law Center encouraged leaders within towns and cities to sign statements denouncing the Klan.

One of the largest formations to emerge during the Reagan years was the National Anti-Klan Network. The network was founded in 1980 after a Klan group—with the assistance of the local police—attacked a demonstration organized by members of the Black community in Decatur, Alabama. The National Anti-Klan Network described its work as "a revival of the civil rights movement" and aimed to counter the resurgence of the Klan by coordinating local efforts to "force elected officials to use our tax dollars to prosecute violent racists and fight racism through education and other affirmative actions."[144]

The National Anti-Klan Network focused on legislation, law enforcement, and community action. Throughout the life of the organization, an average of sixty-five educational, religious, and legal groups were actively involved, including the National Council of Churches, the Southern Christian Leadership Conference, United Methodist Women, Klanwatch, the United Furniture Workers Union, the Center for Constitutional Rights, the United States Student Association, and the National Organization for Women. Many of the member organizations were based in the South, and some had decades of experience fighting the Klan in their regions. The National Anti-Klan Network was critical of mainstream initiatives to minimize or ignore white supremacist activity and made it their mission to expose, ban, and prosecute the Klan and other racist formations.

In February 1981, the National Anti-Klan Network called for a "Spring Offensive" against racism and terror. The reach of the organization was vast, which helped it pull together a series of conferences aimed to coordinate strategies. At the first conference, held at Howard University, a historically Black college, five hundred people came from across the country. One of the most popular topics centered on "why the right has out-organized [progressive social movements]." The most controversial debate during the conference was representative of those being had across the movement: "the extent to which local, state and Federal agencies had encouraged, protected and even participated in Klan activity."[145]

The Committee was one organization among several in the anti-Klan movement that aligned themselves with self-defense politics. This tendency upheld the right of those attacked by white supremacist groups to organize for self-defense. Armed resistance by Black communities in the Freedom movements in Mississippi provided important examples.[146] One such example was the Deacons for Defense and Justice. In 1964, when attempts for Black integration into political life were thwarted by Klan attacks—church and community center bombings—the Deacons organized more than twenty chapters throughout South. Another was the work of Robert F. Williams, a former Marine and an NAACP member who turned his Monroe, North Carolina, chapter into an armed self-defense unit a few years before the Deacons began.[147]

Within this sea of anti-Klan formations, the issue of how to assess and respond to the role of state culpability presented another point of difference among groups on the left during 1980s. By 1983, white power groups such as Aryan Nation and the White Patriot Party had declared war on the U.S. government. Feminist writer and longtime Southern anti-racist activist, Mab Segrest, remembered that the anti-racist strategies that emerged in North Carolina were forged as an effort to making law enforcement and the criminal justice system in the state accountable for responding to the upsurge of far-right organizing and acts of racist, homophobic, and other violence. "I was then—and continue to be—in support of the Fourteenth Amendment principle of 'equal protection under the law.' This strategy brought us into contact with police, district attorneys, sheriff's departments whose behaviors we sought to shift. We were calling out their lack of response to Klan resurgence. The strategy, in which we cooperated with the National Anti-Klan Network (and later became the Center for Democratic Renewal), and the Southern Poverty Law Center eventually ended up with convictions for 17 members of Klan and neo-Nazi groups and the disbanding of two organizations."

In the summer 1983 edition of *Death to the Klan!*, the Committee extensively addressed the issue: "Even at its beginning stages, the anti-Klan movement is being attacked by the same repressive forces (such as the FBI) that are working to destroy the revolutionary leadership of New Afrikan, Puerto Rican, Mexicano, and Native American movements."[148] The Committee warned that tactics of the state, as seen at anti-Klan events in Houston, Kalamazoo, Meriden, San Antonio, and Boston, were part of a strategy to "heighten the risks, intimidate people, and make it a crime for people to fight the Klan and the growth of a fascist movement."[149] These tactics included selective searches of anti-Klan demonstrators, midnight raids of anti-Klan activist's homes, roadblocks preventing anti-Klan activists from protesting the Klan, herding anti-Klan demonstrators behind fences or inside baseball stadiums, and asking Klansmen to identify anti-Klan activists prior to upcoming Klan rallies.

For the Committee, the Klan and the state were intertwined in the political economy of armed white supremacy that began with settler colonialism and the war on Native Americans, and continued to impose itself through the enslavement of Africans, slave patrols, the convict leasing system, and Jim Crow, and deeply shaped the imperialist nature of U.S. foreign policy. In this context, the group warned that a reliance on the Fraternal Order of the Police and state law enforcement agencies would never go far enough to abolish white supremacy, and that such reliance would inevitably serve to enforce subordination of people's movements to authoritarianism and empire. From this argument, the Committee encouraged the anti-Klan movement not to invest in "Ban the Klan" law enforcement measures, but instead to align with local anti-Klan campaigns and the revolutionary demands by movements for self-determination.

Anti-Klan organizations' positions regarding whether or not the First Amendment should protect the activities of white supremacists and fascists varied widely. "It was a regular sticking point," said Carla Wallace, an anti-racist organizer in Kentucky Alliance Against Racist and Political Repression, an organization committed to building an anti-racist majority in Kentucky in the early 1980s. "At this time, it seemed like a contradiction that Klansmen were in the Louisville Police Department. We started a campaign to demand that the Klan not be allowed on the police force, but then the American Civil Liberties Union came in and defended them. It nearly stopped that work." If organizations took the position of defending white supremacist activity on First Amendment grounds, those organizations also often advocated ignoring Klan demonstrations rather than elevating them in the media through protest.

"We would always point to Germany," asserted Laughlin, and how after World War II the German government illegalized public displays of fascism, including Nazi symbols, including swastikas. While the effectiveness of Germany's legal strategy is debatable, the initiative was praised by those that saw a lack of response as far worse. Some, like Amilcar Shabazz from the Black Citizens Task Force, felt that the real issue of why similar public protections against violent ideologies aren't in place in the United States was less because of the primacy of the First Amendment and more due to persistent power of white supremacy: "There has never been the will within the white majority to just say it's out of bounds," said Shabazz.

In 1983, the Committee argued *Death to the Klan!* that defending the First Amendment rights of white supremacists served to fracture the anti-Klan movement by positioning those who engage in confrontational anti-Klan activity as "anti-democratic." They wrote that this dynamic enabled white supremacists and state authorities to use "anti-democratic" charges as leverage to criminalize a wide range of groups, including Black and Brown movements for self-determination.[150]

By the end of Reagan's first term, the Committee was adapting to the shifting political terrain. Two incidents during that period bolstered the group's understanding that the role of white privilege in society wasn't something that could easily be abandoned.

The first incident occurred in July 1983, when Terry Bisson and Lisa Roth rented a van to transport a group from the New York chapter to a national John Brown Anti-Klan Committee national conference that was taking place in Chicago. The conference marked a renewed organizational commitment, established a more unified national organization, and created an opportunity for chapters to network and share strategies from their local campaigns. During the drive home, the van went out of control, crashed into a guardrail, and sent one member through the window.

"It was really scary. Our friend was unconscious and laying on the freeway. We were trying to stop cars from hitting her," recalled Roth. Every John Brown member in the van was wearing a "Death to the Klan!" T-shirt. "There we were," said Roth, "standing in a ditch next to the highway where our van had rolled. A few people were on the highway with the injured woman, all taking our shirts off to turn them inside out." The group grew worried that if police pegged them as militant radicals and potentially dangerous, their injured friend might not be the authorities' first priority at the scene. "We made a choice I think about all the time," said Roth. "In this situation, we had the option to pretend that we were not police-hating revolutionaries so that they would treat us like the white citizens they are sworn to protect. The shocking part was to see how very helpful the police can be to white people they wish to assist." The friend was severely injured but survived because she was able to quickly get to the hospital.

"If anything, the freeway incident underscored that police treat white people better than they treat anyone else. All we had to do was hide our anti-police, pro–Black Liberation views by hiding our T-shirt slogans, and we were treated respectfully and helped by white police officers. White privilege gave us the *option* to do that," explained Roth.

The second incident also occurred in 1983, when the Klan was picketing a movie house in Bel Air, Texas, that was showing a film about the Vietnamese people whom the Klan had recently targeted. Ten John Brown members from the Austin and Houston chapters drove out to the movie house location to counter-protest. The crew quickly became outnumbered. Fifty Klansmen surrounded the contingent, calling out their names and personal information. "It was really scary, I nearly peed myself, because they knew how to make it personal," said Laughlin. One of the members approached the police and requested that they force the Klan to allow them to pass. With police support, the group marched safely past the Klan and scrambled into their cars. Laughlin admitted, "We were self-righteous, and at times really dumb, but we were young and trying to figure it out . . . because you can't let fear stop you. The cops, the Klan, the FBI—they use fear, intimidation, and murder against liberation movements. We weren't going to let fear stop us."

While small encounters, for the Committee these were examples that even if the "cops and Klan go hand in hand," there were critical differences in power and roles. With time, the group became increasingly aware of the state's use of fear, surveillance, and harassment of activists, movement organizers, and revolutionaries.

DEMONSTRATE
STOP POLICE TERROR!

We are demonstrating at the Belmont police station to protest racist police terror in Chicago. In the last 3 months alone the police have murdered 5 Black, Puerto Rican and Mexican people. We say police terror must be stopped and the human rights of Black and Third World people must be defended.

On December 4, 1969 the FBI and Chicago police murdered Black Panther Party leaders Fred Hampton and Mark Clark as part of the FBI's infamous COINTELPRO program designed to crush the Black Liberation movement....Today the FBI continues to attack the New Afrikan (Black) movement through imprisonment and murder. We are demonstrating to remember Fred Hampton who gave his life fighting for the liberation of Black people. We say no to FBI and police attacks on liberation movements.

WEDNESDAY, DEC. 7, 5:00 pm
19th DISTRICT POLICE STATION
BELMONT & WESTERN

DEATH TO THE KLAN AND ALL WHITE SUPREMACY!

LAND & INDEPENDENCE FOR THE BLACK NATION·· NEW AFRIKA!

More info: JOHN BROWN ANTI-KLAN COMMITTEE ** BOX 7239 ** CHICAGO 60680 ** 769-8159
(leave message)

FOUR

CONFRONTATIONS AND CULTURE WARS

> I know you'd kill me if you could
> You hide your head beneath a hood
> I know that you're a closet case
> Afraid to show your fucking face
>   —The Dicks, "Anti-Klan" (Part 1)

> You still think swastikas look cool
> The real Nazis run your schools
> They're coaches, businessmen and cops
> In a real fourth Reich you'll be the first to go
>   —Dead Kennedys, "Nazi Punks Fuck Off"

In the mid-1980s, the far right began using youth counterculture as a recruitment tool. Before this, political synergy with dissident youth culture was something associated with the radical left. But during the Reagan years, white nationalist organizations such as White Aryan Resistance and Aryan Nations began to harness social networks, punk rock culture, and mainstream television in an attempt to turn young people's anger into a political force. They recognized the possibility that the deeply rebellious do-it-yourself sensibility of punk—its music, zines, anti-fashion, and performance networks—lent itself to fighting the intolerance and authoritarianism inherent in white supremacy and neo-fascism. Through the Coalition to Stop Racist Graffiti in Chicago and anti-Nazi campaigns in the San Francisco Bay Area, the John Brown Anti-Klan Committee organized within youth subcultures to counter the influence of fascists. It was also during this time that the organization was targeted by increased FBI surveillance and a series of grand jury investigations. The group began to adjust its approach to militant anti-fascist work, recognizing that if there were to be radical transformation in their time, the fight wouldn't just be physical, but would involve winning hearts and minds as well.

LIKE MISBEGOTTEN WEEDS

Chicago has always been a barometer of volatile political trends in the United States. Only a few short decades after the city's founding in 1833, Chicago became an economic powerhouse. The excesses of the city's industry brought about a radical labor movement best known for the 1886 Haymarket massacre, where police shot and killed workers in the labor movement during a protest against police violence. Following the massacre, eight labor organizers were convicted in a related and controversial trial, and four of them were executed. Ward politics shaped Chicago around a strictly segregated racial order which catalyzed generations of Black organizing.[151] And when Martin Luther King Jr. brought the Civil Rights movement to Chicago to challenge segregation in housing and education in 1966, his efforts were met with a wave of violent reaction from white residents. He remarked, "Swastikas bloomed in Chicago parks like misbegotten weeds."[152]

Popular films reflected and satirized Chicago's racist renaissance. In the *Blues Brothers* (1980) the American Nazi Party was cast as a group of bumbling villains antagonized by fictional white blues musicians Jake and Elwood Blues. In the film, a multiracial group of anti-fascist protesters confronts the Nazis, with the brothers chasing the villains off a bridge using their 1974 Dodge sedan. Elwood, played by comedian John Belushi, coolly utters, "I hate Illinois Nazis." The made-for-TV movie *Skokie* (1981) depicted a real-life 1977 incident in which the National Socialist Party of America mobilized in a Jewish

Original poster by Terry Forman.

enclave bordering northern Chicago.[153] Hollywood took notice, because in real life, hate was all around the Windy City. A variety of far-right organizations regularly converged in Chicago's public parks. This furthered the John Brown group's concern that the Klan was not only becoming "Nazified" but

Demonstration & Ra

SATURDAY, OCTOBER
12 NOON
Wilson & Clifton (near Broadw

OPPOSE THE UPTOWN CROSS-BURNING!

UPTOWN, September 3, 1984: For residents of this northside community, the Labor end ended with an act of racial bigotry and violence. At approximately 9:00 PM, Monday cross was burned as 15-20 people — some dressed in white robes — carried Confederate flags.

The fiery cross and the Confederate flag are symbols of white supremacy that have for over a hundred years to terrorize Black people. The Uptown cross-burning occurred block of Malden, near Wilson. It is an integrated area — many Black, Latin and white fai houses ringing the vacant lot whose charred grass and racist graffitti on nearby buildings reminder that racist violence is not confined to the pages of history books.

We must act NOW to prevent further racist violence and show that the people of Chica tolerate any expression of racial hatred in our communities. We are community, religious progressive organizations and individuals building this united response to the Uptown cr and all forms of racist violence. JOIN US!

Stand Up For The Human Rights Of Black
And All Third World People!

STOP RACIST TERROR!

Partial list of sponsors: John Brown Anti-Klan Committee, Rev. Susan Uptown residents: Bob Bossie, Kathy King, Neil Dunaets.

For more information, call 769-8159 or 528-3548

also actively targeting youth. In Chicago, this was most evident when old-guard organizations such as the Klan and the American Nazi Party collaborated with new upstarts such as Chicago Area Skinheads (CASH), setting a tone of fear and intimidation in one of the most segregated and diverse cities in the United States.[154]

What made Chicago ripe for racist organizing? In the 1970s, a 10 percent decrease in the white population and a similar increase in the Black population contributed to white racial anxiety. The 1983 election of Harold Washington, the city's first Black mayor, dismantled some of the political patronage system that had governed the city for decades.[155] A year after his election, the Save Our Neighborhoods/Save Our City coalition, a collection of white neighborhood groups, created a list of demands articulating the anxieties of those who never anticipated a Black mayor in Chicago. This coalition, consisting of more than a thousand white people, insisted that its efforts had nothing to do with racism. As a way to soft-pedal their objections to Chicago's limited residential integration, they focused much of their anger on the real estate industry. Eileen Vahe, one activist involved in the coalition, commented that she was "tired of watching our neighborhoods collapse like dominoes" and that she was "tired of apologizing for being white."[156]

Underlying white residents' anger was resentment over many key city appointments being given to Black and Latino people, and Chicago's compliance with a federal court order mandating that public housing be integrated throughout the city instead of clustered in ghettos. While many in Chicago's left saw Washington's victory as a mark of progress, through their national newspaper, *Death to the Klan!*, the Committee offered an opposing view: "The massive racist backlash which surfaced recently in the Chicago mayoral race is a clear signal that the Klan has a potentially huge amount of support among disaffected white people." The Chicago Committee asserted that the election had advantaged an extremely organized racist movement while offering false hope that white supremacy could be defeated at the ballot box.[157]

Severe segregation in Chicago helped catalyze an anti-racist presence in the city. In particular, the neighborhood of Uptown, sitting between Lakeview and Rogers Park, was always contested territory in Chicago's desegregation wars, and it continued to be so throughout the 1980s. Known as "Hillbilly Harlem" or "Hillbilly Heaven," in the 1950s and 1960s Uptown had attracted white Southern migrants who came to the area in search of work. During the early 1960s and 1970s, left-leaning groups such as the Young Patriots Organization, Rising Up Angry, and the Intercommunal Survival Committee organized working-class whites in solidarity with groups such as the Illinois Black Panther Party and the Puerto Rican Young Lords Organization. The Patriots worked directly with Southern migrants, while Rising Up Angry recruited greaser youth. The Survival Committee incorporated itself directly under the Black Panther Party's command structure and sold the Panthers' newspaper door-to-door, encouraging all to join the movement against white supremacy.[158]

In 1983, the Prairie Fire Organizing Committee sent a California-based cadre to Chicago to support the Puerto Rican Independence Movement, which was active there through many organizations such as Fuerzas Armadas de Liberación Nacional (FALN) and many other above-ground organizations. Prairie Fire's day-to-day work mainly supported the Puerto Rican Cultural Center. The newly formed Prairie Fire chapter was responding to the 1983 arrests and trials of Puerto Rican community leaders in Chicago. Among the activists arriving in Chicago were Howie Emmer, Bob Wells, and Vicki Legion. Once there, they found that shifting political conditions complicated their plans. Nancy remembered the impact that political organizing in Chicago—particularly the confluence of multiple movements—had on her as a young mother of two. "When I got to Chicago, I realized that we could have a mass presence. And the 'we' was a bigger 'we' than I ever thought it could have been."

Nancy was a veteran of many of the iconic organizations of the 1960s. Her family was also a living link between the Old and New Left. A red diaper baby, her mother was an active member of the Communist Party USA. In the 1960s, Nancy joined the Friends of the Student Nonviolent Coordinating Committee and co-founded the Youth International Party (Yippies) with larger-than-life characters Abbie Hoffman and Jerry Rubin. Howie Emmer had been part of campus organizing against racism at Kent State in the months leading up to the National Guard killing four of his classmates during a May 1970 anti-war protest. Organizing with Kent SDS, the chapter adopted anti-racist and anti-imperialist political priorities early on. In November 1968, Kent SDS and Black Students United (BUS) took over a building on Kent's campus in order to stop the Oakland Police Department (OPD) from recruiting there. The OPD had killed Black Panther Party member Bobby Hutton as he attempted to surrender to them. The university administration brought disciplinary charges against leaders of

SDS and BUS, including Emmer. In response, all of the Black students walked off campus and set up a Freedom School in nearby Akron, Ohio. The administration backed down and withdrew the disciplinary charges after the walkout because it didn't look good for all of the Black students to boycott a state university, especially at a time when the Civil Rights and Black Power movements were putting a spotlight on the racist practices of our the nation's institutions, including the universities. Vicki Legion, a Prairie Fire member who never officially joined a John Brown chapter, was a central member in Women Against Imperialism, an organization that provided material aid for a women's clinic in Sandinista Nicaragua.

This came on the heels of the government's crackdown on Puerto Rican independence militants, particularly those associated with the FALN. Multiple Puerto Rican organizations emerged from 1950 to 1980, some advocating independence and others demanding that the island become the fifty-first state in the union. Founded in 1974, the FALN was a revolutionary organization that had no qualms about using insurgent violence as a tactic in its campaign for release of 1950s-era political prisoners and revolutionary independence. Between 1974 and 1980, the group claimed responsibility for more than one hundred bombings of government sites, and resolutely endorsed revolutionary independence over statehood.[159]

In April 1980, more than a dozen members of the FALN were arrested for "seditious conspiracy" to overthrow the government through illegal means. A year later, Elizam Escobar, Adolfo Matos, Dylcia Pagan, Carlos Alberto Torres, Ida Luz Rodriguez, Alicia Rodriguez, Ricardo Jimenez, Luis Rosa, Alfredo Mendez, and Carmen Valentin were convicted. None of the defendants testified on their own behalf, and all denounced the court proceedings as "illegitimate."[160] In 1981, FALN leader Oscar López Rivera was arrested during a traffic stop, charged with seditious conspiracy against the United States government, and later sentenced to fifty-five years in prison.

In 1983, four Chicago FALN members—Albert Rodriguez, Jose Rodriguez, Eddie Cortes, and Alejandrina Torres—were arrested and charged with plotting to blow up a Marine Corps training center. Around the same time, the FBI raided the Pedro Albizu Campos Puerto Rican High School and Puerto Rican Cultural Center. The crackdown in Chicago came in a long line of efforts against the movement for Puerto Rican independence. According to Howie Emmer, the convictions in the preceding years made it difficult, if not impossible, to carry out joint work. "Here we were saying we were in support of armed struggle, but those who were actually carrying it out were all in prison." While continuing to support the revolutionary Puerto Rican movement, the increase in racist incidents in Chicago provided the Prairie Fire crew with an abundance of reasons to bolster support for the Black community. Rather than return to California, in 1985 they formed the Chicago chapter of the John Brown Anti-Klan Committee.

Individual hate crimes spiked in Illinois during that time. Later in 1985, multiple firebombs incinerated homes purchased by Black families.[161] In the fall, Henry Hampton, a Black man, was killed by a former member of the Uptown Rebels, a white street gang that had been heavily courted by Jack Quinn, the head of Chicago Klan.[162] Cross burnings were also a regular occurrence in and around Chicago. The sheer volume of racist violence at that time drove Prairie Fire's decision to make noise about the fact that it had formed a Chicago chapter of the John Brown Anti-Klan Committee.

Thus, the chapter's early activities included mounting loudspeakers on their cars and driving around Lakeview, a white neighborhood then in the early stages of gentrification, chanting slogans in support of the Black Liberation Army and political prisoner Sekou Odinga. Few Chicagoans seemed moved by people screaming leftist slogans from cars. Emmer recalled, "It didn't take long for us to realize that drive-by outreach wasn't going to bring any white people over to the cause of Black

Liberation." There was a lot to do. Throughout the 1980s, members of the Klan and Nazi skinheads were a public presence in Chicago. The fascists not only frequently held their own rallies, but often confronted and disrupted anti-racist events. Shifting their approach, Chicago's John Brown crew organized teams to do door-to-door canvassing, asking white Chicagoans to attend rallies and sign letters to officials opposing the Klan's right to rally.

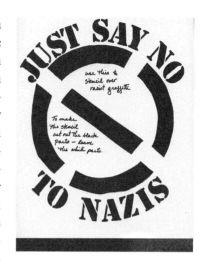

The act of in-person outreach sparked conversations in Chicago's white enclaves about the kinds of values and practices people wanted to support. The letter gained the signatures of more than two hundred individuals, and a wide variety of small businesses and community organizations, including LGBT and faith-based groups. For the Chicago chapter, it added the act of radical listening to their defiant pose, suggesting that anti-Klan politics might develop a louder voice in the Windy City.[163]

GRAFFITI WARS

It wasn't long before the terrain of a racialized culture war revealed itself. White supremacists marked their territory by spray-painting slogans, epithets, and menacing images of Klansmen. They created stickers that read "Death to Race Mixers" and "Communism is Jewish," and weaponized them by embedding the stickers with razor blades in the hope of cutting anyone who tried to tear them down with their fingers. Instead of waiting for officials to remove the stickers and graffiti,

the group saw this as an opportunity to organize through local direct action, and to favorably associate the John Brown Anti-Klan Committee with improving community security and quality of life.

In the late 1970s and early 1980s, politicians around the country waged a war on graffiti. Graffiti was largely viewed as a minor offense until it became associated with Black and Latino urban culture and hip-hop music. Ironically, it was when the practice evolved from simply spraying one's name on a wall to complex and colorful murals that it came to be seen as a source of social disorder. Politicians were more than happy to associate graffiti with unemployment, crime, and the social breakdown of low-income urban areas.[164] By extension, anti-graffiti rhetoric pointed towards a politics of racial containment. Cities weren't just covering up art spray-painted on walls, they were declaring "war" and confronting a "threat." It wasn't just talk. In city after city, authorities surrounded popular graffiti sites with barbed wire, enacted laws that increased prison time for artists and the parents of young people arrested for vandalism. During this time the state response to graffiti contributed to the proliferation of surveillance technology and the criminalization of communities of color. By focusing on *racist* graffiti, the John Brown group demonstrated that it was willing to address everyday community concerns while at the same time exposing the racial dimensions of a "graffiti war" that mostly targeted young people of color. They decided to organize a broad-based front. Building the Coalition to Stamp Out Racist Graffiti, the John Brown Committee successfully brought together a diverse array of groups from Chicago's left, including pacifist organizations, labor unions, and neighborhood and student groups. Nancy Kurshan represented the John Brown group in the Coalition's leadership committee. She felt committed to including as many people as possible. "It was a fairly big turnout for back then," recalled Kurshan. "We sometimes would have 100 to 200 people at our meetings."

On June 21, 1985, the Coalition hit the streets to organize the first Stamp Out Racist Graffiti Day, a free community event where those interested in ending racism could meet like-minded people, clean up racist graffiti in the area, and learn about how to get more involved. Members of the Coalition scouted out locations with racist graffiti and then mapped out a route connecting them. As a result, the actual event was conducted as a mobile demonstration, a clean up, and an outreach campaign during which interested passersby were engaged. The event was a huge success. "It was a really exciting and practical way to get people involved. Here is a paintbrush. Let's walk and talk," said Kurshan.

Building on momentum of the first event, in September 1985 the Committee gathered about 150 people from the Coalition at Aetna Plaza to kick off a second day of eliminating racist graffiti. These events were attracting positive attention and successfully appealing to Chicago's progressive community to get involved against white supremacy. "We were meeting constantly at this time," said Nancy. "Groups within the Coalition didn't necessarily share the same political line, but we would have big meetings about tactics." Chicago's progressives weren't the only one to take notice. While gathering at Aetna Plaza, a group of white supremacists from different local organizations—Klansmen, the Uptown Rebels, and neo-Nazi coalition members—ran up to the rally wielding swords, shields, and sharpened flagpoles, and assaulted Coalition members. The fascists arrived wearing black shirts and swastika armbands, and brought signs that read "Smash Communism in South Africa" and "Racial Purity is South Africa's Security." The John Brown crew pelted them with a barrage of eggs quickly purchased from a store nearby. Television crews captured the melee. With her face covered in blood, Kurshan told the reporters, "These people have no right to be demonstrating out here for white power! They're making attacks against Black people and all progressive people in the country!"[165]

"I remember grabbing one of their anti-Semitic signs and tearing it apart before I thought about what would happen next," said Kurshan. From there, and amidst a cacophony of flying eggs, fists, and weapons, Kurshan suffered serious wounds to her head. Three other people from the Coalition, several of whom were also members of the John Brown chapter, were injured in the confrontation. An article in Prairie Fire's newspaper, *Breakthrough*, noted that the conflict was a turning point, and that new tactics were needed to defend against white supremacist violence. The article concluded that even though white supremacist attacks were increasing in Chicago, the city's police were not expected to crack down or sufficiently intervene. As a result of this analysis, Chicago's John Brown crew believed that elevated risks to members' personal security demanded a women-led model of self-defense. Such an approach called for solid planning, cooperation, and communication to replace male-centered notions of security which were often based on little more than bravado.

These events were attracting positive attention and gaining traction with Chicago's progressive community to get involved against white supremacy. The largest source of criticism came from the police. Officer Donald Eichler opined to the *Chicago Tribune*, "These people are trouble, not the Nazis."[166] Nonetheless, the Coalition amassed a broad list of organizations and individuals willing to sign their names on a full-page ad "Say No to Racist Violence: An Open Letter to the People of Chicago" which was published in the *Chicago Reader*:

> We the undersigned are concerned and angry about the rise of racist activity in Chicago. The ku klux klan and nazis have targeted Chicago as fertile ground for organizing. They have already expanded from their traditional southwest side base to Lakeview, Uptown, and the northwest side. Several new white supremacist groups have established themselves here in recent months.
>
> Two years ago, on the heels of a mayoral campaign marked by overt racism, we saw a sharp increase in racist graffiti and a cross-burning. Today, white-supremacist groups have escalated their violence as they assault people, distribute racist literature to school children, and openly harass those who oppose them. At the same time there has been an alarming increase in the number of fire bombings of Black people's homes and of attacks on Black people

in all-white sections of the city. We need to support the human rights of Black people. This racist violence must stop!

We will not sit idly by as promote white supremacy They have no "right" to organize for race war nor to carry out racist attacks. Bitter experience has shown us that ignoring groups such as the klan and nazis will not make them go away. We call upon the rest of Chicago to join us to say no to racist violence.[167]

Although other John Brown chapters had worked in coalitions, this was the biggest formation to date and the first time a chapter had helped to form a coalition's steering committee. As a result, the group found itself grappling with the complex challenges that came with organizing alliances among a politically diverse spectrum of groups. "There was a fair amount of tensions in the Coalition," said Bob Wells, referring to the fact that each group held different ideas about how the Coalition should confront the white supremacists who were menacing the community. The Sojourner Truth Organization, for example, believed the Coalition was not militant enough. Disagreeing with the proposal to soften the Stamp Out Racist Graffiti Day events in order to broaden public appeal, the Sojourner Truth Organization advocated that direct confrontation with white supremacists was the best path for attracting working-class youth to the movement. This position directly clashed with the Faith Based Center for Peace and Justice which believed that a peaceful, non-confrontational approach should be taken in order to prioritize keeping people safe. An Anti-Imperialist League revival group, originally founded in 1898 in resistance to the U.S. annexation of the Philippines, resigned from the Coalition after raising many of the same security-related concerns.

"We had to have a bit of a tough skin," Kurshan asserted. "We wanted to build a large coalition, and yet at the same time we wanted to hold on to our politics. We didn't want to drive out people who were not ready for revolution. Chicago has a very large pacifist community, including many who were rooted in liberation theology. At this point, we were convinced that we had to build a large front against fascists. The pacifists stuck with the Coalition, even as others peeled away."

Despite the John Brown group's best attempt to build a diverse alliance, not everyone on the left agreed with the anti-graffiti campaign. The Heart of Uptown Coalition, which had been organizing in the neighborhood since the 1960s, believed that the campaign would only serve to escalate racial tensions. In fact, the group even undercut the Coalition's events. The Heart of Uptown group, as Kurshan explained, went out the day before one Stamp Out Racist Graffiti event and cleaned up the racist graffiti themselves, denying the John Brown crew and the Coalition from successfully staging a major public clean-up event.

For the rest of the decade, the far-right continued its assaults in Chicago and the surrounding areas. In a high-profile trial, Joey Isbell was convicted for the 1986 shooting of Fahim Ahmad, a black teenager from Zion, Illinois. Isbell reportedly yelled "Klan! Klan! Klan!" during his attack.[168] Fire bombings of homes in Black communities continued in connection to long-delayed neighborhood integration. The events in Chicago served as a reminder that Klan, and other racist organizations, were not just a problem in the South. Chicago would also become known as the place where traditional white nationalist organizations would eventually meet and find common cause with a younger generation of Nazi skinheads.

UNROMANTIC VIOLENCE

The Punk scene was another theater of combat in which the John Brown group fought the far right. While the organization's

Austin chapter dabbled in cultural organizing, the Chicago and Bay Area chapters deeply engaged with punk culture as a strategy for making the fight against fascism and white supremacy an organic part of punk's anti-authoritarian rebellion. In part, these chapters were responding to conditions on the ground. For instance, among a slew of racist groups operating in Chicago, the Chicago Area Skinheads (CASH) was particularly active. Combining punk's "do it yourself" ethic with persistent recruitment efforts, this white power group literally placed the writing on Chicago walls: stickers, posters, flyers, "calling cards," and graffiti appeared throughout the city, particularly in white neighborhoods. Clark Martell, a former member of the American Nazi Party, was the liaison between the skinheads and more formal organizations on the far right. CASH operated Romantic Violence, a white-power service that helped connect racist musical acts from around the country and overseas.

Nazi skinheads replaced the "God and country" approach of their forefathers with a high-octane outlook rooted in youth culture, punk rock, and white power. They eschewed the white robes and regalia of previous generations for a militarized look of combat boots, flight jackets, and heads shaved close for battle. Christian Picciolini, a former skinhead member of CASH turned anti-racist activist, recalls how music was the catalyst for white power recruitment among young males. "Punk rock has always been a place for disaffected youth, often traumatized ones, to find a release. White supremacist organizations seized on this. It was like saying, 'here is a bunch of secret information about how the world works, stuff that you won't find anywhere else.' Music was the most important thing for the young people. For the Klan and the older racists, it wasn't important at all. White power organizations used music to attract youth who were typically very smart, idealistic and provide them with a sense of purpose and ideology."

The history that brought Nazi skinheads to the United States follows a strange trajectory. Starting in the 1960s, non-racist skinhead culture was rooted in working-class networks of British youth and Caribbean immigrants who loved ska and soul music and created racially integrated bands such as the Specials, English Beat, and The Selector. These bands comprised the Two-Tone sound (later also the name of a music label) and regularly confronted England's racial strife in their lyrics. There was always an anti-authoritarian defiance to the scene, but not much politics at first. In time, the influence of the neoconservative Thatcher years increasingly politicized the bands and pushed them into solidarity with oppressed groups. Surprisingly, some of rock's old guard moved decidedly to the right during this time. Superstar David Bowie told *Playboy* magazine that Britain could benefit from a fascist leader. "Adolf Hitler was one of the first rock stars. . . . You've got to have an far-right front come up and sweep everything off its feet and tidy everything up." That year, musician Eric Clapton, drunkenly declared from stage that Pakistanis needed to leave the United Kingdom. Combined with a series of racist attacks, including the high-profile 1976 slaying of Alab Ali, a garment factory worker, it was clear that the far-right's presence in the U.K. could not be ignored.[169]

The Anti-Nazi League organized the first "Rock Against Racism" concerts. Throughout the United Kingdom, concerts featuring punks, skinheads, and reggae artists opened a powerful cultural front against social intolerance and racism. The concerts consciously brought together punk, reggae and north soul artists to model a popular front and disrupt the right's entry into rebel music. Jon Langford, of the Leeds band the Mekons, remembers how Rock Against Racism fought on both the practical and ideological fronts. "The Rock against Racism campaign in Leeds culminated in the Specials playing Potternewton Park in Chapeltown after a march/parade through the streets of this densely populated immigrant neighborhood. The Specials fused punk rock and ska and fulfill the early promise of Punk's adoption of U.K. Western Indian youths' rebel stance. Their single "Ghost Town" [a song decrying racist violence] was number one in the charts. . . . It seemed obvious at the time that the punks and the rude boys were having a lot more fun than Leeds Nazis. Many Leeds kids who'd fallen under that right-wing spell deserted en masse after this event and much of the street violence went away."

Britain's racists started their own labels such as Resistance Records and a "Rock Against Communism" concert series to promote their ideology and culture. This built a powerful platform for the far-right National Front organization to promote their ideas through the lyrics of bands such as Skrewdriver, No Remorse, and the Ventz. Skrewdriver's "Before the Night Falls" questioned England's opposition to fascism in the 1930s: "Our forefathers fought in two world wars, they thought to keep us free. But I'm not sure that in those wars, who was our enemy."

The politics of both Rock Against Racism and Rock Against Communism found their way to the United States. During the Reagan years, the punk rock subculture in North America was a mostly left-wing affair, so much so that it seemed like it a matter of genuflection for a band to have an anti-Reagan song. Bands such as D.O.A., the Minutemen, Government Issue, and the Crucifucks wrote some of the best-known songs criticizing the president and his authority. Rock Against Racism concerts in the U.S. were tiny in comparison to the massive U.K. shows and anti-Nazi mobilizations. Yet, the decentralized efforts put forward an image of a music scene that was steadfastly anti-racist and anti-establishment. One offshoot, Rock Against Reagan, was organized with heavy influence from John Brown chapters in Houston, Chicago, Washington D.C., and San Francisco. A series of national concerts attracted acts such as Bad Brains, Really Red, and the Dead Kennedys.[170] One Austin band, the Dicks, wrote songs whose lyrics voiced the John Brown ethos almost perfectly. Among these songs were "George Jackson," "Anti-Klan," and "Dicks Hate the Police."

Nazi symbolism always had been part of the scene too. In 1976, British singer Siouxsie Sioux celebrated "Nazi chic" on stage, coupling a swastika-emblazoned t-shirt with bondage clothing. In the film *The Decline and Fall of Western Civilization*, Penelope Spheris's documentary on early punk in Los Angeles, the swastika appears frequently on the clothing of youth. For many, it was simply about shock value, an attempt to unsettle the post–World War II status quo and social norms. For others, it was a propaganda, indoctrination, and recruitment opportunity. For example, Dave Dictor of the band M.D.C.—alternatively known as Multi Death Corporations or Millions of Dead Cops—remembers punk shows where Nazi skinheads gave away free cans of beer stickered with a label that read, "This beer bought for you by the KKK."

Despite stereotypes of punk being an all-white cultural phenomenon, all-Black bands like Death and Bad Brains, along with multiracial acts, were at the forefront of the scene. At the same time, punk, like its rock and roll parent, always had a strained relationship with Blackness. Following in the literary tradition of Norman Mailer's "The White Negro" (1957) and Jerry Farber's "The Student as Nigger" (1967), otherwise progressive acts such as the Avengers and Patti Smith wrote controversial songs deploying racialized language to equate being a white social outsider with the experience of Blackness and racialized oppression.[171]

Racism was always a contested element in U.S. skinhead culture. Besides *Love and Rage*, few radical left-wing publications attempted to give voice to anti-racist youth in the punk scene. The work of Red and Anarchist Skinheads (RASH) aimed to ensure that core left-wing ideas—particularly working-class solidarity and antagonism to racism—were always present in the skinhead and punk scenes. Dan Sabater, a founding member of RASH, believed that the organized left had as much difficulty as mainstream society in telling the difference between racist and anti-racist punks and skinheads. To him, this ultimately helped white supremacists do their work. He credits the John Brown Anti-Klan Committee for their efforts to reach out to young skinheads. Sabater was a working-class skinhead who often found himself at odds with the middle-class sections of the left. "The left's lack of recognition of anti-racist skinheads gave the right carte blanche to hijack the subculture. But I think that's a general problem on the left—not engaging people unless they are perfect. Not engaging people with contradictions that must be worked out. Not engaging people unless they fit some desired ideological bill. Easier to stick to college students and stay in the comfort zone. Which leaves anyone outside that to get eaten by the wolves." The wolves, it turned out, had a strong understanding about the role of culture in fomenting populist rebellion.[172] Thoughts of nation and religion weren't reaching young white supremacists the way that music was. "Underground music was a better vehicle for them," observed Sabater. "It was Tom Metzger who saw that, and he pretty much dragged the whole far right in that direction." The Committee's Chicago chapter helped organized a forum at the University of Illinois, Chicago, for anti-racist skinheads to draw a line between themselves and their fascist counterparts. Skinhead Roman Rokiciak remarked that it was when "nationalists and racists started infiltrating the groups [of skinhead youths] and poisoning their minds," that fascism became a permanent element of the skinhead scene.[173]

BATTLES OF THE BAY

The San Francisco Bay Area, often considered a bastion of progressive lifestyles, was far from immune to organized racism, including the cultural influence operations of the far right during the Reagan years. In the mid-1980s, Bob Heick founded the American Front, a California-based racist skinhead group that espoused anti-Semitism and white supremacy. Heick was born in San Francisco and had been a part of the local punk scene, gradually embracing right-wing politics in reaction to the Bay Area's left-leaning punks. Heick was notorious for doing recruitment outreach to kids outside of schools.

On May 1, 1988, the American Front and others organized a "White Workers Day" on San Francisco's infamous hippy-affiliated Haight Street. The demonstration attracted about fifty supporters who yelled, "We Don't Care What the Commies Say, May First Is White Workers Day!" The skinheads paraded down Haight in packs and claimed the hill on Buena Vista Park, a spot previously popular with street youth and queer people. One young person who had heckled the marchers was beat up the next morning by a half dozen skinheads who warned him to "stay away from skinhead hill."

The skinheads' claims, while grandly pompous, were aligned with years of increased racial violence in the area. In November 1985, the body of Timothy Lee, a young Black man, was found hanging from a tree in the nearby working-class Bay Area suburb of Concord, just 20 miles northeast of Oakland. While local police ruled it a suicide, the NAACP disputed the claim, pointing to the fact his body was found a few hours after hooded Klansmen stabbed two Black teenagers just blocks away.[174] In autumn of 1987, skinheads and the Klan held a joint cross-burning ceremony in nearby Modesto, California, during which 4 of the 13 young skinheads who attended were initiated into the Klan.[175] Only months before and 40 miles away in San Jose, white supremacist Kenneth Lamar Allen had been arrested for an attack on a 54-year-old Black woman. "We are racial, and she was Black, we're into white supremacy" said Allen. All of these incidents underlined the fact that the liberal San Francisco Bay Area could at times be as perilous as the Deep South for people of color.[176]

When skinheads marched through the Haight in 1988, they went virtually unopposed. The following February, the American Front and White Aryan Resistance announced that they would hold a white power concert just north of San Francisco in a rural area between the working-class town of Vallejo and the Napa Valley. The bill featured right-wing skinhead bands such as the Boot Boys, Hammerhead, and New Glory. Over 1,400 law enforcement officers in the area were put on alert. Dubbed "Aryan Woodstock," the concert was planned for March 4, 1989, and became a flash point between white supremacists and anti-racists. This time around, the San Francisco branch of the John Brown Anti-Klan Committee was ready to mobilize and challenge the Nazis.

In the weeks leading up to the concert, American Front organizers sent recruiters to target white youth at high schools and skate parks. During this time, there was a strong suspicion that the Mare Island Naval Shipyard, which supplied a massive amount of jobs in the area, would shutter in the coming years. Racist recruiters exploited the sense of economic uncertainty to incite fear that union jobs would disappear, low-income minorities and immigrants would increase, and the area would go down the toilet. The John Brown crew sent members to conduct street-corner outreach to locals to oppose the event. The chapter popularized a campaign called "Just Say No to Nazis"—a play on Nancy Reagan's anti-drug slogan—in an effort to deny fascists spaces to demonstrate.

San Francisco's John Brown chapter used Napa city council meetings to push a resolution denying the fascists a permit for their concert. "We didn't expect that they would do anything about it but wanted to use the meetings to create a public conversation about the threat of organized racism," remarked

Roth. The tactic of using city council meetings as a site to organize originated with the committee's work in Connecticut years prior. This time, the council responded, and did in fact deny the permits.

When the fascists took the matter to court, Judge W. Scott Snowden allowed the gathering to proceed, but without a sound permit, citing a 1971 law requiring a permit for outdoor concerts. John Brown's counter-organizing efforts directly helped to sabotage the white supremacists' concert. Aryan Woodstock's attendance was under 100, a number far below the 2,000 originally predicted by concert organizers. Many media outlets, including the *New York Times*, portrayed the day of the event as peaceful. Police prohibited parking for miles around the concert site, meaning that protesters and concertgoers had to walk along the same road to assemble. Modesto Klansman Bill Albers was chased back to his car by anti-racists. Albers was a high-profile white supremacist who regularly hosted cross burnings on his private property in the California's Central Valley. Tom Metzger went to great lengths to try to explain that their defeat was actually a victory. To his mind, the "Zionist Occupational Government" lost just by the fact that the event occurred. Speaking in the rain, he boasted that Aryan Woodstock exposed how frightened Jewish people were of the skinhead movement. The event came to be known as "Aryan Woodflop."[177]

Aryan Woodstock was emblematic of the racist right's foray into cultural organizing. It also exposed how working-class towns just outside of major cities were being targeted by white supremacists. Back in San Francisco, the John Brown Anti-Klan Committee decided to mount its own cultural campaign to counter skinhead influence in the Bay Area. The group began by mailing out anti-Nazi kits to people California, but after some months, requests came from as far as Germany and Poland. The kit included a message to recipients that read:

So, here's your Just Say No to Nazis kit! This kit is to USE . . . and we've put in a bunch of things that might come in handy in educating and mobilizing your community against Nazi skinheads and all forms of racist, sexist, anti-gay, anti-Semitic organizing. There are lots of things to do. So, do what feels right, possible, and safe. Don't look for fights! Remember Nazis tend to travel in packs; they might be armed. The best response is an organized campaign by as many people as possible to expose their racism and violence.

Building on tactics from the Chicago chapter's "Stamp Out Racist Graffiti" campaign, the San Francisco Committee's kit offered free stickers, stencils, literature, and a 26-point list of ideas on how to organize locally against fascists. In addition to providing these resources, the kit emphasized building community and provided information about using an "anti-racist hotline" for connecting with other anti-racists in a region and reporting neo-Nazi and white supremacist activities.

The Bay Area chapter of the John Brown Anti-Klan Committee also used punk networks to counter-organize against the neo-Nazi influence. Members Les Gottesman and William Crossman regularly attended regional punk shows at legendary venues such as the On Broadway, the Gilman Street Project, and the Deaf Club. The duo, who were older than most of the punks at the time, recruited bands to be a part of bolstering the anti-racist stance already apparent in many Bay area acts. They regularly organized shows with anti-racist themes featuring the Dead Kennedys, Operation Ivy, the Beatnigs, and the Dicks. As Gottesman recalled, the John Brown Anti-Klan Committee's approach to cultural organizing was simple: "We weren't going to let racists take over youth culture in San Francisco. We recognized that punk was reaching exactly whom we wanted to reach, the disaffected youth. The Nazis knew that, and it would have been foolish for us to ignore it." At their shows, they also

Punk band M.D.C. at the Berlin Wall, late 1980s. Photographer unknown. *From the collection of Jennifer Joseph.*

screened short videos about anti-Klan organizing occurring in other parts of the country.

M.D.C. became the band most identified with the John Brown group's politics. A line from the band's song *Born to Die* was adopted by the organization as its best-known slogan: "No Cops, No KKK, No Fascist USA!" The band directly promoted the John Brown Anti-Klan Committee and invited the organization to table at various shows, including Central American solidarity benefits and the national Rock Against Reagan tour. "We looked up to the John Brown Anti-Klan Committee as they were really smart and serious about what they were doing," recalled M.D.C.'s lead singer, Dave Dictor.[178]

Back in Chicago, violence easily spilled into punk shows from street protests. Vic Bondi, lead singer of the left-wing hardcore band Articles of Faith, described the time when Nazi skinheads arrived at Big Blue, a well-known crash pad and practice space. Most of the bands which came through Chicago slept at Big Blue, a three-story brownstone where they stayed in two apartments on the top floor. The bottom apartments were unoccupied. "We practiced in the attic, and it was a huge space. At one of these shows the son of Tom Metzger, the Nazi leader, showed up with some of his skinhead buddies. We were upstairs, and someone grabbed me and told me they were spray-painting swastikas on the house. So, we bolted downstairs and started wailing on them. We did them substantial damage. Threw that kid down two flights of stairs."

The culture wars against fascists and white supremacists briefly escalated from small punk venues and street protests to national television. As racialized violence was flaring up in Chicago and across the country, Oprah Winfrey, then in her second year as the first Black woman talk show host, invited white fascists on to her *Oprah Winfrey Show*. "My guests today are Skinheads," she began. "They say their heads are shaved for battle. Do you believe that only white people created this country?" Just four months prior to Oprah's show, the Klan organized its largest rally in Chicago to date, with over 500 members and affiliated neo-Nazis, on the anniversary of Martin Luther King Jr.'s "I Have a Dream" speech.

As the *Oprah Winfrey Show* was filmed in Chicago, the situation presented a pivotal organizing opportunity for the Chicago John Brown chapter. "We knew we needed to pack the whole room and really give it to them," recalled Bob Wells. "We didn't know who they were going to bring on, but it turned out that [White Aryan Resistance chief] Tom Metzger was in the audience, also using Oprah's show to get his message out." For the John Brown crew, the show offered an opportunity to mobilize people in Chicago to turn out against a local neo-Nazis and white supremacists. The occasion also represented a massive opportunity to publicly spotlight one of the most pressing objectives for the organization: to educate the nation that many white people strongly supported the abolition of white supremacy. To disrupt the racists' message, they reached out directly to anti-racist skinheads in Chicago and urged them to be a part of the studio audience. To do this, the group relied on the outreach they had done in the punk scene, tabling until all hours of the night outside of the Metro, a popular underground club on North Clark.

It's not clear what Winfrey had hoped to accomplish. The episode was chaotic and provided the panel of Nazis a chance to promote everything from anti-Jewish conspiracy theories to aspirations for a racially pure white nation. During the show the Nazis referred to Black people—and Oprah, in particular—as monkeys. Tom Metzger, dressed in a black suit and tie, was frequently handed the microphone. When Howie Emmer introduced himself as a member of the John Brown Anti-Klan Committee, he was met with applause from the audience. "As a white person, I am here to tell you that these people do not speak for me!" Giving Metzger the chance to retort, he said, "John Brown's main claim to fame was exterminating white men, women, and children at Harpers Ferry. It is a Marxist group that don't have the guts to call themselves Marxist." Having none of it, Emmer countered, "John Brown was a white man who before the Civil War gave his life for the cause of Black Liberation."

During the question and answer portion of her show, Oprah picked a John Brown member to comment: "I'm from the John Brown Anti-Klan Committee and I want to make it clear that our group has a lot of support, we have done a lot of activity against white supremacists. As a white person, these people definitely do not stand for me!" After a number of forced commercial breaks, Oprah asked a skinhead who was in the audience: "So apparently there are two different factions of skinheads, can you tell me what they are?" The Skinheads replied, "The faction of Skinheads sitting up on stage right now are just being used by white power organizations for the muscle. A lot of these groups were white power before, but now they just shave their heads and use this identity to recruit." The episode caused a national sensation, but the subsequent discussion missed an important point: anti-racist skinheads associated with crews such as the Pitbulls and Skinheads of Chicago vastly outnumbered Oprah's racist guests. From the audience, person after person denounced racism and its corrosive influence within the scene.

The *Geraldo Rivera Show* aired an episode called "Teen Hatemongers." Rivera brought John Metzger of White Aryan Resistance, Bob Heick of the American Front, and Michael Palish of the Skinheads of the National Resistance. The first half of the show consisted of Rivera and his guests trading barbs, with Heick calling Adolf Hitler a hero and declaring that it didn't matter if the Holocaust happened or not. Roy Innis of the Congress of Racial Equity and Rabbi A. Bruce Goldman of the Center for Jewish Living were invited to provide a counter-perspective. If Rivera wanted a spectacle, he got exactly what he wished for. All hell broke loose when Metzger called Innis an Uncle Tom, resulting in Innis attempting to choke Metzger. Soon, the entire studio audience was engulfed in a chair-throwing fracas that left Rivera with a broken nose.

The rise of the television talk shows gave the white power movement a national platform and an opportunity to reach hundreds of thousands of people at once. Up to that point, skinhead organizations had built a base through informal mail-order networks such as Romantic Violence, and late-night cable TV shows. "Before the internet, white power bands relied on face-to-face-social networks to organize. It was all about phone calls, P.O. boxes, and festivals. Few of the clubs would book us, so we would play in people's homes, or sometimes we would find a V.F.W. Hall that would let us perform," recalled Picciolini. Thanks to Oprah Winfrey and Geraldo Rivera, the movement's bullhorn was louder than ever before.[179]

The work to counter fascist influence in music scenes brought out some of the best aspects of the John Brown Anti-Klan Committee. It was here that they developed the ability to work far outside of previous comfort zones and go toe-to-toe with the right for the hearts and minds of working-class youth. Their work also acknowledged how culture can be used to influence individuals to interpret the cause of material inequalities in their lives. Economic hardship can set the stage for far-right recruitment as much as it can spark a desire for social justice. The John Brown crews in Chicago and San Francisco recognized this reality.[180]

During the Reagan years, punk culture provided spaces for young people to respond to the social and political crises of the time. For organized white supremacists and fascists, punk was used to amplify the grim diagnosis that social problems could only be solved by a full embrace of white power, something that the social and cultural movements of the 1960s and 1970s had unsettled just enough to catalyze a backlash. For anti-racists, punk was a rebellion against meaningless consumer culture, militarism, racism and the authorities that enforced them.[181] The John Brown Anti-Klan Committee was a significant voice helping to make anti-racism cool within music subculture by supporting artists who were unambiguous in their rejection of white supremacy.

John Brown Anti-Klan Committee protests the Klan's use of a public library for a recruiting drive. Photo by Liz Hafalia/*San Francisco Chronicle*.

FIVE

SMALL STEPS ON A LONG ROAD

"Too often, our standards for evaluating social movements pivot around whether or not they 'succeeded' in realizing their visions rather than on the merits or power of the visions themselves. By such a measure, virtually every radical movement failed because the basic power relations they sought to change remained pretty much intact. And yet it is precisely these alternative visions and dreams that inspire new generations to struggle for change."
　　　　　　　　　　　　　　　—Robin D.G. Kelley

In 1988, Terry Bisson published a small book, *Fire on the Mountain*, which imagined how the United States might have evolved if John Brown's raid at Harpers Ferry had successfully catalyzed a wave of rebellions against slavery. In Bisson's novel, John Brown succeeds because he listens to Harriet Tubman's counsel on matters of strategy. Without the shackles of white supremacy, a sovereign Black nation—New Afrika—emerges and advances so far that by 1959, it launches a space program to explore the solar system. A white nation, centered in Appalachia, emerges as a developing socialist democracy.

Bisson's novel poignantly expressed key aspects of the John Brown Anti-Klan Committee's abolitionist vision. Lasting thirteen years, the organization enjoyed a longer life than many radical left-wing organizations in the United States. By the early 1990s, the group's membership slowly waned as members moved on to other projects, began families, or pursued careers deferred by lives spent at the front lines. There was no dramatic end, written summation, or even a final meeting to call it quits. As the organization waned, the political activism of its members continued in new directions throughout the next decade and beyond.

The Committee was always concerned with incarceration. The organization came into being in response to an urgent call from incarcerated people of color seeking to expose Klan infiltration of New York prisons. Toward the organization's end, as many former members and allies faced long prison sentences, the Committee increased its focus on confronting the politics of the carceral state. Doing so led many to address the emerging AIDS-related health crisis by organizing for better HIV treatment programs for incarcerated people and supporting the nonviolent direct action group ACT UP.

The political aftermath of the John Brown Anti-Klan Committee is an essential part of the organization's story. Understanding what came next situates the organization within a constellation of tributaries that have shaped today's movements and shows the arc of people's political commitments to anti-imperialism, anti-racism, and anti-fascism through time.

This chapter follows the stories of former members who integrated the lessons of their time in John Brown into new projects confronting the HIV/AIDS crisis and the growth of mass incarceration in the United States. Former members Judy Siff and Judy Berger relocated to Atlanta to take part in the fight against HIV/AIDS in the South. Committee members in Chicago and San Francisco also worked in broad coalitions to confront the plague. Former member Linda Evans served a prison sentence while others such as Nancy Kurshan and Pam Fadem built grassroots organizations to support incarcerated people. All worked to sound the alarm on the racist nature of what would come to be called the prison industrial complex.

ACT UP, FIGHT BACK

AIDS activism began receiving international visibility in 1987 as a result of dramatic direct actions by the AIDS Coalition to Unleash Power's (ACT UP). The group's interventions disrupted the stock exchange, live media broadcasts, National Health Institute offices, homophobic churches, and political events staged by politicians who had no real interest for the issue. The organization was also relentless in its research in immunology and sex education as forms of direct action. Although the organization favored nonviolent acts of civil disobedience, ACT UP's uncompromising approach to fighting AIDS was similar in spirit to the John Brown Anti-Klan Committee's stance against white supremacy. Members of both organizations shared a conviction that civil disobedience was required to motivate state forces to change. As chapters of the Committee began to dissolve, many of their members collaborated with ACT UP chapters in Atlanta, Chicago, and the San Francisco Bay Area.[182]

First reported on in 1981, AIDS quickly became known as the "Gay Plague," as it systematically destroyed the gay male population and made its way to many others, including women, incarcerated people, and intravenous drug users. As increasing numbers of people became diagnosed with HIV/AIDS, the emerging crisis transformed the politics of the 1980s. President Reagan initially refused to acknowledge the national threat posed by the epidemic, delaying urgently needed federal research, prevention, and treatment programs. His administration's neoconservative position was summed up when Secretary of Education William Bennett said, "Everyone detected with AIDS should be tattooed in the upper forearm, to protect common-needle users, and on the buttocks, to prevent the victimization of other homosexuals."[183] By the beginning of Reagan's second term, 5,596 people in the United States had died from the disease. By the time he finally addressed the issue, he was safely into his second term and focused on his skepticism of sex education in the schools. By the end of Reagan's second term, more than 61,816 people had died from the epidemic in the United States. False rumors that AIDS could be transmitted through mosquito bites or casual contact with infected people created a climate of fear and increased stigmatization of both the disease and LGBTQ people. In 1986, far-right gadfly Lyndon LaRouche launched a ballot measure in California attempting to mandate mass testing for HIV/AIDS and quarantining of those determined to be infected.[184]

Evans and other incarcerated activists and militants were confronted with abysmal health services and nonexistent HIV/AIDS-prevention programs. For them, medical conditions inside the prisons were glaring examples of genocide against Black and Brown communities. As they became more conscious of the health crisis, they began AIDS education and support inside the prisons. Judy Siff and Judy Gerber were dispatched to Atlanta by the Prairie Fire Organizing Committee to support building anti-racist politics in the South. During this time, it was common for left political organizations to send members to different cities to support the group's political priorities. "We were very clear we could not go be carpetbaggers. We could not drop ourselves, these two Northern Jewish Lesbians, into the South and present ourselves as *the* anti-racist organizers," recollected Gerber. There, they supported anti-Klan mobilizations by the New Afrikan Peoples Organization, the American Friends Service Committee, Concerned Black Clergy, and Atlanta's broader progressive community.

They also played a pivotal role in the southern front of the AIDS movement. They helped to organize the January 9, 1990, direct action against the Centers for Disease Control (CDC) that resulted in fifty arrests. Protesters showered the CDC library with ping-pong balls to symbolize human T cells; others dropped a banner from the side of the building that read "CDC Kills." They accused the CDC of killing through bureaucracy, as its narrow definition of AIDS excluded many who had the disease from receiving social benefits such as Medicare and housing assistance.[185]

Siff and Gerber also played a central role in raising funds and awareness for the legal challenge to Georgia's anti-sex laws in the case of *Bowers v. Hardwick*, in which the U.S. Supreme Court ultimately backed laws criminalizing anal and oral sex. Siff recalls, "AIDS was hidden in Atlanta because the gay population was largely hidden. Our work was to push for the movement to come out." The duo also helped to organize and promote the annual Pride gatherings, where attendance soared from hundreds to thousands in a few years time. As Gerber explained, the John Brown ethos shined through: "We needed to be bold, we needed to be out, and we didn't need permission or permits. We always had to develop an international perspective, however small the immediate project."

In Chicago, former Committee members played an important role in the local ACT UP chapter and in an early coalition called Dykes and Gay Men Against Racism and Repression. Moncada Library member Mary Patton was among the coalition's founding members. The group held a twenty-four-hour vigil and committed civil disobedience on the front lawn of Governor James Thompson in an attempt to urge him to vocally oppose proposals to quarantine people diagnosed with AIDS. They campaigned against a local pharmaceutical company, Lyphomed, over price gouging for life-saving drugs.

Throughout this period, race and class conflicts repeatedly surfaced. Darrell Gordon, a Chicago ACT UP member, noted that one faction of mostly white gay men insisted on staying singularly focused on HIV/AIDS. Former members of the John Brown Anti-Klan Committee not only demanded that race and class be on the table, but that Black and white people should organize in their own communities.[186]

Ingrid Nelson of ACT UP San Francisco remembers meeting members of the John Brown Anti-Klan Committee and how closely aligned their anti-racist commitments were.

Before the San Francisco chapter of the Committee folded, it invited ACT UP San Francisco to protest Aryan Woodstock, and both groups hit the streets together to demonstrate against the Rodney King verdict. The two organizations also studied together, focusing on past protest movements and the writings of Angela Y. Davis and Assata Shakur. They also joined forces to support campaigns by incarcerated people to improve conditions behind bars. "I feel like those ACT UP and John Brown folks were my mentors," said Nelson, "and I got a lot of education and inspiration from them."

AIDS activism linked former John Brown members both inside and outside of prison. After leaving the Austin chapter in 1980, Linda Evans took part in clandestine resistance groups, a trajectory often taken by those dedicated to radical leftist politics in the period between the Civil Rights era and the first Gulf War. On May 11, 1985, Linda Evans was arrested in Dobbs Ferry, New York, alongside Marilyn Buck, who had been on the run since Assata Shakur's escape from prison. After an initial mistrial, a jury of eight white people and four Black people convicted Evans of possessing a firearm and harboring the fugitive Buck. Sentenced to five years in federal prison, she soon faced additional trials in Connecticut and Louisiana. The Connecticut case (about false ID) was dismissed because of government misconduct. In Louisiana, she was convicted and sentenced to forty years for making false statements to purchase legal firearms and ammunition. Later, her Louisiana sentence was reduced to thirty years on appeal.

In 1988, additional charges were filed against Evans. This time, authorities stitched her into cases being brought against several others—Buck, Betty Ann Duke, Timothy Blunk, and Alan Berkman—who were also already imprisoned for their alleged roles in a series of bombings of domestic military and police sites. The trial was labeled the Resistance Conspiracy Case. In an effort to add several decades to their sentences, federal prosecutors made the argument that the six conspired to execute or support a string of bombings claimed by the Armed Resistance Unit, United Freedom Front, and the Red Guerrilla Movement. The ordeal came to an end on September 8, 1990. Buck, Whitehorn, and Evans decided to plead guilty to bombing charges in exchange for charges against Berkman, Blunk, and Rosenberg being dropped. Despite being locked up for half of the John Brown Anti-Klan Committee's life span, Evans continued to be allied with the organization's politics and programs from inside prison.

While awaiting trial in Washington, D.C., she took part in what might have been her most effective political project up to that point: organizing behind bars against the spread of AIDS. She connected with Judy Greenspan, the AIDS Information Coordinator for the ACLU's Prison Project. Through the chaplain's office at the D.C. Jail, they brought HIV/AIDS-prevention materials into the prison to dispel myths surrounding the epidemic, like the possibility of infection through sharing toilets.[187]

Initial AIDS prevention outreach in D.C. consisted of passing information informally between incarcerated people, and ad hoc peer counseling. Many of the women inside the D.C. Jail were visibly ill, but HIV+ prisoners had little support or medical treatment. The women political prisoners did what they could to provide accurate information and emotional support.

In 1990, Evans was transferred to FCI-Pleasanton, a federal women's prison in the San Francisco Bay Area. There, she followed the example of both men and women political prisoners in New York State who actively educated their fellow prisoners about HIV/AIDS and provided peer counseling. In the California prison, Evans co-founded an organization called Pleasanton AIDS Counseling and Education (PLACE). With the help of Judy Greenspan, PLACE modified Alison Bechdel's comic book *Dykes to Watch Out For*, and turned it into an educational poster with HIV/AIDS information in the dialogue bubbles.[188] An official prison "club," PLACE gained permission to accompany women to receive HIV test results, and to provide peer-based counseling.

PLACE connected with a progressive Catholic from the local community, and she was to bring in craft materials. Women in PLACE crocheted toys for HIV+ children in local hospitals and sponsored a Prisoners Fight AIDS Walkathon similar to walkathons that took place in other federal prisons. "People walked literally thousands of miles around the [prison's running] track," said Evans. "We raised thousands of dollars." During this time, Prisoners Fight AIDS also drafted solidarity statements with organizations such as ACT UP and advocated for better health care and medications. One of the walkathons benefited residents of San Francisco's Ambassador Hotel, a single-room occupancy establishment where the city sent impoverished people diagnosed with AIDS. The women learned about the hotel through a television documentary, *Life and Death at the Ambassador Hotel.* "Everybody in the prison participated," said Evans. "Even if they only walked around one time, we counted it, it went into the totals. People raised money. We raised a lot of money because we had connections in the progressive Catholic community, but we got a lot of donations from all kinds of people. The women inside donated so generously—offered their lousy prison wages." Evans's HIV/AIDS work mirrored that of other radicals serving time in prison, notably John Brown Anti-Klan Committee co-founder Susan Rosenberg and Brink's defendants David Gilbert and Judith Clark.[189]

San Francisco activist Val Robb and Ambassador Hotel manager Tom Calvanese traveled to Dublin to thank the women. Recalled Calvanese, "They made some incredible gifts for the residents, including a Christmas nativity scene made entirely of stuff they were able to utilize from prison materials such as tongue depressors and tampons. When they asked me what they could make for the residents, I told them almost everybody had lost their keys on multiple occasions, so they made like 150 individual key chains out of home-made clay, and the residents loved them!"

In 1985, longtime queer activist Cleve Jones started organizing the AIDS Memorial Quilt. The project involved stitching together panels featuring the names of those lost to the epidemic. The quilt became a powerful and visible reminder of the damage done by the disease and Reagan's refusal to devote federal resources to research and prevention. Growing daily, by 1988 the quilt contained more than eight thousand panels and was displayed in front of the White House.

In the summer of 1993, Pleasanton AIDS Counseling and Education received permission to sew panels in Dublin. They added two large panels, which they made from recycled fabric and prison uniforms. Unexpectedly, this created a rare moment of solidarity between the prisoners and the prison guards. Evans remembered, "The quilt just blew everybody's mind. Everybody in the compound went into that building. The whole floor was covered with the quilt panels. They put the quilt panels for people in law enforcement who had died up in the loft, for the guards to view. And it was very deep to recognize that HIV had affected every single person at the compound. It was really important. It was great that we were able to bring that there."

On January 20, 2001, Linda Evans and Susan Rosenberg were pardoned by President Bill Clinton and released from prison. The grant of clemency came as a surprise to Evans, even though her attorney, Debra Katz, had strongly advocated for release. Ms. Katz also discovered a connection to Clinton's chief of staff, John Podesta through a mutual friend—the owner of a local women's bookstore. She brokered a two-and-a-half-hour conversation between Podesta and Katz. Soon after Evans's release, a well-placed source in the administration confided that he believed was the real reason for her release was that Clinton wanted to send a "fuck you" to the FBI for their handling of the Whitewater case, a real estate scandal that had sullied the Clintons' reputation.[190] While back-channel

AIDS quilt, Washington, D.C. Photograph by Carol M. Highsmith.
Library of Congress Prints and Photographs Division.

connections to the White House may have contributed to the pardons, Evans credits her defense committee for keeping her connected to a larger community while she was behind bars. With assistance from her supporters, Evans was able to earn degrees from New College of California and California State University at Dominguez Hills while incarcerated.

Today, Evans lives in Santa Rosa, California, and organizes around prison abolition and the rights of incarcerated people, particularly women. She was a co-founder of All of Us or None, a grassroots civil rights organization of formerly incarcerated people and their families. All of Us or None initiated the "Ban the Box" campaign, which has now eliminated discrimination based on prior convictions in thirty-eight states and over 150 cities and counties. Her politics haven't softened much; she is still an anti-imperialist stalwart. She actively supports other political prisoners and serves on multiple defense committees. What has changed is her ability to see value in the slower processes of changing people's hearts and minds.

ABOLITIONIST SPIRIT: CONFRONTING MASS INCARCERATION

Because of their connections to imprisoned friends and comrades, members of the John Brown Anti-Klan Committee had a unique vantage point to witness the disturbing growth of mass incarceration in the United States. John Brown members Nancy Kurshan and Pam Fadem founded important grassroots organizations responding to the growing crisis. The prison population grew from about 330,000 in 1972 to more than two million in 2000.[191] The organization's view that all imprisoned people had a political aspect to their condition guided much of the work former members dedicated themselves to after the Committee folded. As time progressed, many former members joined the growing movement against mass incarceration, police brutality, and the criminalization of Black and Latino people.

The line between being "political" and "social" incarceration had always been thin, and was made more so by the passage of the Violent Crime Control and Law Enforcement Act of 1994, bipartisan legislation that provided new federal funding for prisons, identified fifty new federal crimes, eliminated student aid for incarcerated people, and fortified mandatory minimum sentencing. As these policies hardened the imposition of maximum sentences on the federal level, many state and local laws soon did so too.

Former John Brown member Nancy Kurshan and her husband at the time, Steve Whitman, gave presentations to challenge the liberal assertion that prisons were attempting to rehabilitate people. They argued that prisons instead served to subordinated and control communities of color. They correlated the rise of mass incarceration as a government response to the rebellions of the 1960s and 1970s, particularly uprisings by Black people. This belief was bolstered by the writings of Samuel Harrington, who blamed the "ungovernable sectors as the cause of decline of the United States."[192] Whitman was one of the first scholars to demonstrate how the growth of prisons disproportionately impacted Black people. His research found that between 1972 and 1986 the overall prison population more than doubled, and that a Black person was six times more likely than a white person to go to prison.

> It is no coincidence that the rise in black imprisonment accompanies the rise of the Klan and the Nazis, attacks on black people in Howard Beach, Queens; in Forsyth County, Ga.; and in Marquette Park, Uptown and other areas of Chicago. It is not surprising that these events coincide with the term of a President who is endorsed by the Klan, who has undermined civil rights advances and decimated social programs. It is no coincidence that all of this occurs while the proportions of black doctors, lawyers and professors remain tiny, while the black infant mortality which already in some communities is at levels associated with the Third World, remains twice the white rate; while the black maternal mortality rate is three times the white rate; and while black poverty intensifies. None of this could happen without the implicit, and far too often complicit, agreement of white people. We are caught up in a law-and-order ideology generated not by reality but by hysteria. Imprisoning more black people will not stop the decay of our social system. In fact, the opposite is true. Until whites confront racism, and stop using blacks as the scapegoats for our failing social system, the situation will only get worse.[193]

Transitioning from the John Brown Anti-Klan Committee, Kurshan founded the Committee to End the Marion Lockdown, which had a larger mission regarding prison reform. "We felt that we had to struggle, even with those on the left, to not only focus on political prisoners, but to broaden that to see that there were all these political dimensions to imprisonment," said Kurshan. "There were all these debates about whether the mass of prisoners were political or not. We really didn't get into the debate so much, because we were interested in showing imprisonment in general and revealing how that had to do with racism. We thought we had to do the work around racism, not just [express] a humanistic concern for prisoners. We had a humanistic concern, of course, but wanted to show the systematic side of the problem." Throughout its entire existence, the John Brown Anti-Klan Committee had advocated that white supremacy be fought as an international system. The Marion Lockdown campaign revisited the terrain where the Committee had begun—prisoner support—but took the conversation a step forward by turning its attention to the consequences of carceral public policy.

Kurshan and the other members of Committee to End the Marion Lockdown regularly protested outside of Marion, a control unit prison, which had been in a state of perpetual lockdown since 1983. Marion also housed many political prisoners, including Oscar Lopez-Rivera and Sundiata Acoli. The Marion Lockdown Committee published a book, *Can't Jail the Spirit*, that explained that political prisoners were those "who have made conscious political decisions, and acted on them, to oppose the United States government and who have been incarcerated as a result of those actions. These actions are taken in response to economic, social, and political conflicts within our society." They pointed out that prisoners of war were people who were members of oppressed nations who believed that their nations were at war with the United States or were building toward such a war. *Can't Jail the Spirit* articulated the growing understanding of the connectedness between social and political incarceration:

> More importantly, we recognize that prisons are instruments of population control for people of color. The act of incarcerating huge numbers of prisoners is a fundamental political act by the United States. This is an act which is central in sustaining the system of white supremacy, a system we are dedicated to destroying. Many people are sent to prison for "crimes" that are acts of self-defense or survival. These would include women who attack or even kill men who brutalize them, people who steal to survive, prostitutes, and other similar groups of people. Although these people are not political prisoners according to our definition, they deserve our support for their struggle to survive and, in many cases, resist.[194]

Nationally recognized prison abolition organizer Rachel Herzing considers the work of Kurshan and the Campaign to End the Marion Lockdown a pivotal moment in the evolution of today's prison abolition movement. "They presented an ethos that recognized how the fates of political prisoners, prisoners of war, and those caught up in the push toward punishment were interrelated. They sounded the alarm that imprisonment was growing exponentially. Unfortunately, they were right, and many people didn't listen at the time. Their work was foundational for many of the activists who came after." Kurshan later wrote *Out of Control—A Fifteen Year Battle Against Control Unit Prisons*, a book about the Campaign to End the Marion Lockdown.

After being released from prison for refusing to cooperate with a grand jury, another former John Brown member, Pam Fadem, co-founded the California Coalition of Women Prisoners (CCWP). Fadem and CCWP assisted a campaign for improved health care in women's prisons that coalesced around a class-action lawsuit by Charisse Shumate, who was serving seventeen-to-life for killing her abuser. The lawsuit challenged the California Department of Corrections for its complete lack of adequate medical care in women's prisons. The group mustered considerable outside support and mobilized dozens of formerly incarcerated women to speak up in demonstrations and public hearings. The lawsuit was dismissed, but resulted in a settlement enabling women in prison to request medical care, higher professional standards of confidentiality for medical records, and screenings for contagious diseases.

The California Coalition of Women Prisoners remains one of a handful of organizations that continues to prioritize the needs of women in prison and organizes with both incarcerated and formerly incarcerated people. Fadem regularly participates in mobilizations and speaks out against mass incarceration. Her work has shifted slightly in recent years. Decades of organizing against mass incarceration have shifted the debate and made policy makers and politicians more open to limited reforms to reduce the prison population. It's up to grassroots organizers such as Fadem to ensure that "reform" doesn't simply translate into freedom for some, while relegating others to lifelong incarceration. "In California, Governor [Gavin] Newsom has come out against the death penalty, and the conversation has definitely changed for the better," Fadem observed. "Yet the state wants to replace the death penalty with automatic life without parole, which we have always said was a hidden death sentence."

Today, most veterans of the John Brown Anti-Klan Committee continue to embody the group's original abolitionist spirit through a wide spectrum of social justice activism. While their approaches have changed with time, their principles have not. Some are teachers, working to undermine racial disparities in education. Many continue to speak to young people about the lessons of their work at activist conferences. Others continue on the front lines. In 2018, on the anniversary of the Charlottesville atrocity, a group of Committee veterans living in the San Francisco Bay Area reunited to take part in counter-protests against white nationalist mobilizations in Berkeley and Oakland. The group marched under a banner that showed the face of John Brown, inviting all to once again, "*Take a Stand Against White Supremacy.*"

SIX

LESSONS FOR TODAY'S MOVEMENTS

"Policies change, and programs change, according
to time. But objective never changes. You might
change your method of achieving the objective, but
the objective never changes. Our objective is complete freedom, complete justice, complete equality,
by any means necessary."

—Malcolm X, 1964

On February 15, 2019, a forty-nine-year-old U.S. Coast
Guard lieutenant, Marine Corps veteran, and white nationalist named Christopher Hasson was arrested for plotting to as-
sassinate high-profile politicians, media figures, and civilians.
From his desk at Coast Guard headquarters in Washington,
D.C., Hasson spent hours researching killing techniques used
by far-right mass murderers. According to prosecutors, Hasson was inspired by Norwegian terrorist Anders Behring Brei-
vik and abortion clinic bomber Eric Robert Rudolph. In his
basement apartment, Hasson had amassed a stockpile of guns,
ammunition, and body armor worth approximately $13,000.
Hasson was a longtime neo-Nazi who wrote that he preferred
"focused violence" to marches and rallies. He drafted letters
to friends speculating how to cause the maximum amount of
damage to society. The purpose of Hasson's violence was to
incite a race war.[195]

Media outlets pondered the significance of a white nationalist with twenty-eight years of military service: Was he an

indicator or an anomaly? Does serving in the U.S. military in-crease or decrease the probability of white men being radical-ized? What is the Department of Defense doing to prevent the problem of white supremacists in the armed forces? What most media missed was that groups like the John Brown Anti-Klan Committee had warned us about the Hassons of the world de-cades ago. White supremacists are not outliers living off the grid in rural areas; they are organizing all around us and serve in the military, in police departments, on prison staffs, and in the offices of elected officials. Taken together with the increas-ing frequency of far-right violence, Hasson's intended attacks served to fulfill the prophecy of the John Brown Anti-Klan Committee: If not directly confronted, the influence of white nationalists will spread.

White supremacists have historically existed in all branch-es of government, but have only been tracked in the military since the 1980s.[196] This coincided with white nationalists' dec-laration of war against the U.S. government and an increase in armed attacks. The questions journalists ask are necessary, but often fail to address the scope of the threat posed by white na-tionalists organized within the military and law enforcement. The problem is not just how many white nationalists hold posts in the armed forces or what actions the Department of Defense will or will not take. Instead, we must interrogate what com-mon historical interests remain between state authorities and right-wing vigilantism. What is required of anti-racist people, organizations, and movements during political moments such as the current era, when white nationalist and far-right agen-das are all but sanctioned by officials at the highest levels of government?

The uptick in racialized violence isn't an anomaly, but a recurring historical backlash to the political, social, and eco-nomic advancement of people of color. It can be seen in the Ku Klux Klan's emergence as a reaction to the Black community gaining access to state power during Reconstruction, and in the inception of the "Southern Strategy" to retrench segregationist policies in the mid to late twentieth century.

Today, more far-right groups have entered the White House to provide counsel on federal policy than ever before. Similarly, more far-right politicians hold office than ever before. In 2018, the number of hate groups recorded in the United States rose to 1,020, an all-time high. The number of white nationalist groups grew nearly 50 percent, from 100 to 148. And, in 2018 alone, the "alt-right" was responsible for killing forty people in the United States and Canada. While the Trump administration was far from the only cause of this spike in activity, the Southern Poverty Law Center reported that approximately 6 percent of the 198 million people living in the United States "have beliefs consistent with the racist right worldview, meaning that they broadly believe that politics should promote white interests above those of other racial groups."[197]

While those committed to abolishing white supremacy may differ on how to do it, the John Brown Anti-Klan Committee's understanding of the severity of the situation can be a starting point for any discussion on how to confront the crisis of violence plaguing the country. Moreover, the experience of the Committee offers numerous valuable lessons for today's anti-racist and anti-fascist movements. This final chapter explores what we can learn from the Committee's strengths and weaknesses.

SOLIDARITY IS POWER

A key strength of the John Brown Anti-Klan Committee was the intense level of solidarity the organization developed, both among members and with other anti-imperialist organizations. Such relationships can be an activist organization's greatest asset. In the absence of traditional resources like material wealth, solidarity is power, and the Committee was able to accomplish much because of members' dedication to one another and the vision of liberation they had in common.

Throughout the thirteen-year existence of the organization, every action taken, chapter founded, newspaper written, and network developed, was an attempt to confront and abolish white supremacy and the imperialist politics in which it was embedded. By forging strong and lasting relationships within the organization, members of the Committee established resilience against pressures and threats. Intense emphasis on solidarity, said founding member Bob Boyle, "was always part of the strategy. . . . We never would have done it just on our own." As a result, the Committee was able to take action and withstand backlash from vigilante groups, including acts of intimidation, death threats, and misinformation campaigns. Internal solidarity also enabled the organization to stand up to pressures from government surveillance, harassment, grand jury investigations, and threat of arrest and imprisonment. "We understood that the state disappears people. Our politics wouldn't let us let our friends disappear," explained Donna Willmott, a friend of the group. When members and allies did end up in prison, the Committee kept in constant touch with them, mailing photos, articles, books, and information about what was going on in the movement.

Members of the John Brown Anti-Klan Committee often lived and worked together, connecting their personal and political lives to a degree that had lasting impacts. "It was the relationships in John Brown Anti-Klan Committee that have stayed with me the longest. We raised children together and have been family through all these years," noted Pam Fadem, a founding member of the New York chapter.

In the winter of 1985, members' solidarity came under sharp duress. Four Committee members—Sandra Roland, Steven Burke, Julie Nalibov, and Christine Rico—were held in contempt of court for refusing to testify about a bombing at Washington, D.C.'s, Capitol Building. Two years prior, the Committee had described the bombings as a "response to the invasion of Grenada and other armed actions in solidarity with El Salvador and Nicaragua."[198] Christine Roland, a former D.C. chapter member, said publicly, "Our subpoenas are part of an escalated use of the grand jury which has jailed more than 40 people for refusing to betray their principles and political work by informing the government about their movements."[199] This indicated how the group saw the subpoenas: as an intimidation tactic. What's more, they knew that they had been targeted for supporting Puerto Rican Independistas and Black Liberation activists.

Even though they had moved on from the D.C. chapter, Roland, Burke, Nalibov, and Rico remained dedicated to one another throughout the ordeal. They published newsletters with pictures of themselves together with information about their legal process and advice for others who might be approached by government authorities. They made a point of reminding activists that they had no legal obligation to talk with investigators, that they should demand search warrants if law enforcement showed up at their door, and that they should *not* lie to federal agents in order to avoid charges.

In July 1984, the four, under the name of the John Brown Anti-Klan Committee, joined a national campaign of non-collaboration with grand juries, and signed on to a public letter that was published in *The Guardian*. More than one hundred people and organizations declared, "We, the undersigned, are grand jury resisters, former grand jury resisters, people who have been targets of grand jury investigations, and people who have consistently fought for non-collaboration with the grand jury. We are united now to protest the current escalation of grand jury attacks."[200] The signers cited the role that grand juries had played over the previous fifteen years in the political repression of the "anti–Vietnam war movement, the women's and lesbian movement, the Black liberation movement, the Native American movement, the Catholic left, the Mexicano struggle and the Puerto Rican Independence movement, and the current anti-imperialist and anti-war movement."[201] With this campaign, the Committee worked to turn the grand jury trials into an opportunity to build a broad movement against state repression.

The ways previous movements practiced the defiant pose of non-cooperation are relevant today because activists of all kinds—including those committed to Black Liberation, Puerto Rican independence, Palestinian human rights, Indigenous sovereignty, peace, animal rights, freedom of the press, and ecological sustainability—continue to be targeted by federal grand juries. In 2016, a federal grand jury convened during the height of nonviolent protests targeting the Dakota Access Pipeline at Standing Rock in an effort the Water Protectors Legal Collective called "a broader effort to criminalize Water Protectors and to unfairly target individuals in an effort to divide the movement."[202]

When anti-racist activists who were targeted by the car attack in Charlottesville were subpoenaed to testify at a grand jury, they were unsure whether or not the investigation was fishing for information about their comrades in the movement. The resilience needed to withstand pressure of a grand jury is not always a given within social justice movements. Rather, it must be consciously developed. The John Brown Anti-Klan Committee's extensive cultivation of political and personal solidarity was an essential part of the organization's successful development and growth as a national network for over a decade. The strength that came with such solidarity enabled the organization to take the very real risks that come with confronting vigilante groups historically associated with acts of violence. It also empowered them to refuse to divulge information about fellow activists to grand juries. The value of such solidarity offers important lessons for today's movements.

DISRUPTING FASCIST MESSAGING

Another notable strength of the John Brown Anti-Klan Committee was the organization's commitment to "no-platforming"—actively disrupting racists and fascists from publicly promoting their ideas. This confrontational approach emerged in response to white supremacy's record of atrocities inside the United States, and its connections to fascistic violence throughout the world. If white supremacists' history of perpetrating atrocities was intolerable, then messaging and platforms used for propagating narratives validating those histories and acts of violence should also be considered intolerable.

As a tactic, no-platforming has been rooted in the idea that ignoring fascist and racist formations, no matter how small, does not prevent them from growing. Even though over one hundred years of European anti-fascist history has fully established this point,[203] the position remains controversial in the United States today.[204] The controversy pivots around the First Amendment's protections of freedom of speech, expression, and assembly. Complexity arises when the far right insists that the First Amendment protects their right to publicly propagate their ideas—including notions of social intolerance, exclusion, and racial domination. On multiple occasions, white supremacists have walked away untouched from serious criminal charges by successfully arguing that their right to free speech was violated.

In August 2017, three members of the Rise Above Movement (RAM), a martial arts–based skinhead group, were acquitted of charges of inciting a riot in Berkeley, California, on First Amendment grounds.[205] And Christopher Hassan, the "domestic terrorist" Coast Guard lieutenant accused of stockpiling weapons, has, so far, successfully been defended on a First Amendment basis. While arguments for increased government control over speech or judicial prosecution of white supremacists often led to the conclusion that this would permit a similar crackdown on left movements, struggles around First Amendment rights for white supremacists raise important questions. Heidi Beirich, director of the Southern Poverty Law Center's Intelligence Project, said that although the First Amendment creates some challenges for prosecutors, the deeper problem is a lack of political will to pursue far-right extremists.[206] The question remains, how can anti-racist and anti-fascist movements leverage legal strategies without being stifled within them?

Given the numerous examples of far-right gatherings escalating into violence against marginalized communities, the John Brown Anti-Klan Committee considered disrupting such events as a legitimate form of augmenting the security of targeted populations. Given the long history of police and legal systems supporting white supremacists, the Committee never expected authorities to protect communities of color from the threats posed by the far right. Instead, the Committee went to locations where white supremacists were demonstrating in order to directly support communities threatened by the gatherings. "The public needs to see a voice of opposition. We were showing that there are white people who are against what [the Klan and other white supremacist groups] stand for," D.C. member Julie Nalibov asserted. "We were showing a clear opposition to having a public building used for white supremacy."

Today, the politics of no-platforming is a widely accepted tactic of anti-fascist movements. In 2017, prominent members of the alt-right, such as Milo Yiannopulos and Alex Jones, were met with fierce protests at separate public speaking events at college campuses. Anti-fascist protesters, continuing in the tradition of the Committee, did everything possible to disrupt the events. The results were decidedly mixed. Conservative media outlets seemed to savor the confrontations as opportunities to make their case that it was the left, not the right, that suffered from intolerance and anti-democratic beliefs. Liberal commentators further warned that militancy would help those on the far right reinforce their claim that they were misunderstood patriots.

What actually happened in the cases of Yiannopulos and Jones was that mainstream sentiment turned against both men and contributed significantly to undermining their influence. Under growing scrutiny, Yiannopulos had his book contract cancelled, partially owing to the fact that previous comments he had made seemed to endorse pedophilia. Jones, known for combining wild conspiracy theories with old-school racism, was banned from most major social media platforms.

The John Brown Anti-Klan Committee fought relentlessly against the normalization of white supremacy in U.S. state and social institutions. Committee members at times referenced Germany's post-WWII prohibition against all expressions of Nazism. This is why German Chancellor Angela Merkel expressed horror at the racist marches that roiled Charlottesville in 2017. "It is racist, far-right violence, and clear, forceful action must be taken against it, regardless of where in the world it happens," she said on German television.[207] While the effectiveness Germany's anti-racist and anti-fascist policies have not curtailed the resurgence of the racist right there, it points to an important question: What happens when the state is unable or unwilling to respond to racist violence? No-platforming is one such form of forceful action that the John Brown Anti-Klan Committee waged to successfully deny racist ideas from spreading. Though controversial, it remains a strategy worth studying and learning from today.

Activists who want to confront the right on these terms should do so with an understanding of how racists have adapted their own strategies over time. Through the use of social media, they have honed victimization to an art. They continue to portray their political opponents as intolerant authoritarians, and themselves as patriotic defenders of civil liberties. This position has become harder to defend as right-wing terrorism has escalated. The most effective method to deprive them of this propaganda tool is through strategic flexibility. There are times when physical self-defense is absolutely critical and others when mass mobilizations are truly the most effective approach. Following the example of the John Brown Anti-Klan Committee, the surest way to know the difference is to build organizations able to make strategy, analyze conditions, and recuperate from mistakes.

THE POWER OF BUILDING DIVERSE ALLIANCES

Despite its initial go-it-alone militancy, the John Brown Anti-Klan Committee gradually embraced working within diverse coalitions, and often had the most impact when it did. The shift coincided, in part, with the influx of Prairie Fire members. It was also a direct response to the far right's forays into coalition building following the Greensboro massacre. In Chicago, the Committee juggled confrontational militancy and coalition building. Its efforts to eliminate racist graffiti through community action effectively brought together more than two hundred organizations to collectively combat the influence of white supremacists and fascists. It was moments like these, similar to anti-Klan mobilizations in Austin and the Stop Killer Cops work in Richmond, that showed the potential of building alliances. The coalition approach was always a challenge for a group with such precise politics. But when it worked, it worked well. Coalition building successfully brought communities together, made a show of unifying diverse forces, and often helped to normalize community resistance to the surge of racism from the far right. Such alliances only bolstered the Committee's core strength, the capacity and willingness to stage rapid mobilizations against white nationalist gatherings and threats. The John Brown Anti-Klan Committee established networks of people who were committed to taking action at a moment's notice and shared agreements about messaging, conduct, and orientation. Flyers, banners, pamphlets, talking points, and an outreach plan were gradually developed and eventually became essential elements used during rapid response mobilizations.

When, for example, Klan members in the U.S. Marine Corps began using an effigy of Dorothy Turner of the Black Citizens Task Force as target practice, the Austin chapter mobilized housing defense for Task Force members. The chapter circulated flyers describing the incident and ways to support the Task Force community. These rapid-response tactics furthered three important aspects of challenging organized racism. First, they described the event as part of the legacy of white terror against communities of color. This served an educational function by acknowledging the extent of white supremacists' role in U.S. history. Second, they offered ethical counter-narratives to racism and social intolerance. Third, they suggested concrete ways people could engage in collective action locally.

THE IMPORTANCE OF CULTURAL WORK

There are lessons to be learned from the way the Committee's cultural work magnified its visibility, message, and impact. The organization understood that music and other forms of counterculture can guide young people's raw anger toward the politics of anti-racism and social solidarity, as well as toward their opposites. When the Committee organized events at punk venues, it was an active attempt to go head-to-head with the far right in the battle for the hearts and minds of young people. By embracing youth culture, the John Brown Anti-Klan Committee worked with artists and organizers who helped make emancipatory politics more exciting, interesting, and promising than the oppressive ideas offered by white supremacists. Today's activists would do well to emulate this work, the U.K. Rock Against Racism movement, and the domestic Rock Against Reagan concerts. Working with youth in terms of their own cultural spaces and forms can be a powerful method to increase education, organizing, and resistance to the social intolerance and racial violence of the far right.

DISTORTED JUSTICE, UNEQUAL CRACKDOWNS

There are lessons to be learned regarding how the state has used grand juries to investigate activists on the left and how that treatment has differed from the state's posture toward violent white supremacists. In the case of the John Brown Anti-Klan Committee, the state knew that there was no evidence that members of the organization had committed the crimes it was investigating: bombings of government sites that resulted in no casualties. Historically, revolutionaries in movements on the left have received harsher sentences than racist militants on the far-right. Leftists are detained more often in isolating and inhumane conditions, and more are prosecuted as groups or movements, rather than as individual offenders. Two cases from the 1980s—the Greensboro massacre and Fort Smith trial—provide clear lessons for today's activists. Between 1980 and 1984, the two criminal trials held against Nazis and Klansmen who murdered five anti-Klan protestors at a rally in Greensboro, North Carolina each turned out acquittals by all-white juries. Through the trials, and the pending civil suit, it was revealed that the F.B.I. and the Bureau of Alcohol, Tobacco, and Firearms (ATF) were fully aware of the Klan and Nazi plan to attack the rally. The police also had an informant working inside the Klan who participated in inciting heated confrontations between the Klan and their opponents in China Grove months earlier.

Prior to what came to be known as the Greensboro massacre, police had provided intelligence to the Klan regarding the anti-racists' parade route, ensuring that the Klan knew where their enemies would be and when. Setting the scene for targeted one-sided violence, Bernard Butkovich, and agent with the federal Bureau of Alcohol, Tobacco, and Firearms, had previously infiltrated the Nazi group. With active knowledge and consent of his superior officers, Butkovich overtly encouraged the Klan to bring bombs and guns to the rally, while the press and general political milieu pressed leftist organizers to leave any weapons at home. Setting the scene for targeted one-sided violence, a federal officer with the Bureau of Alcohol, Tobacco, and Firearms, with active knowledge and consent of his superior officers, overtly encouraged the Klan to bring bombs and guns to the rally, while pressing leftist organizers to leave any weapons at home. While the Klan got away with murder in the criminal trials, on June 7, 1985, families of the victims and the Greensboro Justice Fund won a last-resort civil suit brought against eight Nazis and Klansmen involved in the massacre.

Between 1987 and 1988, a trial in Fort Smith, Arkansas provided another prominent example of acquittals for the right-wing militants and marked a shift in the terms of prosecution right-wing militants would face, if found guilty, for decades to come. Fourteen white supremacists, including key figures known for bridging racist movement sectors—Louis R. Beam, a Klan leader in Texas; Robert E. Miles, a Klan and Christian religious leader in Michigan; and Richard G. Butler, founder of Aryan Nations from Idaho—were indicted and stood trial for conspiracy to overthrow the United States government.[208] Prosecutors attempted to prosecute "white power as a coherent social movement."[209] The defendants were charged with sedition, interstate transport of stolen money, conspiracy to manufacture illegal weapons, as well as conspiracy to kill a federal judge and an F.B.I. agent. Despite the prosecution's overwhelming evidence that included recorded conversations about near successful plans to poison the drinking water in New York City, Chicago, and Washington, the all-white jury (a similar feature as to the two criminal trials at Greensboro) took only three days to reach their acquittal. This meant that the white supremacists not only walked away scot-free, but that their illegal firearms were returned to them. Had they been found guilty, the "maximum penalties would have included 20 years and a $20,000 fine for seditious conspiracy and life for conspiracy to murder."[210]

According to researcher Kathleen Belew, following the acquittals "the F.B.I. decided that white power violence would be prosecuted only at the scale of individual actions, rather than attempting to portray them as part of a social movement."[211] This would be a defining feature of future "lone wolf" cases like Timothy McVeigh in the Oklahoma City bombing that killed 167 people, and Dylann Roof's mass murder in Charleston, South Carolina, that killed 9 Black people during church services. Instead of arguing for fair treatment, members of the John Brown Anti-Klan Committee and other New Left militants believed that, while the structure and the messaging of the Klan, the police, and the F.B.I., were at times different, the reason for such uneven handling of left and right forces was simple: the far right's agenda, more or less, was in alignment with that of the state. In other words, the underlying imperatives between the extra-judicial far-right and the right that holds state power were integrated. As elements of that integration clearly persist today, so too does the need to eradicate it through the abolition of white supremacy. For this reason and many others, there remains an urgent need for today's social justice networks to learn from the past and carry on the work of anti-racist formations like the John Brown Anti-Klan Committee.

LIMITATIONS AND SHORTCOMINGS

Like any other organization, the John Brown Anti-Klan Committee had its shortcomings, and learning from these can be just as useful as studying its strengths. In our interviews, many former members offered critical reflections. At times, we agreed with their hindsight. The shortcomings that we believe offer lessons for today's movements concern self-righteousness, organizational limitations around class, and missed opportunities regarding confronting anti-Semitism.

Self-righteousness

Self-righteousness was a glaring weakness of the John Brown Anti-Klan Committee. In its early years, the Committee often turned differences between progressive groups into points of antagonism and competition. "We tended to out-left each other," said Laura Whitehorn. For example, as the Committee waged anti-gentrification campaigns in Brooklyn in 1978, it also picked fights with other organizations that were fighting the same forces but did not advocate the same political line. Fissures like these were rampant. Opportunities to cultivate diverse coalitions, however strategic, were dismissed by members. It took years before members consciously chose a more collaborative orientation. To this day, sectarianism and self-righteousness have remained defining features of the organization's reputation.

For much of its life, the Committee did not mix well with other movement sectors on the radical left. This was most often due to the Committee investing in a maximalist vision where achieving Black liberation was espoused as the one and only way to abolish white supremacy, and armed struggle the only revolutionary solution to imperialism. While such a vision had its merits, it also came at a cost. This cost, at times, meant dismissing political tendencies that approached transformational efforts from other angles, such as electoral work and campaigns for reform. Julie Nalibov reflected, "We wanted revolution. If you only want revolution, then you don't want reform, because it prolongs a system that has to go." Even though many liberals were anti-racist and also wanted to live in a world without white supremacy and fascism, "at the time, it was as if 'liberal' was the most insulting thing you could call somebody," said Nalibov. "The idea of no compromise was a flaw in our whole perspective." Thus, the John Brown Anti-Klan Committee's very militancy hobbled the group's potential power with self-imposed social and political rigidity.

More precisely, the Committee did not mix well with other primarily white organizations doing anti-racist work. It was, in part, contending with other such groups that were also supporting aspects of the Black freedom movement, a movement that at times was at odds with the Republic of New Afrika and elements of the Puerto Rican Independence movement. Nalibov reflected, "We were in your face. We made sure nobody thought we were racist. We needed to prove to the Black Liberation movement that we were righteous white people." In some ways, they did need to prove themselves. They needed to be different from the numerous other political groups that fractured when pressured by the types of government surveillance, infiltration, and harassment common at the time.

Today, it is clear that no one group of activists can push back against the far right on its own. An organization's ability to amplify its impact through broad-based coalitions tactically advantages it over those unable or unwilling to do so for reasons of sectarianism and political righteousness, as was often the case with the John Brown Anti-Klan Committee.

Low-income and working-class issues

The John Brown Anti-Klan Committee's dedication to abolishing white supremacy and supporting armed resistance to imperialism severely limited its ability to address other political concerns, particularly those rooted in economic injustice and class divisions within the communities where it was organizing. Although the Committee was deeply influenced by apartheid resistance movements in South Africa, the organization often focused its attention on abolishing white supremacy solely, rather than attempting to do so while also confronting white working-class willingness to serve the interests of the wealthy. The Committee was dedicated to reaching out to working-class sectors as potentially valuable anti-racist groups, but not ready to organize those populations to revolt against the economic injustices imposed by the wealthy. Bob Boyle explained that they were simply not prepared to incorporate working-class issues into their programs and campaigns.

According to Boyle, in the late 1970s there were numerous breaks within the radical left, particularly at the Hard Times Conference, where it seemed people were forced to make an impossible choice: fight racism or organize the working class. To radicals at that moment, the tendency to foreground class and worker organizing often led to ignoring politics of race, gender, and sexuality. These were telltale signs of the old-guard communist franchise, and the John Brown Anti-Klan Committee was not biting. "Communist movements were really terrible about feminism, race, homophobia. We weren't right, but we were moving toward intersectionality," said China Brotsky, a Bay Area member. The Committee's line fell more along the position raised in the early 1980s in *Settler: The Mythology of the White Proletariat*, in which J. Sakai argued that the white sector of the U.S. working class was unlikely to become revolutionary due to the profound ways that the settler-colonial process had indoctrinated society. Sakai pointed to the root causes of racial chauvinism, which prevented white radicals from doing the hard, necessary work in working-class communities. The John Brown Anti-Klan Committee's organizing focused on confronting the mechanisms of white supremacy from the inside out. It was a shortcoming that they did not also expose and incite rebellion against the ways that white supremacy is inextricably interconnected with mechanisms of economic injustice perpetrated by the wealthy few.

Anti-Semitism and anti-Zionism

From its beginning, the John Brown group was always an anti-Zionist organization. The organization regularly criticized Israeli policies through its newspaper and called for the support of Palestinian people's right to resist occupation and self-govern. Given the dispossession of Palestinian land and the massive displacement after 1948, the Committee equated the establishment of Israel with other colonial projects. In 1980, it wrote, "Zionism is an ideology and a strategy designed to create, establish, and defend a white settler colony in the Middle East against the national liberation struggle of the Palestinian people."[212]

This position earned them the enmity of the far-right

Jewish Defense League (JDL), which equated *any* critique of Israel with anti-Semitism. Tensions between the Committee and the JDL came to a head in 1983, in the Los Angeles suburb of Sunland, when the Committee organized a picket at the local fire department to protest its negotiations with the Klan over fire permits for a cross burning. At the picket, JDL members assaulted the Committee members. In the Winter 1984 issue of *Death to the Klan!*, the Committee wrote:

> The Aryan Nations and the Klan are both virulently antisemitic. JBAKC opposes antisemitism and all forms of anti-Jewish bigotry. But the JDL is not fighting antisemitism. They are trying to convince people that Jewish and Zionist are the same thing, and using the issue of antisemitism to build their own reactionary movement. JBAKC opposes the JDL because we support Black liberation here, and because we support the struggle of the Palestinian people to win their liberation. Zionism is racism, a pro-imperialist ideology that attacks all national liberation struggles. An anti-Klan movement must also be an anti-Zionist movement.

Indeed, the Jewish Defense League had little credibility as a voice against white supremacy. After its founding in 1968, early JDL pamphlets warned against the imagined violence of Black and Puerto Rican people against Jewish people. Jewish Defense League members were arrested for bombing mosques and for harassing Jewish people who were not "Jewish enough." The group's violent campaigns against Arab and Muslim targets suggested an ideological overlap with groups such as White Aryan Resistance. The Jewish Defense League claimed responsibility for the bombing of an Iranian bank in San Francisco, a Lebanese restaurant in Brooklyn, and the Iraqi mission to the United Nations.[213]

Many members of the John Brown group were themselves Jewish. More than one had relatives who had survived the Holocaust and described their family's experience as contributing to their anti-fascist politics. Despite this, they did not lead with this position in their anti-racist work. The Committee cared very little about criticism of the organization's politics when it came from those on the right, especially accusations from the Jewish Defense League that the John Brown organization was an anti-Semitic organization. It wasn't. "Of course, we got the whole 'self-hating Jews' thing," Lisa Roth recalled.

What bears closer examination, and serves as a lesson for today, is not the conflict with the Jewish Defense League, but critiques of how the John Brown group approached the question of anti-Semitism originating from Jewish allies who were themselves supporters of Palestinian self-determination. When criticism came from trusted organizers in the movement, the John Brown group listened. In the late 1980s, the Committee exchanged a series of letters with Matthew N. Lyons, a longtime activist who is known today for his writing on right-wing politics and history. Lyons pushed the Committee to engage anti-Semitism with more nuance. He reflected, "They didn't have the worst framework, but it left a lot to be desired."

For example, the group relied on a simplified portrayal of the complex relationship between Jewish and Black organizations in the Civil Rights movement. Its position criticized Jewish donors for severing financial support for radical Black organizations that pursued self-determination and rejected imperialism. Many white-led organizations that had supported the Civil Rights movement withdrew support for the Black Power movement after major organizations such as the Student Nonviolent Coordinating Committee (SNCC) moved away from reform and became more militant. The Committee wrote: "As long as the struggle was for civil rights and integration, the white liberal community, including many Jewish organizations, was willing to back it financially and politically to some degree. But as soon as Black people demanded to control their own struggle, let alone their own lives and destiny, liberal support vanished. More and more, Zionism replaced liberalism as the dominant position of Jewish people in the United States."[214] The assertion reflects the unsettled debates and divisions of the Civil Rights era. The Committee was absolutely correct in its description of how non-Black supporters of the Civil Rights movement often distanced themselves from the sections of the Black Freedom movement that embraced self-determination. However, when Committee statements made overgeneralizations about Jewish people, it often raised questions as to whether the Committee had sufficiently grappled with the legacy of anti-Semitism and was itself perhaps engaging in forms of racism.

Missing from the Committee's critiques of the far right were how racist groups spread anti-Semitism through conspiracy theories and Jewish scapegoating. In his 2017 article "Skin in the Game: How Antisemitism Animates White Nationalism," Eric Ward, a civil rights strategist, underlines this point:

> White supremacism through the collapse of Jim Crow was a conservative movement centered on a state-sanctioned anti-Blackness that sought to maintain a racist status quo. The White nationalist movement that evolved from it in the 1970s was a revolutionary movement that saw itself as the vanguard of a new, whites-only state. This latter movement, then and now, positions Jews as the absolute other, the driving force of white dispossession—which means the other channels of its hatred cannot be intercepted without directly taking on antisemitism.[215]

By not fully confronting the white supremacists' new and virulent anti-Semitic focus described by Ward, the Committee's contribution to anti-Zionist and anti-racist political work was stunted. Without confronting anti-Semitism directly, the

Committee could not contend with the Christian right's use of anti-Jewish ideology during the Reagan years, nor the tendencies of some left activists to overgeneralize and equate all Jewish people with Zionism. The Committee limited its contribution to this discussion by omitting the role of anti-Semitism in animating white nationalist movements of the time, as well as the ways anti-Semitism persisted in various forms within left movements.

Over time, the organization began to confront anti-Semitism with more focus and depth. This entailed creating an internal study group on anti-Semitism as well as inviting Lyons and others to write articles on Israel, the Gulf War, and anti-Arab racism in the autumn 1991 edition of its newspaper, then called *No KKK! No Fascist USA!* In many ways, this shift within the Committee was reflective of other political developments happening at the time. For instance, the New Jewish Agenda was founded in 1980. As a multi-issue, chapter-based organization, New Jewish Agenda had a major influence on feminist discussions about anti-Semitism and Zionism, and helped to establish the precedent that criticism of the Israeli government is not an anti-Jewish position.

Today, with anti-Semitic forces again on the march, it is critical for social justice movements to grapple with the details of its resurgence. Some perpetuate old tropes in contemporary packages, such as the assumption that all Jewish people are fair-skinned, wealthy, and supportive of Israel's military occupation and settlements in Palestine. It must be recognized that anti-Semitism is a crucial building block in the far right's explanation of the world to its adherents. During times of social anxiety and insecurity, xenophobia and anti-Semitism often spike. During the Great Depression, for example, the demagogue Father Coughlin and other right-wing leaders propagandized against Jewish people.[216]

That tumultuous decade, however, also showcased the potential of multi-racial unity. A diverse coalition of World War I veterans occupied the Capitol to demand promised wartime bonuses. Anti-lynching legislation was heard in Congress, and unemployed workers' movements demanded full employment and an end to evictions. Radicals built defense committees for the Scottsboro Boys—Black men falsely accused of rape.

The critiques that anti-Zionist Jewish allies offered the John Brown Anti-Klan Committee decades ago are still instructive today, particularly for those doing solidarity work for Palestinian self-determination. Being open to constructive criticism from allies and willing to actually apply it—as was the John Brown Anti-Klan Committee—is an essential prerequisite for realizing the emancipatory social relations for which one is struggling. And by exposing and challenging the anti-Semitism of white nationalist groups, today's social justice organizations can do much to weaken the far right.

TODAY'S MOVEMENTS

Perpetrators of racist violence today operate in a very different context compared to those of previous generations. Today the far right does not need to rely on a network of fringe newspapers and late-night cable access television shows to propagate its messages. The strategic use of the internet enables white nationalists to radicalize disaffected people gradually, pulling them into silos of resentment and intolerance. This is reinforced by a network of online platforms such as *Breitbart* that invest in ways to commercialize hate-fueled politics while simultaneously portraying their opponents as the ones with the intolerance problem.

While Reagan's bigotry was clear, his public statements rarely approached the enthusiasm for belittlement and ridicule embraced by Trump, the alt right, and today's Republican Party, which assert false equivalence between "both sides" and constantly redirect criticism by pointing to violence within communities of color. Combined, these forces have served to further normalize bigotry and violence. Today, many attacks are as likely to be carried out by individuals incited by online discourse as they are by organized groups.

The ongoing crisis of racialized violence lends credence to the Committee's conviction that simply ignoring the far right will not make it go away. Inaction—and insufficient action—will continue to produce more Christopher Hassons and events like El Paso. Counter-mobilization is a matter of self-defense and community security, and should be strengthened. However, changes in the alt-right's strategies point to the idea that communities must respond to actions of the far right in ways that constantly experiment and evolve with the times. One simple approach that has proven quite effective is the return of mass counter-mobilizations. Just two weeks following Charlottesville, far-right forces attempted to organize a "Free-Speech" rally in Boston. Organizers of the rally were described as "in step with the alt-right in their hatred of feminists and immigrants, among others."[217] However, anti-fascists managed to mobilize thousands of people; aerial photos of the march showed the counter-protesters easily outnumbering a paltry number of far-right demonstrators. Thanks, in part, to that strength in numbers, there were few injuries or arrests. In the months that followed, this model was used to counter fascist mobilizations in the San Francisco Bay Area and other cities. In contrast, similar efforts that failed to attract the same kinds of numbers often devolved into violence. Mass mobilization of this sort also allows anti-racists to avoid being trapped into the right's fairly successful efforts to depict them as anti-American threats to sacred First Amendment freedoms of speech and assembly.

Today's anti-racist and anti-fascist movements have many strengths. Among them is a willingness to describe white supremacy in open terms. It is far more common now than it was in the 1980s to identify the mechanisms of white supremacy in all their historical and present-day forms. Contemporary social justice groups and liberation movements can and should draw on decades of organizing by those who came before. As a result, it's much easier now to connect seemingly separate issues into a coherent intersectional analysis of systemic oppression. The bravery necessary to directly confront organized racism and structural injustice is another strength evident in movements today. The challenge is to move toward ever more diversity, depth, and nuance, while winning hearts, minds, and communities with the common dream that a better world *is* possible.

Finally, today's movements must contend with a national political environment that is increasingly polarized and defined by far-right policy. There is much to resist: Muslim travel bans; mass raids, detentions, and deportations of undocumented peoples; militarization of police, increased surveillance and criminalization of social movements, tax cuts for the rich, privatization of public services, attacks on unions, pro-corporate anti-climate policies, attacks on LGBTQI rights, defunding access to reproductive health, and the normalization of an authoritarian political culture that itself increasingly resembles a nascent form of fascism.

There is a continuous need to build broad, diverse, and effective forms of mass opposition that creatively allows for many ways to engage. Far-right street action and reactionary public policy reinforce each other. Curbing the right in the manner that the John Brown Anti-Klan Committee envisioned continues to be necessary and urgent. But if we are to succeed in abolishing white supremacy, we must also heed the lessons learned from the shortcomings of those who came before us. It is essential, for example, to include coalition building and electoral organizing in our strategies. We must become comfortable with being uncomfortable confronting violence and intolerance, but we must also practice embodying the non-oppressive social relations we envision as an essential quality of a more liberated world. A world outside the two-party system. A world that acknowledges the legacies of enslavement, genocide, and land theft. A world that seeks to repair, reconstruct, and heal. A world of dignity and community. A world with ever more humanity and flickers of light.

ACKNOWLEDGMENTS

We give heartfelt thanks to everyone at City Lights Publishing and Open Media. Greg Ruggiero combined an understanding of the politics of the book with an ability to spot the stories hidden within stories. It has been a joy to work with, and at times be challenged by his astute insight. In a time when the independent book industry is facing daily assaults on its well-being, we are especially grateful to Elaine Katzenberger for taking a risk on publishing this book. Elizabeth Bell expertly coaxed out the nuances of words. Her fine attention to detail vastly improved our final draft. Since nothing is more painful to an author than a book that never finds its way onto bookshelves, we are grateful to have the skilled and dedicated Stacey Lewis and Chris Carosi on our promotion team. Thanks to Linda Ronan for making our book look beautiful.

A special thank you to Robin D.G. Kelley, whose work, with steadfast grace and uncompromising precision, continues to tune the political compass of movements for liberation. Thank you for your enthusiasm and investment in this project.

This book would not have been possible without archivists and librarians, who, like independent publishers, are a ray of decency in the tattered world. Claude Marks and Nathaniel Moore, the catalysts behind the Freedom Archives, have gone above and beyond for us in every way possible. Randy "Arm the Spirit" Smith's generosity in time and resources has been indispensable. Bradley Duncan's voluminous collection of New Left materials in Philadelphia is a resource for all looking to uncover the past in order to plot a better future. Thanks to G.A. Matiasz for digging into the Maximum Rock and Roll archives for us. We also extend sincere thanks to the Tamiment Library of New York University and Penelope Houston of the San Francisco Public Library. Thanks to Matt Dineen, Mick Ward, Z! Haukeness, and Tiffany Criswell (Austin) for saving us trips to Philadelphia, Madison, and Austin by going through archives with expert eyes. We are very eager to read forthcoming books from two scholar-activists—Susan Reverby and Edward Onaci. While we have been writing this book, they have been studying different parts of the activist family tree near the John Brown Anti-Klan Committee. We have benefited from their generosity with source material and political insight.

Dan Berger, Matthew N. Lyons, Chris Dixon, and Walter Hergt read early drafts of our chapters and gave valuable feedback and criticism. We know that sharing one's memories is sometimes a fraught process, often uncovering regret and revisiting unfinished personal business. Agreeing to speak with us for this book is never as easy as recalling a few old war stories and sharing some political insight. Our most heartfelt thanks goes out to: Linda Evans, Terry Bisson, Lisa Roth, Julie Nalibov, Judy Siff, Judy Gerber, Trella Laughlin, Akinyele Umoja, Claude Marks, Pam Fadem, Laura Whitehorn, Donna Wilmott, Rob McBride, Bob Wells, Nancy Kurshan, Richard Roth, Bob Boyle, Susan Richardson, Jon Langford, Dan Sabater, Amilcar Shabazz, Christian Picciolini, Mickey Ellinger, Vicki Legion, Howie Emmer, Michael Novick, Shelley Miller, China Brotsky, Les Gottsman, and William Crossman as well as Carla Wallace, Mab Segrest, Cate Fosl, Elizabeth Ross, Claire Goldstene, Cleve Jones, Linda Gordon, and Dan Sabater.

Hilary Moore thanks Chris Dixon for years of encouragement and for modeling the ways we write with movements. Carla Wallace for always finding the lessons in life and for movement. Claude Marks for sharing your steadfast commitment to liberation and always having a seat for me. Also, big thanks to adrienne maree brown, David Trealeaven, ASK+, and the Apabiz archive in Berlin, Germany.

James Tracy thanks Juliette Torrez for her encouragement, brainstorming, and constantly calling my attention to relevant articles and debates. Alicia Garza for the silent writing at Hasta Muerte Cafe in Oakland, and Rachel Herzing for the sharp analysis, always graciously offered.

ENDNOTES

Unattributed quotes are from original interviews with the authors.

FOREWORD

1. Adam Serwer, "The President's Pursuit of White Power," *The Atlantic*, January 13, 2019, www.theatlantic.com/politics/archive/2019/01/ trump-embraces-white-supremacy/579745/; David Neiwert, *Alt-America: The Rise of the Radical Right in the Age of Trump* (London: Verso Books, 2017); Vegas Tenold, *Everything You Love Will Burn: Inside the Rebirth of White Nationalism in America* (New York: Nation Books, 2018); Jon Wiener and Start Making Sense, "The Trump Family's History with the KKK: Linda Gordon on Fred Trump, plus Nancy MacLean on the roots of the right," *Nation*, January 4, 2018, www.thenation.com/article/the-trump-familys-history-with-the-kkk/; Maureen Dowd, "Trump, Neo-Nazis and the Klan," *New York Times*, August 19, 2017, www.nytimes.com/2017/08/19/ opinion/sunday/trump-neo-nazis-and-the-klan.html; Charles Bethea, "What a White Supremacist Told Me After Trump was Elected," *New Yorker*, August 17, 2017, www.newyorker.com/news/news-desk/ what-a-white-supremacist-told-me-after-donald-trump-was-elected.

2. See Kat Chow, "Tracing the Dark Origins of Charlottesville's KKK," *Code Switch*, National Public Radio, August 19, 2017, www.npr. org/sections/codeswitch/2017/08/19/543968997/tracing-the-dark-origins-of-charlottesvilles-kkk. Even the Charlottesville Syllabus, an incredibly astute and comprehensive project, focuses on the Klan in the 1920s and says nothing of the third Klan, beyond a sentence to the effect that it did not entirely disappear. See Catherine Halley, "Charlottesville Syllabus: Readings on the History of Hate in America," *JSTOR Daily*, August 19, 2017, daily.jstor.org/charlottesville-syllabi-history-hate-america/; Tara McAndrew, "The History of the KKK in American Politics," *JSTOR Daily*, January 25, 2017, daily.jstor.org/history-kkk-american-politics/; Kelly J. Baker compared the rise of the second Klan to the popularity of Trump in her essay "Make America White Again?," *Atlantic Monthly*, March 12, 2016, www.theatlantic.com/politics/archive/2016/03/ donald-trump-kkk/473190/.

3. See for example, Linda Gordon, *The Second Coming of the KKK: The Ku Klux Klan of the 1920s and the American Political Tradition* (New York: Liveright Publishers, 2017); Felix Harcourt, *Ku Klux Kulture: America and the Klan in the 1920s* (Chicago: University of Chicago Press, 2017); Kelly J. Baker, *Gospel According to the Klan: The KKK's Appeal to Protestant America, 1915–1930*, (Lawrence: University of Kansas Press, 2011); and the classic work by Nancy MacLean, *Behind the Mask of Chivalry: The Making of the Second Ku Klux Klan* (Oxford, UK: Oxford University Press, 1995).

4. This was not the only lynching in the 1980s, but it received notoriety not only because the perpetrators were convicted (one was executed—the only Klansman in the 20th century to be executed for killing a Black person), but because Michael Donald's mother, Beulah Mae Donald, successfully sued the United Klans of America for wrongful death and was awarded $7 million. The award drove the organization into bankruptcy. Morris Dees, founder of the Southern Poverty Law Center, represented Ms. Donald. "Donald v. United Klans of America - Case Number 84-0725;" Laurence Leamer, *The Lynching: the Epic Courtroom Battle that Brought Down the Klan* (New York: William Morrow, 2016).

5. Of course, there are exceptions. Perhaps the most noteworthy, besides this book, is Kathleen Belew's *Bring the War Home: The White Power Movement and Paramilitary America*, (Cambridge, MA: Harvard University Press, 2018); Branko Marcetic, "Fighting the Klan in Reagan's America," *Jacobin*, August 25, 2017, jacobinmag.com/2017/08/ greensboro-massacre-ku-klux-klan-far-right. There has been much more written about the Greensboro massacre, since it was the bloodiest and most consequential attack by the Klan on protesters. See Signe Waller, *Love and Revolution: A Political Memoir, A People's History of the Greensboro Massacre, Its Setting and Its Aftermath* (New York: Rowman and Littlefield Publishers, 2002); Sally Avery Bermanzohn, *Through Survivors' Eyes: From the Sixties to the Greensboro Massacre* (Nashville, TN: Vanderbilt University Press, 2011); and the first scholarly treatment of the incident and subsequent trials, Elizabeth Wheaton, *Codename Greenkil: The 1979 Greensboro Killings* (Athens: University of Georgia Press, 1987).

During the 1980s, Black scholars certainly paid attention to the resurgence of the Klan and anti-Black violence during the late 1970s and 1980s. Two influential texts exposing this trend back then were Manning Marable, *How Capitalism Underdeveloped Black America* (Chicago: Haymarket Books, 2015 reprint ed., orig. 1983); and Gerald Gill, *Meanness Mania: The Changed Mood* (Washington, D.C.: Howard University Press, 1980).

6. Micki McElya, *Clinging to Mammy: The Faithful Slave in the Twentieth Century* (Cambridge. MA: Harvard University Press, 2007).

AUTHORS' STATEMENTS
7. Sam Levin, "Revealed: FBI Investigated Civil Rights Group as 'Terrorism' Threat and Viewed KKK as Victims," *The Guardian*, February 1, 2019, www.theguardian.com/us-news/2019/feb/01/ sacramento-rally-FBI-kkk-domestic-terrorism-california.

PREFACE: PAST AS PROLOGUE
8. P.R. Lockhart, "Supporters of Confederate Monuments had a very bad week," *Vox*, January 19, 2019, www.vox.com/

identities/2019/1/18/18185501/confederate-monuments-birmingham-alabama-north-carolina.

9. Not all city officials sided with the white supremacists. Charlottesville city councilor Kristin Szakos received multiple death threats for simply raising the question of the removal of statues. The city's vice mayor, Wes Bellamy, championed removal efforts. Jacey Fortin, "The Statue at the Center of Charlottesville's Storm," *New York Times*, August 13, 2017, www.nytimes.com/2017/08/13/us/charlottesville-rally-protest-statue.html.

10. The John Brown Anti-Klan Committee, *The Dividing Line of the 80's: Take a Stand Against the Klan, a pamphlet on the fight against white supremacy* (New York: The John Brown Anti-Klan Committee, 1980), freedomarchives.org/Documents/Finder/DOC37_scans/37.StandvsKlan. pdf. Formed in 1933, Immigration and Naturalization Service (INS), was a part of the Department of Justice. In 2003, under Bush Jr.'s presidential administration, the Homeland Security Act reorganized this branch of government, transferring the investigative, deportation, and intelligence functions of the department to three agencies, the most well-known of which is Immigration and Customs Enforcement (ICE). In this transition, ICE was granted heightened civil and criminal authority.

11. Ibid.

12. Loch K. Johnson, *A Season of Inquiry Revisited: The Church Committee Confronts America's Spy Agencies* (Lawrence: University Press of Kansas, 2015).

13. Susan Rosenberg, *Bridges* 5, No. 1 (1995), pp. 104–08, www.jstor. org/stable/40358907.

14. *The Dividing Line of the 80's*, pp. 16–18.

15. John Brown Anti-Klan Committee, "Who We Are," *No KKK! No Fascist USA! Newspaper of the John Brown Anti-Klan Committee*, Spring/Summer 1989, www.freedomarchives.org/Documents/Finder/DOC37_scans/37.nokkk.spr89.pdf.

16. The original concept of the New Boundaries plan maintained, in part, the colonial legacy of the United States, relegating Native Americans to a nation in the northern tip of Canada, arguably the coldest region on the continent, issuu.com/mickeyellinger/docs/nb.newbound5.81.

17. The National Association for the Advancement of Colored People, "A History of Lynchings," NAACP.org, www.naacp.org/history-of-lynchings/. Between 1882 and 1968 there were 4,743 recorded lynchings; 72.7 percent of those murdered were Black people; 27.3 percent were white people believed to be helping Black people or taking anti-lynching positions. Additionally, the New Orleans massacre and the Memphis massacre, both in 1866, were two notable events in which Black neighborhoods and groups of Black delegates were attacked by mobs of white men.

18. History.com editors, "Black Leaders During Reconstruction," *HISTORY*, A&E Television Networks, June 24, 2010, www.history.com/topics/american-civil-war/black-leaders-during-reconstruction.

19. Brian Stevenson and the staff of the Equal Justice Initiative, *Lynching in America: Confronting the Legacy of Racial Terror, Third Edition*, Equal Justice Initiative; lynchinginamerica.eji.org/report/.

20. "Ku Klux Klan: A History of Racism," Southern Poverty Law Center, February 28, 2011, www.splcenter.org/20110228/ku-klux-klan-history-racism#the%20terror%20is%20born.

21. Linda Gordon, "Populism, Fascism, and the Ku Klux Klan of the 1920s," Marcus Bierich Lecture, Berlin, April 4, 2019, www.americanacademy.de/videoaudio/populism-fascism-and-the-ku-klux-klan-of-the-1920s/.

22. Mike Wallace, "Madison Square Mayhem," *New York Times*, January 11, 2003, www.nytimes.com/2003/01/11/opinion/madison-square-mayhem.html.

23. Linda Gordon, *The Second Coming of the KKK: The Ku Klux Klan of the 1920s and the American Political Tradition* (New York: Liveright Publishing Corporation, 2017).

Linda Gordon notes, "The Johnson-Reed Act of 1924, named for Washington Klansman Albert Johnson in the House and Pennsylvania's David Reed in the Senate, ensconced into law the Klan's hierarchy of desirable and undesirable 'races' by assigning quotas for immigrants in proportion to the ethnicity of those already in the United States."

24. The "Third Wave" of the Klan became known for its emphasis on violence, led by the Imperial Wizard Bill Wilkinson.

25. Ben A. Franklin, "Klan Faction's 'Recruiting' Efforts Pose a Policy Problem for the Navy," *New York Times*, October 7, 1979, www.nytimes.com/1979/10/07/archives/klan-factions-recruiting-efforts-pose-a-policy-problem-for-the-navy.html; Dave Phillips, "White Supremacism in the U.S. Military, Explained," *New York Times*, February 27, 2019, www.nytimes.com/2019/02/27/us/military-white-nationalists-extremists.html.

26. John Brown Anti-Klan Committee, "Principles of Unity," *Death to the Klan! Newsletter of the John Brown Anti-Klan Committee* (Volume 1, No. 3, Jan./Feb. 1980).

27. Phil McCausland, "White Nationalist Leads Torch-Bearing Protestors Against Removal of Confederate Statue," *NBC News*, May 14, 2017, www.nbcnews.com/news/us-news/white-nationalist-leads-torch-bearing-protesters-against-removal-confederate-statue-n759266.

28. Joanna Walters, "Militia Leaders who descend on Charlottesville condemn 'right wing lunatics,'" *The Guardian*, August 15, 2017, www.theguardian.com/us-news/2017/aug/15/charlottesville-militia-free-speech-violence.

29. Joe Heim, "Recounting a day of rage, hate, violence and

death," *Washington Post*, August 14, 2017, www.washingtonpost.com/graphics/2017/local/charlottesville-timeline/?noredirect=on.

30. Amy Goodman, "Cornel West & Rev. Traci Blackmon: Clergy in Charlottesville Were Trapped by Torch-Wielding Nazis," *Democracy Now!*, August 14, 2017, www.democracynow.org/2017/8/14/cornel_west_rev_toni_blackmon_clergy.

31. A.C. Thompson and Robert Faturechi, "Police Stood By As Mayhem Mounted in Charlottesville," *ProPublica*, August 12, 2017, www.propublica.org/article/police-stood-by-as-mayhem-mounted-in-charlottesville.

32. Adam Johnson, "In Month After Charlottesville, Papers Spent as Much Time Condemning Anti-Nazis as Nazis," Fairness & Accuracy in Reporting, September 13, 2017, fair.org/home/in-month-after-charlottesville-papers-spent-as-much-time-condemning-anti-nazis-as-nazis/.

33. Marc Theissen, "Yes, Antifa Is the Moral Equivalent of Neo-Nazis," *Washington Post*, August 17, 2017, www.washingtonpost.com/opinions/yes-antifa-is-the-moral-equivalent-of-neo-nazis/2017/08/30/9a13b2f6-8d00-11e7-91d5-ab4e4bb76a3a_story.html?utm_term=.07967e772a31; James S. Robbins, "Trump Is Right—Violent Extremists on Both Sides Are a Threat," *USA Today*, August 30, 2017, www.usatoday.com/story/opinion/2017/08/17/condemn-all-extremists-all-political-stripes-dot-pick-and-choose-james-s-robbins-column/574235001/; Alan Dershowitz, "The Hard Right and Hard Left Pose Different Dangers," *Wall Street Journal*, September 10, 2017, www.wsj.com/articles/the-hard-right-and-hard-left-pose-different-dangers-1505073662.

34. Chip Berlet and Matthew Lyons, *Right Wing Populism in America: Too Close for Comfort* (New York: The Guilford Press, 2000).

35. Anti-Defamation League, "Imagine a World Without Hate," www.adl.org/sites/default/files/documents/assets/pdf/combating-hate/David-Duke.pdf.

36. *Regents of the University of California v. Bakke*, 438 U.S. 265 (1978).

37. Daniel Kreiss and Kelsey Mason, "Here's what white supremacy looks and sounds like now. (It's not your grandfather's KKK.)," *Washington Post*, August 17, 2017, www.washingtonpost.com/news/monkey-cage/wp/2017/08/17/heres-what-white-supremacy-looks-and-sounds-like-now-its-not-your-grandfathers-kkk/.

38. Ruth Wilson Gilmore, *Golden Gulag: Prisons, Surplus, Crisis, and Opposition in Globalizing California* (Berkeley: University of California Press, 2007).

39. Matthew Lyons, "What Is Fascism?," Political Research Associates, www.politicalresearch.org/2016/12/12/what-is-fascism-2/.

ONE LONG REIGN OF TERROR

40. Civil and federal lawsuits greatly contributed to the Klan's decline in membership in the 1970s. Making them "wary of organizing into chapters, naming officers and expanding across state lines." See Branko Marcetic, "Fighting the Klan in Reagan's America," *Jacobin Magazine*, August 25, 2017, jacobinmag.com/2017/08/greensboro-massacre-ku-klux-klan-far-right.

41. Pete Wagner, "Eddie Ellis 1941–2014," Prison Policy Initiative, July 25, 2014, www.prisonpolicy.org/blog/2014/07/25/eddie/. Eddie Ellis was instrumental in shaping the early moments of the movement of formerly incarcerated people in the United States. As Black Panther member, and former target of the COINTELPRO, Ellis became a lifelong supporter of education for people incarcerated. He also pushed the movement to adapt its language to reflect the power relations and humanity of those on the inside more clearly. Instead of saying inmate or prisoner, he urged the use of the term "incarcerated person." Many of the historical texts quoted in this book were part of this shifting moment, and therefore the reader will see a range of terms used. As authors, we use the contemporary phrase to align with the evolving politic.

42. Brian Kates, "We still haven't kicked the Klan," *New York Daily News*, February 1, 1979, www.newspapers.com/image/484986518/?terms=New%2BYork%2BDaily%2BNews%2C.

43. Everett T. Holles, "Marines in Klan Openly Abused Blacks, Panel Hears," *New York Times*, January 9, 1977, www.nytimes.com/1977/01/09/archives/marines-in-klan-openly-abused-blacks-at-pendleton-panel-hears.html.

44. Robert Lindsey, "Marines Transfer Leader of Klan to Ease Tension," *New York Times*, December 4, 1976, www.nytimes.com/1976/12/04/archives/marines-transfer-leader-of-klan-to-ease-tension-at-camp-pendleton.html; Bill Richards, "ACLU Role in Klan Suit Against Marines Provokes Dispute," *Washington Post*, January 29, 1977, www.washingtonpost.com/archive/politics/1977/01/29/aclu-role-in-klan-suit-against-marines-provokes-dispute/ae2d433e-cdc5-439e-b197-3a082346a2ac/.

45. Assata Shakur and Sundiata Acoli, two Black Liberation Army activists, were imprisoned following a 1973 shootout that left a BLA member, Zayd Shakur, and a New Jersey state trooper, Werner Foerster, dead. Forensic evidence indicated that Shakur did not fire a gun.

46. Barbara Ransby, *Ella Baker and the Black Freedom Movement: A Radical Democratic Vision* (Chapel Hill: University of North Carolina Press, 2004), pp. 340–342.

47. Chana Lee, "Anger, Memory and Personal Power: Fannie Lou Hamer and Civil Rights Leadership," in *Sisters in the Struggle African American Women in the Civil Rights–Black Power Movement*, ed. Bettye

Collier-Thomas and V.P. Franklin (New York: New York University Press, 2001), pp. 160–164.

48. Martin Luther King Jr., "Letter From a Birmingham Jail," in *The Autobiography of Martin Luther King Jr.*, ed. Claybourne Carson (New York: Warner Books reprint edition, 2011), pp. 187–204.

49. John Brown, "John Brown's Last Speech," Charlestown, West Virginia, November 2, 1859, Zinn Education Project, www.zinnedproject.org/materials/john-brown-last-speech.

50. Tony Horwitz, *Midnight Rising: John Brown and the Raid That Sparked the Civil War* (New York: Henry Holt and Company, 2011).

51. Malcolm X, "On Afro-American History," speech, January 24, 1965, www.marxists.org/history/etol/newspape/isr/vol28/no02/v28n02-w179-mar-apr-1967-int-soc-rev.pdf.

52. Michael T. Kaufman, "Upstate Prison Teacher Defends His Klan Role," *New York Times*, December 23, 1974, www.nytimes.com/1974/12/23/archives/upstate-prison-teacher-defends-his-klan-role.html. Schoonmaker's Klan affiliation had been public since at least 1974.

53. Juanita Diaz-Cotto, *Gender, Ethnicity and the State: Latina and Latino Prison Politics* (Albany: State University of New York Press, 1996), p. 231.

54. Jeffrey B. Perry. "The Developing Conjuncture and Some Insights From Hubert Harrison and Theodore W. Allen on the Centrality of the Fight Against White Supremacy," *Cultural Logic*, July 2010, www.jeffreybperry.net/blog/posts/28646.

55. Robin D.G. Kelley, "What Did Cedric Robinson Mean by Racial Capitalism?," *Boston Review*, January 12, 2019, bostonreview.net/race/robin-d-g-kelley-what-did-cedric-robinson-mean-racial-capitalism.

56. Peggy McIntosh, "White Privilege: Unpacking the Invisible Backpack," National Consortium of Interpreter Education Centers, www.interpretereducation.org/wp-content/uploads/2016/03/white-privilege-by-Peggy-McIntosh.compressed.pdf.

57. J. Sakai, *Settlers: The Mythology of the White Proletariat* (city unknown: Morning Star Press, 1983), p. 49.

58. Ibid, Diaz-Cotto, pp. 21–22.

59. We use the term Latino to reflect its use during this period in social movement history. However, today many people use the term Latinx. It is a recent language shift beginning in the 2000s that disrupts the binary of gender representation in the Spanish language. Those in favor say that this term is more open to include transgender and gender-nonconforming people from Latin America. As culture and language evolve, conversations about accessibility and representation push the conversation forward.

60. Clara Bingham, "An Oral History of the 1968 Columbia Uprising," *Vanity Fair*, March 26, 2018, www.vanityfair.com/news/2018/03/the-students-behind-the-1968-columbia-uprising.

61. John F. Kennedy, "Address on the First Anniversary of the Alliance for Progress," speech, March 13, 1962, www.jfklibrary.org/asset-viewer/ archives/JFKPOF/037/JFKPOF-037-026.

62. Discussion of the expulsion of whites from SNCC remains controversial and painful even today. To understand the strategic thought behind it, see Stokely Carmichael and Charles Hamilton, *Black Power: The Politics of Liberation in America* (New York: Vintage Books, 1967). For further reading, Faith S. Holsaert, Martha Prescod, Norman Noonan, Judy Richardson, Betty Garman Robinson, Jean Smith Young, Dorothy M. Zellner, *Hands on the Freedom Plow: Personal Accounts by Women in SNCC* (Chicago: University of Illinois Press, 2010); and Clayborne Carson, *In Struggle: SNCC and the Black Awakening of the 1960s* (Boston: Harvard University Press, 1995).

63. Michael Staudenmaier, *Truth and Revolution: A History of the Sojourner Truth Organization 1969–1986* (Oakland, CA: AK Press, 2012); Jennifer Frost, *An Interracial Movement of the Poor: Community Organizing and the New Left in the 1960s* (New York: NYU Press, 2005); Amy Sonnie and James Tracy, *Hillbilly Nationalists, Urban Race Rebels and Black Power: Community Organizing in Radical Times* (Brooklyn, NY: Melville House, 2011).

64. More than 40,000 copies of *Prairie Fire* were eventually distributed. Dan Berger, *Outlaws of America: The Weather Underground and the Politics of Solidarity* (Oakland, CA: AK Press, 2006).

65. Noam Chomsky, *The Vietnam War with Noam Chomsky*, Working Class History Podcast, October 29, 2018, workingclasshistory. com/2018/10/31/e14-the-vietnam-war-with-noam-chomsky/.

66. Malcolm X, quoted in speech delivered by Ahmad Obafemi to the John Brown Anti-Klan Committee Teach-in, San Francisco, May 21, 1983. Ahmad Obafemi, *The Legacy of Malcolm X and the Struggle to Defeat the Ku Klux Klan: a Speech by Ahmad Obafemi*, pamphlet of the John Brown Anti-Klan Committee, publication date unknown, freedomarchives.org/ Documents/Finder/DOC37_scans/37.LegacyMalcolmX.pdf.

67. Freedom Archives, *COINTELPRO 101*. Directed by Claude Marks. Oakland, CA: PM Press, 2010. Also, Jim Vander Wall and Ward Churchill, *The COINTELPRO Papers: Documents from the FBI's Secret Wars Against Dissent in the United States*, (Boston: South End Press, 1990).

68. FBI memo, March 4, 1968, p. 3.

69. Jeffrey Haas, *The Assassination of Fred Hampton: How the FBI and the Chicago Police Murdered a Black Panther* (Chicago: Lawrence Hill Books, 2010).

70. For more on the Attica and other aspects of the radical prisoner movements of the 1960s and 1970s see, Heather Ann Thompson, *Blood in the Water: The Attica Prison Uprising of 1971 and Its Legacy* (New York: Vintage Books, 1971); and Dan Berger, *Captive Nation: Black Prison*

Organizing in the Civil Rights Era (Chapel Hill: University of North Carolina Press, 2016).

71. Murray Kempton, *The Briar Patch: The Trial of the Panther 21* (New York: Da Capo Press, 2007). The Panther 21 case still shapes the tone and tenor of radical Black politics, and the response to government repression.

72. Harvey Klehr, *The Heyday of American Communism: The Depression Decade* (New York: Basic Books, 1985), and Robin D.G. Kelley, *Hammer and Hoe, Alabama Communists During the Great Depression* (Chapel Hill: University of North Carolina Press, 1990). In 1928, the Communist Party USA decided that Black people in the United States consisted of a separate distinct nation within the United States, and they had the right of self-determination within the South.

73. Joshua Bloom and Waldo E. Martin Jr., *Black Against Empire: The History and Politics of the Black Panther Party* (Oakland: University of California Press, 2016); Alondra Nelson, *Body and Soul: The Black Panther Party and the Fight Against Medical Discrimination* (Minneapolis: University of Minneapolis Press, 2013); Elaine Brown, *A Taste of Power: A Black Woman's Story* (New York: Pantheon Books, 1994); Huey Newton. *Revolutionary Suicide* (New York: Harcourt Brace Jovanovich,1973).

74. Assata Shakur, *Assata: An Autobiography* (London: Zed Books, 1987).

75. Bernardine Dohrn, Bill Ayers, and Jeff Jones, eds., *Sing a Battle Song: The Revolutionary Poetry, Statements, and Communiqués of the Weather Underground, 1970–1974* (New York: Seven Stories Press, 2006).

76. Bobby Seale, *A Lonely Rage* (New York: Times Books, 1978); Angela Davis, *The Autobiography of Angela Davis* (New York: International Publishers Co; later edition, 2013).

77. Ronald P. Formisano, *Boston Against Busing: Race, Class and Ethnicity in the 1960s and 1970s* (Chapel Hill: University of North Carolina Press, 2004); Queers United in Support of Political Prisoners, *Dykes and Fags Want to Know* (Toronto, 1995).

78. Edward B. Fiske, "After 8 Years of Open Admissions City College Still Debates Effect," *New York Times*, June 19, 1978, www.nytimes.com/1978/06/19/archives/new-jersey-pages-after-8-years-of-open-admissions-city-college.html.

79. Ibid.

80. Robert B. Moore, *Violence: The Ku Klux Klan and the Struggle for Equality* (Washington, D.C.: Council on Interracial Books for Children, 1983); Sandra Gardner, "Schools Seeking To Counter Ku Klux Klan," *New York Times*, September 13, 1981, www.nytimes.com/1981/09/13/nyregion/schools-seeking-to-counter-ku-klux-klan.html.

81. *Clark et al. vs. the United States of America*. Also, the Committee for the Suit Against Government Misconduct, *COINTELPRO-Domestic Subversive Warfare*, pamphlet.

82. Op. cit., *Outlaws of America*, Berger, pp. 100–101.

83. Not all radical Black organizations were down with the Days of Rage. Chairman Fred Hampton of the Illinois Panthers denounced the actions. "We do not support people who are anarchistic, opportunistic, adventuristic, and Custeristic." Sam Green, director, *The Weather Underground*, 2002, Doc Club.

84. Cathy Wilkerson, *Flying Close to the Sun: My Life and Times as a Weatherman* (New York: Seven Stories Press, 2007). The "action faction" refers to the part of the Students For a Democratic Society that preferred direct-action protest tactics.

85. Stanford University Martin Luther King Jr. Research and Education Institute, "White Citizens Councils," kinginstitute.stanford.edu/encyclopedia/white-citizens-councils-wcc.

86. Anti-Defamation League, "Extremism in America, Council of Conservative Citizens," Wayback Machine Internet Archive, web.archive.org/web/20110804231655/www.adl.org/learn/ext_us/CCCitizens.asp?xpicked.

87. Emily Hobson, *Lavender and Red, Liberation and Solidarity in the Gay and Lesbian Left.* (Oakland: University of California Press, 2016) p. 2; New York Women's School, *The Lavender Papers Vol. 2., An Analysis of Lesbian Oppression,* June, 1975, www.freedomarchives.org/Documents/Finder/DOC46_scans/46.LavenderPapers2.pdf.

Historian Emily Hobson points out that the lesbian and gay left of the era saw "sexual liberation and radical solidarity as constituted within each other rather than wholly separate." The John Brown Anti-Klan Committee's leadership was largely comprised of white lesbians. Their presence was a part of a growing lesbian and gay anti-imperialist tendency. In step with many other parts of the movement, they identified U.S. imperialism as the common enemy of all oppressed people. In 1975, the New York Women's School (in which some early John Brown members participated) published *Lavender Papers*, which attempted to situate lesbian liberation in relationship to empire, racism and class oppression. Political repression was one of the catalysts for solidarity. The FBI grand juries following Assata Shakur's escape targeted a large number of lesbians and their organizations.

The approach of anti-imperialist lesbian politics shaped the worldview of many John Brown members. As articulated by the papers, this began with a long view of lesbian oppression through the development of the church, the nuclear family, and the emergence of capitalism. It briefly acknowledged that feminists from developing countries faced the additional reality of racism, and criticized women who did not take racism seriously enough. Critically, they linked economic crisis, fueled by imperialist expansion as one of the cornerstones of gender oppression. Throughout the 1980s this analysis led the left edge of the lesbian movement towards solidarity work with international movements facing down U.S. intervention.

This allowed them to seek alliances with groups who were not wholly on board with queer liberation, such as parts of the Black Nationalist community. The anti-imperialist lens was not accepted by all parts of the women's liberation movement. Laughlin recalls being accused that lesbians in the Austin John Brown chapter were "being controlled by Black men."

88. William K. Stevens, "Klan Inflames Gulf Fishing Fight Between Whites and Vietnamese," *New York Times*, April 25, 1981, www.nytimes.com/1981/04/25/us/klan-inflames-gulf-fishing-fight-between-whites-and-vietnamese.html.

89. Starring Ed Harris and Amy Madigan, *Alamo Bay* (Louis Malle, director, Tri Star Pictures 1985) portrayed a fictionalized story based on the tensions in Galveston Bay. The film attempted to sympathize with multiple perspectives. Ed Harris plays a Vietnam veteran financially struggling after the war. Amy Madigan plays Ed Harris's girlfriend, who ends up resisting the racist attacks and riding in the boat with Ho Ngyuen, who plays Dinh, a Vietnamese refugee looking for a bright future. Although the film received mediocre reviews, the release of *Alamo Bay* stoked the controversy still present in Texas. So much so that the Klan held rallies at any theater showing the film, preventing people from seeing the film.

90. Austin History Center, "ACAC Historical Footage, 1976–1995," video compilation, www.youtube.com/watch?v=Ah_0W0MGf38.

91. Associated Press, "Scout Post Is Denied Charter," *New York Times*, November 27, 1980, www.nytimes.com/1980/11/27/archives/scout-post-is-denied-charter.html?searchResultPosition=1.

92. Associated Press, "Scouts Deny Charter: Probe of Klan asked," *Quad City Times*, November 27, 1980, p. 15A.

93. Barbara Casey, *Assata Shakur: A 20th Century Escaped Slave* (Rock Hill, SC: Strategic Media Books, 2017).

94. Signe Waller, *Love and Revolution: A People's History of the Greensboro Massacre and its Aftermath* (New York: Rowman & Littlefield Publishers, 2002).

95. Assata Shakur, *Statement from Assata Shakur, National Human Rights Day*, broadside, November 5, 1979, freedomarchives.org/Documents/Finder/DOC513_scans/Assata_Shakur/513.StatementfromAssata.Nov.5.1979.pdf.

96. The first publications from the Committee were a series of pamphlets called *Smash the Klan!* This preceded their long running newspaper *Death to the Klan!* In 1989, members changed the name to *No KKK! No Fascist USA!* The newspaper had many contributors and was edited by Terry Bisson and Lisa Roth.

ROOTS, RADICALS, AND REAGAN

97. "Transcript of Reagan's 1980 Neshoba County Fair Speech," *Neshoba Democrat*, November 15, 2007, neshobademocrat.com/Content/ NEWS/News/Article/Transcript-of-Ronald-Reagan-s-1980-Neshoba-County-Fair-speech/2/297/15599.

98. Jesse Jackson, "Reagan: A Legacy of States' Rights," *The Nation*, June 17, 2004, www.thenation.com/article/reagan-legacy-states-rights/. Notably, the 1873 Supreme Court ruling following the Slaughterhouse cases were foundational to "states' rights" arguments over one hundred years later. McBride, Alex, n.d. "Slaughterhouse Cases (1873)," *The Supreme Court*, Thirteen, www.thirteen.org/wnet/supremecourt/ antebellum/landmark_slaughterhouse.html.

99. Suzanne Pharr, *In the Time of the Right: Reflections on Liberation* (Oakland: Chardon Press, 1996), p. 10.

100. Sue Anne Pressley, "Klan Gains Higher Visibility in Md.," *Washington Post*, November 10, 1985, www.washingtonpost.com/archive/ local/1985/11/10/klan-gains-higher-visibility-in-md/8a881d4e-19ab-414f-b4a5-ee4a4bd1a9fc/.

101. The Klan last openly marched in Washington, D.C., in 1925, with 35,000 Klansmen in robes taking to Pennsylvania Avenue for "Americanism," stoking fears in a moment of high immigration. Reagan was silent about the Klan's endorsement of his 1980 and 1984 campaigns, and was not the first president (think Coolidge) to leverage silence for votes.

102. Since the end of the Reconstruction Era (1862–1877), at which point Black politicians were extracted from office and replaced with all-white, conservative governments, a political campaign known in racist history as "redemption," the question of Klansmen holding political office has long been a target of abolition movements. Whether politicians are active Klan members, like Louisiana State Representative David Duke, or passive members, like President Harry S Truman, abolitionist politics have understood that the structures of U.S. government and legislative proclamations complement, if not actively align with, a Klan agenda.

103. Manning Marable, *How Capitalism Underdeveloped Black America: Problems in Race, Political Economy, and Society* (Cambridge, MA: South End Press, 2000), pp. 218–219.

104. Author unknown, "Klan Members Recruit Saturday in Damascus," *The Sentinel*, September 23, 1982, www.newspapers.com/searc h/#query=Klan+Members+Recruit+Saturday+in+Damascus.

105. Kathleen Belew, *Bring the War Home: The White Power Movement and Paramilitary America*, (Cambridge, MA: Harvard University Press, 2018).

106. Lori Santos, "An Anti-Ku Klux Klan Group Thursday Announced Plans," *United Press International*, February 10, 1983, www.

upi.com/Archives/1983/02/10/An-anti-Ku-Klux-Klan-group-Thursday-announced-plans-to/7542413701200/.

107. Associated Press, "'White Pride' Celebrated," *Pensacola News*, November 4, 1983.

108. *National Socialist White People's Party et al., Appellants, v. Joseph Ringers, Jr., and Witcher N. Beverly, Appellees*, 473 F.2d 1010 (4th Cir. 1973).

109. Phil Gailey, "Violence Erupts Over Small Klan Rally in Capital," *New York Times*, November 28, 1982, www.nytimes.com/1982/11/28/us/violence-erupts-over-small-klan-rally-in-capital.html. The day after the demonstration, the *New York Times* reported, "The Klan's brief appearance in the nation's capital had an impact far out of proportion to the numbers at the rally. Much of downtown Washington between Capitol Hill and the White House was closed to traffic; miles of snow fence was put up to contain spectators and anti-Klan protestors; hundreds of local and Federal police officers lined the streets to maintain order; tear gas smoke wafted through downtown streets where tourists were caught up in the retreat of anti-Klan activists."

110. Herman J. Obermeyer, *American Nazi Party in Arlington, Virginia 1958–1984*, (Createspace Independent Publishing, 2012), p. 32.

111. James Hershberg and William E. McKibben, "Klan Burns Cross In Connecticut," *The Crimson*, September 15, 1980, www.thecrimson.com/article/1980/9/15/klan-burns-cross-in-connecticut-pscotland/.

112. Daniel Leon, "The Ku Klux Klan in Yankee Country," *United Press International*, October 28, 1981, www.upi.com/Archives/1981/10/28/The-Ku-Klux-Klan-in-Yankee-country/3805373093200/.

113. Joe Verrengia and Stuart Karle, "Visions of Klan America Clash at KKK Rally in Connecticut," *Colombia Daily Spectator*, September 15, 1980, spectatorarchive.library.columbia.edu/cgi-bin/columbia?a=d&d=cs19800915-01.2.5.

114. Ibid., James Hershberg and William E. McKibben.

115. Mathew Wald, "Klan Is Jeered at 2D Meriden Rally," *New York Times*, March 21, 1982, www.nytimes.com/1982/03/21/nyregion/klan-is-jeered-at-2d-meriden-rally.html.

116. Associated Press, "7 Are Injured by Rocks as Connecticut Rally by Klan Is Broken Up," *New York Times*, March 22, 1981, www.nytimes.com/1981/03/22/nyregion/7-are-injured-by-rocks-as-connecticut-rally-by-klan-is-broken-up.html.

117. Samuel Zipp, *Manhattan Projects: The Rise and Fall of Urban Renewal in Cold War New York*, (Oxford: Oxford University Press, 2012).

118. May 19th Communist Organization, *War In America. Fight White Supremacy, Support the Black Liberation Army*, pamphlet (New York: May 19th Communist Organization, 1981), freedomarchives.org/Documents/Finder/DOC37_scans/37.May19.WarinAmerikaaa.pdf.

119. The John Brown Anti-Klan Committee, "Tom Metzger: An American Fascist," *No KKK! No Fascist USA!*, Spring 1989, www. freedomarchives.org/Documents/Finder/DOC37_scans/37.nokkk.spr89. pdf.

120. Joel Kotkin, "Calif. Klansman Nominated for Congress as Democrat," *Washington Post*, June 8, 1980, www.washingtonpost.com/ archive/politics/1980/06/08/calif-klansman-nominated-for-congress-as-democrat/3a2ea72c-c105-44b4-ac2f-b8d9b3d58372/.

121. The John Brown Anti-Klan Committee, "Tom Metzger: An American Fascist," *No KKK - No Fascist USA!*, Spring 1989, www. freedomarchives.org/Documents/Finder/DOC37_scans/37.nokkk.spr89. pdf.

122. The John Brown Anti-Klan Committee, "California Klan Leader Tom Metzger," *Death to the Klan*, July/August 1983, freedomarchives.org/ Documents/Finder/DOC37_scans/37.dttk.jul83.pdf.

123. Associated Press, "Los Angeles Police Reconsider Using Choke Hold," *Los Angeles Times*, September 3, 1991, www.nytimes. com/1991/09/03/us/los-angeles-police-reconsider-using-choke-hold.html.

124. The John Brown Anti-Klan Committee, "Klan Rally in LA: Aryan Nations and KKK Build Racist Alliance," *Death to the Klan!*, Winter 1984.

125. Michael D. Harris, "Criminal Charges Dropped Against KKK, Nazi Party Members," *United Press International*, June 21,1984, www.upi. com/Archives/1984/06/21/Criminal-charges-dropped-against-KKK-Nazi-party-members/3850456638400/.

AFTER WINTER MUST COME SPRING: THE ANTI-KLAN MOVEMENT

126. The John Brown Anti-Klan Committee, "Victory in Austin, On to Meridien and Boston!," *Death to the Klan!*, April/May 2003, freedomarchives.org/Documents/Finder/DOC37_scans/37.dttk.apr83. pdf.

127. Ron Jacobs, *Which Way the Wind Blew, A History of the Weather Underground* (London: Verso Books, 1997). The botched robbery resulted in the death of security guard Peter Paige, Sgt. Edward O'Grady, and Officer Waverly "Chipper" Brown. May 19th members Judith Clark, David Gilbert, and Kathy Boudin were arrested and later convicted and given long sentences for their roles.

128. Frank Jannuzi, "Klan TV Appearance Triggers Protest," *The Daily Texan*, August 2, 1982.

129. East Town Lake Citizens, Black Citizens Task Force, Brown Berets, "Austin Minority Coalition Announcement," press release, Austin, University of Texas Archive.

130. The John Brown Anti-Klan Committee, *Death to the Klan! Free the Land!*, pamphlet, Austin, 1983.

131. The John Brown Anti-Klan Committee, "2000 Demonstrate Against Klan in Austin," *Death to the Klan!*, April/May 1983.

132. Racist organizations' targeting of Black people, Indigenous people, and Chicano people in the state of Texas was not a new occurrence. Controlling the border has a long history of racist motivation and violent acts. The first was Texas Rangers, a paramilitary formation created to seize the "Republic of Texas" through the murder and forced removal of Native Americans beginning in 1836. Texas laws today state that the Texas Rangers cannot legally be disbanded. The next significant border control formation was Klan Border Watch. Founded in 1977 by Knights of the Ku Klux Klan leaders David Duke and Tom Metzger, with volunteers from four states driving from Texas to the coast of California, the group reported suspicious people to the United States Border Patrol. So when the Klan called for a rally at the State Capitol on February 21, 1983, the Austin Minority Coalition positioned this Klan rally within a long history of racist organizations sanctioned by the state.

133. Brown Berets, leaflet, Austin, TX, 1983.

134. "The Day the Klan Marched: Anti-KKK Protesters Beaten by Racist Austin Police," video, Paula Manley, John Fulton, Jane & Gilberto Rivera and Jim Cullers producers, March 26, 2011, www.mobilebroadcastnews.com/NewsRoom/Jeff-Zavala/Day-Klan-Marched-Anti-KKK-Protesters-Beaten-Racist-Austin-Police.

135. John Montgomery, director, *Protest Against KKK at State Capitol 1983*, Texas Archive of the Moving Image, February 2018, www.texasarchive.org/library/index.php/2014_00070.

136. Op. cit., "The Day the Klan Marched: Anti-KKK Protesters Beaten by Racist Austin Police."

137. Black Citizen's Task Force, press release, February 24 1983.

138. Rick Dyer, "Hernandez found guilty of resisting arrest," *Austin Daily Texan Archives*, February 1, 1984.

139. The John Brown Anti-Klan Committee, "Fighting the Klan: Houston, Meriden, San Antonio, New Britain, Kalamazoo, Hartford," *Death to the Klan!*, July/August 1983, freedomarchives.org/Documents/Finder/DOC37_scans/37.dttk.jul83.pdf.

140. Wallace Turner, "Anti Police Suit Focuses on Town's Ills," *New York Times*, February 13, 1983, www.nytimes.com/1983/02/13/us/antipolice-suit-focuses-on-a-town-s-ills.html.

141. The John Brown Anti-Klan Committee, "Richmond, CA: 'Cowboys' Are Killer Cops," *Death to the Klan!*, April 1983, freedomarchives.org/Documents/Finder/DOC37_scans/37.dttk.apr83.pdf.

142. Ibid.

143. Author unknown, "Bigotry Backlash," *Brownsville Herald*, February 20, 1983, www.newspapers.com/image/379285350/?terms=Brownsville%2BHerald.

144. National Anti-Klan Network, *Organizing Effective Local Responses to the KKK*, position paper (Atlanta: 1982).

145. Author unknown, "Anti-Klan Group Plans Action Against Racism," *New York Times*, February 2, 1981, timesmachine.nytimes.com/timesmachine/1981/02/02/248317.html?pageNumber=12.

146. Akineyele Omowale Umoja, *We Will Shoot Back: Armed Resistance in the Mississippi Freedom Movement* (New York: New York University Press, 2013).

147. Robert F. Williams, *Negroes with Guns* (Detroit: Martino Publishing, 1983).

148. The John Brown Anti-Klan Committee, "Criminalizing the Anti-Klan Movement," *Death to the Klan*, July/August 1983, p. 13.

149. Ibid.

150. Ibid.

CONFRONTATIONS AND CULTURE WARS

151. Paul Kleppner, *Chicago Divided: The Making of a Black Mayor* (DeKalb: Northern Illinois University Press, 1985).

152. Martin Luther King Jr., quoted in Claybourne Carson, ed., *The Autobiography of Martin Luther King Jr.* (New York: Time Warner Books, 1998).

153. Popular films offered many portrayals of the racist right, mostly through the lens of camp or revenge films. See *The Omega Syndrome* (1986) and *Surf Nazis Must Die* (1987).

154. Christian Piccolini, *White American Youth: My Descent Into America's Most Violent Hate Movement—and How I Got Out,* (New York: Hachette Books, 2017).

155. Op cit., Kleppner, *Chicago Divided*.

156. E.R. Shipp, "Chicago Group Demands Black Mayor Heed Whites' Concern," *New York Times*, May 2, 1984, www.nytimes.com/1984/05/02/us/chicago-group-demands-black-mayor-heed-whites-concern.html.

157. The John Brown Anti-Klan Committee, "The Chicago Election, A No-win Situation," *Death to the Klan!*, July/August 1983, freedomarchives.org/Documents/Finder/DOC37_scans/37.dttk.jul83.pdf.

158. Jakobi Williams, *From the Ballot to the Bullet, The Illinois Chapter of the Black Panther Party and Racial Coalitions in Chicago* (Raleigh: University of North Carolina Press, 2013); Amy Sonnie and James Tracy, *Hillbilly Nationalists, Urban Race Rebels and Black Power: Community Organizing in Radical Times* (Brooklyn, NY: Melville House Publishing, 2011).

159. In 1898, following the defeat of Spain in the Spanish-American War, the island of Puerto Rico became a colony of the United States. People from Puerto Rico are formally U.S. citizens, yet they cannot vote for president and their Congressional Representative cannot cast votes.

160. Author Unknown, "10 Convicted in Chicago FALN Trial," *New*

York Times, February 12, 1981, www.nytimes.com/1981/02/12/us/10-convicted-in-chicago-faln-trial.html.

161. John Schmeltzer, "Firebomb Victims Sue Ex-Neighbor," *Chicago Tribune*, January 8, 1985. www.chicagotribune.com/news/ct-xpm-1985-01-08-8501020490-story.html.

162. Christopher Hewitt, *Political Violence and Terrorism in Modern America* (Westport: Praegue Security International, 2005).

163. The John Brown Anti-Klan Committee and the Ad Hoc Committee Against Racist Violence, "Say No to Racist Violence" An Open Letter to the People of Chicago," full-page advertisement, *Chicago Reader*, June 20, 1986, freedomarchives.org/Documents/Finder/DOC37_scans/37.JBAKCChicago.SayNoToRacistViolence.pdf.

164. Julian Heuertas, "It's Out of Control and Spreading: Graffiti as the Supposed Cause of the Urban Crisis in 1970s–1980s New York City," paper, Bowdoin College, 2016, www.academia.edu/13322527/_It_s_Out_of_Control_and_Spreading_Graffiti_as_the_Supposed_Cause_of_Urban_Crisis_in_1970s-1980s_New_York_City.

165. NBC Channel 5, "No Arrests, No Investigation," September 28, 1985.

166. Jess Bravin, "Protesters Fight Paint with Paint," *Chicago Tribune*, June 22, 1986, freedomarchives.org/Documents/Finder/DOC37_scans/37. JBAKCChicago.ProtestersFightPaintWithPaint.pdf.

167. The John Brown Anti-Klan Committee and the Ad Hoc Committee Against Racist Violence, "Say No to Racist Violence" An Open Letter to the People of Chicago," full-page advertisement, *Chicago Reader*, June 20, 1986, NBC Channel 5, "No Arrests, No Investigation," September 28, 1985.

168. Robert Enstad, "Gunman Gets Life for Racial Killing," *Chicago Tribune*, December 24, 1986, www.chicagotribune.com/news/ct-xpm-1986-12-24-8604060035-story.html.

169. Daniel Rachel, *The Walls Came Tumbling Down: The Music and Politics of Rock Against Racism, 2 Tone and Red Wedge 1976–1992* (London: Picador, 2016); David Renton, *Never Again, Rock Against Racism and the Anti-Nazi League* (New York: Routledge, 2012); David Widgery, *Beating Time: Riot Race and Rock and Roll* (London: Chatto Press, 1987).

170. David A. Ensminger, *The Politics of Punk: Protest and Revolt From the Streets*, (New York: Rowman & Littlefield, 2016).

171. Listen to Patti Smith, "Rock and Roll Nigger," on the 1978 album *Easter* and The Avengers, "White Nigger" on the 1983 album *The Avengers.*

172. Shane Burley, *Fascism Today, What It Is and How to End It* (Oakland, CA: AK Press, 2017), pp. 198–199. The John Brown Anti-Klan Committee and R.A.S.H. were not the only groups to encourage skinheads to move away from racist currents and/or to the left. Minneapolis-based group The Baldies organized to kick Nazis out of the

punk scene through violent confrontation and later became Anti-Racist Action (A.R.A.). Like JBAKC, much of their work is deeply influential to the tenor and tactics of sections today's anti-fascist movements.

173. Joelle McGinnis, "Local 'skinheads' clear up Nazi misconceptions," *Northern Star*, March 8, 1988, northernstar.info/city/local-skinheads-clear-up-nazi-misconceptions/article_af4a9dde-66c2-5fa3-966e-6c98cda93bcf.html.

174. Mark Steinem, "Racial Friction in Concord: Lynching or Suicide? A City Is Gripped by Tension," *Los Angeles Times*, February 11, 1986, www.latimes.com/archives/la-xpm-1986-02-11-mn-23152-story.html.

175. Author unknown, *Los Angeles Times*, "The State," October 20, 1987.

176. Katherine Bishop, "Neo-Nazi Activity Is Arising Among U.S. Youth," *New York Times*, June 13, 1988, archive.nytimes.com/www.nytimes.com/library/national/race/061388race-ra.html.

177. Robert Forbes and Eddie Stampton, *The White Nationalists Skinhead Movement: UK & US 1979-1993* (Los Angeles: Feral House, 2015).

178. Shortly after the inauguration of Donald Trump as president, the band Green Day resurrected the "No Cops" slogan at the American Music Awards as "No Trump, No KKK, No Fascist USA." This gave the slogan new life as a popular chant in anti-Trump mobilizations. www.youtube.com/watch?v=58H406jATDE.

179. In 2006 Oprah Winfrey said, "I realized in that moment that I was doing more to empower them than to expose them. Since that time, I've never done a show like that again." In 2011, she invited the two skinhead spokespeople back to the show, where they renounced white supremacy. Dave Adela attributed his change of heart to a stint in prison for vandalizing a synagogue where Black prisoners "treated me like a human being even though my past was literally written all over my back in swastikas." Mike Barrett recruited the group of Portland skinheads later responsible for the murder of an Ethiopian man, which caused him to break from organized racism. www.reddit.com/r/videos/comments/3wezua/the_oprah_winfrey_show_gang_of_skinheads_return/

180. Antonio Gramsci, *Selections for the Prison Notebooks* (New York: International Publishers, 1971). Italian theorist Antonio Gramsci, writing from Mussolini's prisons in fascist Italy, recognized that economic conditions were rarely enough to cause revolts and revolutions. Gramsci pointed to the roles played by the church, the press, and schools in upholding the forms of domination perpetrated by the ruling class. In this sense, the anti-racist campaign for the hearts and minds of punk rockers could be seen as a classic "war of position"—resistance to cultural forms being used as vehicles for racial domination of youth and a process that develops the strength of a new and diverse social foundation.

181. John Sinclair, *Guitar Revolution with MC5 and the White Panther*

Party (Los Angeles: Process Media, 2007). The war for ideas in punk culture existed long before the John Brown Anti-Klan groups' activities. Early in the 1970s, John Sinclair, a member of the White Panther Party and the MC5 rock band, declared a "total assault on culture." The White Panther Party promoted cultural activism as a way to spread pro–Black liberation messages among white youth, particularly working-class ones, attracted to the drop-out aspects of hippie counterculture. They actively celebrated Black revolution and called for the release of imprisoned Black Panthers.

SMALL STEPS ON A LONG ROAD

182. Emily K. Hobson. *Lavender and Red: Liberation and Solidarity in the Gay and Lesbian Left* (Oakland: University of California Press, 2016); Deborah B. Gould, *Moving Politics: Emotion and ACT UP's Fight Against AIDS* (Chicago: University of Chicago Press, 2009).

183. William F. Buckley Jr., "Crucial Steps in Combating the Aids Epidemic; Identify All the Carriers," *New York Times*, March 18, 1986, archive.nytimes.com/www.nytimes.com/books/00/07/16/specials/buckley-aids.html.

184. Thomas Oliphant, "Looking at the World as Lyndon LaRouche Sees It; His Enemies List an Eclectic Mix," *Boston Globe*, April 6, 1986.

185. Press release, "AIDS Activists to March on CDC to Demand Expanded AIDS Definition and Improved Epidemiology" (January 8, 1990), Georgia State University Library Digital Collection; press release, "AIDS Activists Storm CDC Headquarters: 50 Arrested," January 9, 1990, Georgia State University Library Digital Collection.

186. Darrell Gordon, "30 Years Later: AIDS activism and ACT UP Chicago," *News and Letters* (Nov–Dec 2011), newsandletters.org/30-years-later-aids-activism-and-act-up-chicago-2/.

187. Colman McCarthy, "45 Years of Working for Prison Reform," *National Catholic Reporter* (September 16, 2017), www.ncronline.org/news/justice/change-system-being-part-it.

188. Allison Bechdel, *The Essential Dykes to Watch Out For* (New York: Houghton-Mifflin, 2008).

189. Susan Rosenberg, *An American Radical: Political Prisoner in My Own Country* (New York: Citadel Press, 2011).

190. Marilyn Thompson, "Caught in the Whitewater Quagmire," *Washington Post*, August 28, 1995, www.washingtonpost.com/wp-srv/politics/special/whitewater/stories/wwtr950828.html.

191. Jenni Gainsborough and Marc Mauer, "Diminishing Returns: Crime and Incarceration in the 1990s," report, (Washington, D.C.: Sentencing Project, September 2000), www.prisonpolicy.org/scans/sp/DimRet.pdf.

192. J. Lopez. "Political Incarceration," in *States of Confinement*, Joy James, ed. (New York: St. Martin's Press, 2000).

193. Steve Whitman, "The Crime of Black Imprisonment," *Chicago Tribune*, May 28, 1987, www.freedomarchives.org/Documents/Finder/DOC3_scans/3.chicago.tribune.whitman.black.imprisonment.5.28.1987.pdf.

194. Committee to End the Marion Lockdown, "Can't Jail the Spirit: Political Prisoners in the U.S., A Collection of Biographies," 1988.

LESSONS FOR TODAY'S MOVEMENTS

195. Dave Phillips. "Christopher Hasson, "Coast Guard Officer, Plotted Attacks at His Desk, Filings Say," *New York Times*, February 21, 2019, www.nytimes.com/2019/02/21/us/coast-guard-christopher-hasson-terrorist-attack.html.

196. Today, unlike in the 1980s, it is more widely documented that the armed forces and the police serve, at times, as training grounds for the far right. "If you look at the list of domestic terrorism attacks, you see a lot of veterans," said Heidi Beirich, director of the Southern Poverty Law Center's intelligence project. This is not a new development, either. In 1986, then–Defense Secretary Casper Weinberger ordered a purge of white supremacists from the military. In 1991, a federal judge determined that a group of Los Angeles Police Department officers had established a "neo-Nazi, white supremacist gang" within the Lynwood station. Also in 1991, Timothy McVeigh, a U.S. Army veteran, blew up a federal building in Oklahoma City, killing 168 people and injuring more than 680 others. In 1995, James Burmeister and Malcolm Wright, two neo-Nazi skinhead paratroopers in the elite 82nd Airborne Division at Ft. Bragg, shot and killed a couple near the base just because they were Black. The trial prompted an internal investigation by the Army that turned up an additional twenty-two racist skinheads in his unit. In 1996, the Department of Defense, shaken by the events in Oklahoma City, issued a complete ban on service people's membership in white supremacist groups. The orders had little impact. As the *New York Times* articles described, still in 2019 Beirich lamented, "We've had a hard time convincing the military of the seriousness of this problem."

197. Southern Poverty Law Center, "Intelligence Report," 2019, p. 40.

198. John Brown Anti Klan Committee, "Stop the Grand Jury!," November 1984.

199. Associated Press, "Activists say they will refuse to testify," January 16, 1985.

200. Multiple Signers, *The Guardian*, "To All Progressive People," July 11, 1984.

201. Ibid.

202. Water Protector Legal Collective, "Press Release: Federal Subpoena Dropped Against Grand Jury Resister Steve Martinez," February 28, 2017, waterprotectorlegal.org/?s=grand+jury.

203. The uncompromising nature of the Committee resonated with classical anti-fascist oppositional struggles like the T.I.G.R.'s resistance to Mussolini's regime; formations opposing fascist political groups in Spain, France, and the United Kingdom through the 1930s; and the alliance of Social Democrats, Communists, and others called *Antifaschistische Aktion* against Hitler's Nazi Germany before the start of World War II.

204. Philosophical arguments for speech, rooted in the Enlightenment, were developed to challenge the Church in Europe in monopolizing claims to truth. From this tradition, the right to freedom of speech is part of the ongoing, contested pursuit of truth. United States legal history is punctuated by important cases that refined, morphed, and adapted the contents of freedom of speech, expression, and assembly. Read David Rabban's *Free Speech in Its Forgotten Years* for a fascinating early history and Anthony Lewis's *Freedom of the Thought We Hate: A Biography of the First Amendment* for a contemporary history of the First Amendment and its use in stifling repression.

205. A.C. Thompson, "Federal Judge Dismisses Charges Against 3 White Supremacists," *ProPublica*, June 4, 2015, www.propublica.org/article/federal-judge-dismisses-charges-against-3-white-supremacists.

206. Luke Barnes, "Judge says that white supremacists charged in violent riots are protected by First Amendment," *Think Progress*, June 4, 2017, thinkprogress.org/white-supremacists-riots-free-speech-f3c644e8386a/.

207. Sarah Wildman, "Why You See Swastikas in America but Not Germany," *Vox*, August 16, 2017, www.vox.com/world/2017/8/16/16152088/nazi-swastikas-germany-charlottesville.

208. Associated Press, "13 Supremacists Are Not Guilty of Conspiracies," *New York Times*, April 8, 1988, www.nytimes.com/1988/04/08/us/13-supremacists-are-not-guilty-of-conspiracies.html?login=email&auth=login-email.

209. Kathleen Belew, *Bring the War Home: The White Power Movement and Paramilitary America* (Cambridge: Harvard University Press, 2018).

210. Bill Simmons, "13 White Supremacists Acquitted in Arkansas Murder and Sedition Trial," *The Washington Post*, April 8, 1988, www.washingtonpost.com/archive/politics/1988/04/08/13-white-supremacists-acquitted-in-arkansas-murder-and-sedition-trial/21c30cbe-c120-40ac-8fec-33420d1b0d2e/?noredirect=on.

211. Interview with Kathleen Belew, "Q. And A: The History of White Power," *New York Times*, May 19, 2018, static.nytimes.com/email-content/RR_2235.html?nlid=72002091.

212. John Brown Anti-Klan Committee, "The Dividing Line of the

1980s, Take a Stand Against the Klan," pamphlet, 1981, freedomarchives. org/Documents/Finder/DOC37_scans/37.StandvsKlan.pdf.

213. Bruce Hoffman, *Terrorism in the United States and the Potential Threat to Nuclear Facilities*, Rand Institute, January 1986, www.rand.org/ pubs/reports/R3351.html.

214. Op cit., "The Dividing Line of the 1980s."

215. Eric Ward, "Skin in the Game: How Antisemitism Animates White Nationalism," Political Research Associates, June 29, 2017, www. politicalresearch.org/2017/06/29/skin-in-the-game-how-antisemitism-animates-white-nationalism/.

216. During the Great Depression, the demagogue Father Coughlin, a Roman Catholic priest, used his weekly radio sermons to propagandize against Jewish people. Leo Ferguson, Dove Kent, Keren Soffer Sharon, "Understanding Antisemitism: An Offering to Our Movement," Jews for Economic and Racial Justice, jfrej.org/wp-content/ uploads/2018/04/JFREJ-Understanding-Antisemitism-November-2017-v1-3-2.pdf.

217. Melinda Warner, "After Charlottesville Violence, Alt-Right Plans Another Weekend of Hate," Right-Wing Watch, A Project of the People for the American Way, August 18, 2017, www.rightwingwatch.org/post/ after-charlottesville-violence-alt-right-plans-another-weekend-of-hate/.

ABOUT THE AUTHORS

 Hilary Moore is an anti-racist political education trainer and teaches with generative somatics. She works on the Leadership Team of Showing Up for Racial Justice, and is the co-author of *Organizing Cools the Planet: Tools and Reflections to Navigate the Climate Crisis*. Her writing has been featured in *Waging Nonviolence*. She lives in Berlin, Germany.

James Tracy is an Instructor of Labor and Community Studies at City College of San Francisco. He is the co-author of *Hillbilly Nationalists, Urban Race Rebels and Black Power: Community Organizing in Radical Times* and the editor of *The Civil Disobedience Handbook: A Brief History and Practical Guide for the Politically Disenchanted*. He lives in Oakland, California.

ALSO AVAILABLE IN THE OPEN MEDIA SERIES

American Nightmare
Facing the Challenge of Fascism
By Henry A. Giroux

Loaded
A Disarming History of the Second Amendment
By Roxanne Dunbar-Ortiz

Death Blossoms: Expanded Edition
By Mumia Abu-Jamal

Torn from the World
A Guerrilla's Escape from a Secret Prison in Mexico
By John Gibler

Narrative of the Life of Frederick Douglass, an American Slave,
Written by Himself: A New Critical Edition
By Angela Y. Davis

Border Patrol Nation
Dispatches from the Front Lines of Homeland Security
By Todd Miller

Redefining Black Power
Reflections on the State of Black America
Edited by Joanne Griffith
Featuring Michelle Alexander, Julianne Malveaux, Dr. Vincent
Harding, Ramona Africa

CITY LIGHTS BOOKS | OPEN MEDIA SERIES
ARM YOURSELF WITH INFORMATION